LIFE AND LETTERS IN THE ANCIENT GREEK WORLD

From the first 'murderous symbols' scratched on a tablet instructing the recipient to kill the one who delivered it, to the letters of St Paul to the early Church, and to later literary experiments, this comprehensive study examines the range of letter-writing in the ancient Greek world. Containing extensive translated examples from both life and fiction, it looks at personal and private letters, providing a glimpse into the lives of ordinary people, letters used in administration and government, letters used as vehicles for the dissemination of philosophy and religion, and letters which played a part in the development of several literary genres. It considers the way in which letters were written and with what materials, how they were delivered, and how it is that, for certain limited periods and locations, so many of them have survived, and how they were rediscovered.

By placing these letters in their social, political and intellectual contexts, *Life and Letters in the Ancient Greek World* draws attention to both familiar topics, such as young soldiers writing home from basic training and the choice of flowers for a wedding, and more alien events, such as getting rid of baby girls and offhand attitudes to bereavement.

This is the first guide in English to provide commentary on such a broad range of letters and will be essential reading for anyone interested in the ancient Greek world.

John Muir taught at King's College London, becoming Senior Lecturer and Vice-Principal. His interests include Greek education, the development of literacy, and early rhetoric. His publications include *Greek Religion and Society* (Cambridge University Press, 1985, co-edited with P.E. Easterling) and editions of Virgil, Homer and Alcidamas.

LIFE AND LETTERS IN THE ANCIENT GREEK WORLD

John Muir

LONDON AND NEW YORK

First published in 2009
by Routledge
2 Park Square, Milton Park, Abingdon, Oxfordshire OX14 4RN

Simultaneously published in the USA and Canada
by Routledge
711 Third Avenue, New York, NY 10017

Routledge is an imprint of the Taylor & Francis Group, an informa business

First issued in paperback 2012

Typeset in Times New Roman by
Taylor & Francis Books

British Library Cataloguing in Publication Data
A catalogue record for this book is available from the British Library

Library of Congress Cataloging in Publication Data
Muir, J. V. (John Victor)
Life and letters in the ancient Greek world / John Muir.
p. cm.
Includes bibliographical references and index.
1. Letter writing, Classical. 2. Greek letters–History and criticism. I. Title.
PA3042.M85 2008
886′.01–dc22
2008016455

ISBN13:978-0-415-39130-6(hbk)
ISBN13:978-0-415-51837-6(pbk)
ISBN13:978-0-203-88952-7(ebk)

CONTENTS

PREFACE

Most of the main areas of ancient Greek literary creativity have had the benefit of general surveys in English; poetry, drama, history, philosophy, oratory are all well served, and indeed have received encyclopedic treatment. I first became aware of the lack of such a thing so far as letters were concerned at a Colloquium in Amsterdam planned by the late Professor A.D. Leeman, to whom I remain always grateful. Letters were very much a part of the ancient Greek world and surprising numbers of them have survived. They offer glimpses of ordinary people and ordinary life in a way that even archaeology finds it hard to rival: they show people at work, directing and being directed, ruling and being ruled; they became vehicles for philosophy and religion; and they formed the framework for adventures in literary imagination which – if not always successful – pointed the way to much fruitful growth and reincarnation.

The project therefore needs, I believe, no apology; its execution certainly does. Anyone who sets out to look over such a wide, fascinating and absolutely varied field soon becomes aware that he is a Jack-of-all-trades and master of none of them. I owe a huge debt to many scholars, and especially to those papyrologists of many nations whose expert and extraordinarily devoted labours have made so much material available and opened our eyes to so many corners of ancient life. My recent debts to Professor Naphthali Lewis, Professor P.J. Parsons, Dr A.K. Bowman and the late Professor E.G. Turner will be obvious, but there are many more. If I have misused their work in any way, I am very sorry. Professor Michael Trapp's scholarship in his exemplary edition of a selection of Greek and Latin letters has been invaluable and, as always, an inspiration. In the field of literary letters I have learnt more than I can say from the scholarly, sympathetic and lively books of Professor Patricia Rosenmeyer; her work has already provoked much further research and she made my task much easier and more agreeable. I should like to thank Mrs Costa and the Oxford University Press for permission to use some of her late husband's splendidly urbane translations of some literary letters, and Professor Ken Dowden and the University of California Press for allowing me to use some translations from *The*

Alexander Romance in B.P. Reardon's *Collected Ancient Greek Novels.* Unless otherwise indicated, all other translations are my own. The late Professor Malcolm Willcock discussed my ideas for a book at an early stage, and with typical simplicity put his finger on one of the basic difficulties of which I have been ruefully aware ever since. I should like to thank Dr John Taylor, Dr Michael Spencer, Mrs Margaret Stylianides and Mr Richard Woff for particular help and encouragement, and the kindly staff of the Sackler Library in Oxford in whose Papyrology Room I have spent many happy and enlightening hours. The Joint Library of the Hellenic and Roman Societies has, as ever, been a great support and I am grateful to the Librarian and his staff for much patient and cheerful help. I am also grateful to Mrs T. Stiff of the City Parochial Foundation, London, for her readiness to listen to my computer problems and her ability to solve most of them so easily. Chris Hook, Lalle Pursglove, Amy Laurens and Liz Jones have seen the book through to production with exemplary courtesy and prompt efficiency; they deserve and have my gratitude. Finally I should like to thank my wife, Helen, who has not only read the typescript and encouraged me, but has also put up with the creative but disgraceful chaos of my study, and a retirement which has often been remarkably busy.

ABBREVIATIONS

AP	*Anthologia Palatina* = *The Greek Anthology*, Vols I–V, ed. W.R. Paton, Loeb Classical Library (Cambridge, Mass., and London, 1916–18)
Austin	*The Hellenistic World from Alexander to the Roman Conquest*, ed. M.M. Austin (Cambridge, 1981)
BGU	*Aegyptische Urkunden aus den Staatlichen Museen zu Berlin – Griechische Urkunden* (Berlin, 1895–1976)
BW	*Royal Correspondence in the Hellenistic Period*, C. Bradford Welles (New Haven, 1934)
CAH and *CAH*^{2}	*The Cambridge Ancient History*, first and second editions (Cambridge, 1924–39 and 1970–2007)
CHCL i	*The Cambridge History of Classical Literature*, Vol. 1, ed. P.E. Easterling and B.M.W. Knox (Cambridge, 1985)
GPE	*Greeks in Ptolemaic Egypt*, N. Lewis (Oxford, 1986).
I. Cret.	*Inscriptiones Creticae*, ed. M. Guarducci, 4 vols (Rome, 1935–50)
Kassel-Austin	*Poetae comici Graeci*, Vol. IV, ed. R. Kassel and C. Austin (Berlin, New York, 1983)
Nauck^2	*Tragicorum Graecorum Fragmenta*, ed. A. Nauck, second edition (Leipzig, 1889)
OCD^3	*The Oxford Classical Dictionary*, ed. S. Hornblower and A. Spawforth, third edition, revised (Oxford, 2003)
OGIS	*Orientis Graeci Inscriptiones Selectae*, ed. W. Dittenberger (Leipzig, 1903–5)
PECS	*The Princeton Encyclopedia of Classical Sites*, ed. R. Stillwell (Princeton, 1976)
PZA	*Greek Papyri in the British Museum*, Vol VII, *The Zenon Archive*, ed. T.C. Skeat (London, 1974)
SB	*Sammelbuch griechischen Urkunden aus Ägypten* (Strasbourg, Berlin, Heidelberg, 1915–)
SIG^3	*Sylloge Inscriptionum Graecarum*, ed. W. Dittenberger and (in part) H. von Gaertringen, third edition (Leipzig, 1915–24)

SP i and ii	*Select Papyri*, Vols I and II, ed. and trans. A.S. Hunt and C.C. Edgar, Loeb Classical Library (Cambridge, Mass., and London, 1932 and 1934)
Suidas (Adler)	*Suidae Lexicon*, ed. A. Adler (Leipzig, 1928–35)
UPZ	*Urkunden der Ptolemäerzeit* I, ed. U. Wilcken (Berlin and Leipzig, 1922–7)

COLLECTIONS OF PAPYRI AND *OSTRACA* REFERRED TO IN THE TEXT

P. Ant.	*The Antinoopolis Papyri*, 3 vols (London, 1950–66)
P. Athen.	*Papyri Societatis Archaeologicae Atheniensis*, ed. G.A. Petropoulos (Athens, 1939)
P. Beatty Panop.	*Papyri from Panopolis in the Chester Beatty Library, Dublin*, ed. T.C. Skeat (Dublin, 1964)
P. Bon.	*Papyri Bononienses*, ed. O. Montevecchi (Milano, 1953)
P. Cair.	*Greek Papyri. Catalogue général des antiquités égyptiennes du Musée du Caire*, ed. B.P. Grenfell and A. S. Hunt (Oxford, 1903)
P. Cair. Zen.	*Catalogue général des antiquités égyptiennes du Musée du Caire; Zenon Papyri*, 4 vols, ed. C.C. Edgar (Cairo, 1925–31); Vol. V, ed. O. Guéraud and P. Jouguet (Cairo, 1940)
P. Ent.	*ENTEUXEIS: Requêtes et plaintes adressées au roi d'Égypte au IIIe siècle avant J-C*, ed. O. Guéraud (Cairo, 1931–2)
P. Giess.	*Griechische Papyri im Museum des oberhessischen Geschichtvereins zu Giessen*, ed. O. Eger, E. Kornemann and P.M. Meyer (Leipzig/Berlin, 1910–12)
P. Grenf. ii	*New Classical Fragments and other Greek and Latin Papyri*, ed. B.P. Grenfell and A.S. Hunt (Oxford, 1897)
P. Hal.	*Dikaiomata: Auszüge aus Alexandrinischen Gesetzen und Verordnungen*, ed. Graeca Halensis (Berlin, 1913)
P. Hamb.	*Griechische Papyrus Urkunden der Hamburger Staats- und Universitätsbibliothek*, ed. P.M. Meyer (Leipzig/ Berlin, 1911–24)
P. Hib.	*The Hibeh Papyri*, Part I, ed. B.P. Grenfell and A.S. Hunt (London, 1906); Part II, ed. E.G. Turner and M.T. Lenger (London, 1953)
C.P. Jud.	*Corpus Papyrorum Judaicarum*, 3 vols, ed. V.A. Tcherikover and A. Fuks (Cambridge, Mass., 1957–64)
P. Lond.	*Greek Papyri in the British Museum*, 7 vols (London, 1893–1974)

P. Mich.	*Papyri in the University of Michigan Collection*, 13 vols (Ann Arbor, Michigan, 1931–77)
P. Mil. Vogliano	*Papiri della Università degli Studi di Milano*, 5 vols (1961–77)
P. Oxy.	*The Oxyrhynchus Papyri* (1898–in progress)
P. Par.	*Notices et textes des papyrus grecs du Musée du Louvre et de la Bibliothèque imperiale*, ed. A.J. Letronne and W. Brunet de Presle (Paris, 1865)
P. Petrie	*The Flinders Petrie Papyri*, 3 vols, ed. J. Mahaffy and J. G. Smyly (Dublin, 1891–1905)
P. Ryl.	*Catalogue of the Greek Papyri in the John Rylands Library, Manchester* (Manchester, 1911 – in progress)
PSI	*Papiri greci e latini*, Publicazzioni della Società Italiana per la ricerca dei Papiri greci e latini in Egitto (Firenze, 1912–in progress)
P. Tebt.	*The Tebtunis Papyri* (London, 1902–in progress)

*****

O. Claud.	*Mons Claudianus: ostraca graeca et latina*, ed. J. Bingen, A. Bülow-Jacobsen, W.E.H. Cockle, H. Cuvigny, L. Rubinstein and W. van Rengen (Cairo, 1992)
O. Flor.	*The Florida Ostraka*, ed. R.S. Bagnall (Durham, North Carolina, 1976)
O. Tait	*Greek Ostraca in the Bodleian Library and Other Collections*, 2 vols, ed. J.G. Tait (London, 1930 and 1955)

Fuller details of the main collections of papyri and *ostraca* can be found in Turner (1980), 154–79. A more complete and up-to-date listing can be found in J.F. Oates, R.S. Bagnall, S.J. Clackson, A.A. O'Brien, J.D. Sosin, T.G. Wilfong and K.A. Worp, *Checklist of Editions of Greek, Latin, Demotic and Coptic Papyri, Ostraca and Tablets*, fifth edition (Oxbow for the American Society of Papyrologists, Oakville CT and Oxford, 2001).

DATES IN THE PAPYRUS LETTERS

The dates given in the letters sometimes identify the year by giving the regnal year of the king (or later of the emperor). Mostly, however, the dating is in terms of days of a month, and it is rather typical of the mixed society in Egypt that the months are sometimes Greek (i.e. those of the Macedonian calendar), sometimes Egyptian and occasionally both. Before the end of the second century BC the correspondence between the Macedonian calendar and the Egyptian is not always clear, but the following table is reasonably accurate from that period.

There were also periodic intercalary adjustments since the Egyptian year was about a quarter of a day shorter than the true year.

Egyptian	*Macedonian*	*Contemporary*
Thoth 1	Dios 1	29 August
Phaophi 1	Apellaios 1	28 September
Hathyr 1	Audnaios 1	28 October
Choiak 1	Peritios 1	27 November
Tubi 1	Dystros 1	27 December
Mecheir 1	Xandicos 1	26 January
Phamenoth 1	Artemisios 1	25 February
Pharmouthi 1	Daisios 1	26 March
Pachon 1	Panemos 1	26 April
Pauni 1	Loios 1	26 May
Epeiph 1	Gorpiaios 1	25 June
Mesore 1	Hyperberetaios 1	25 July

Note: Table based on *SP* i.xv–xvi.

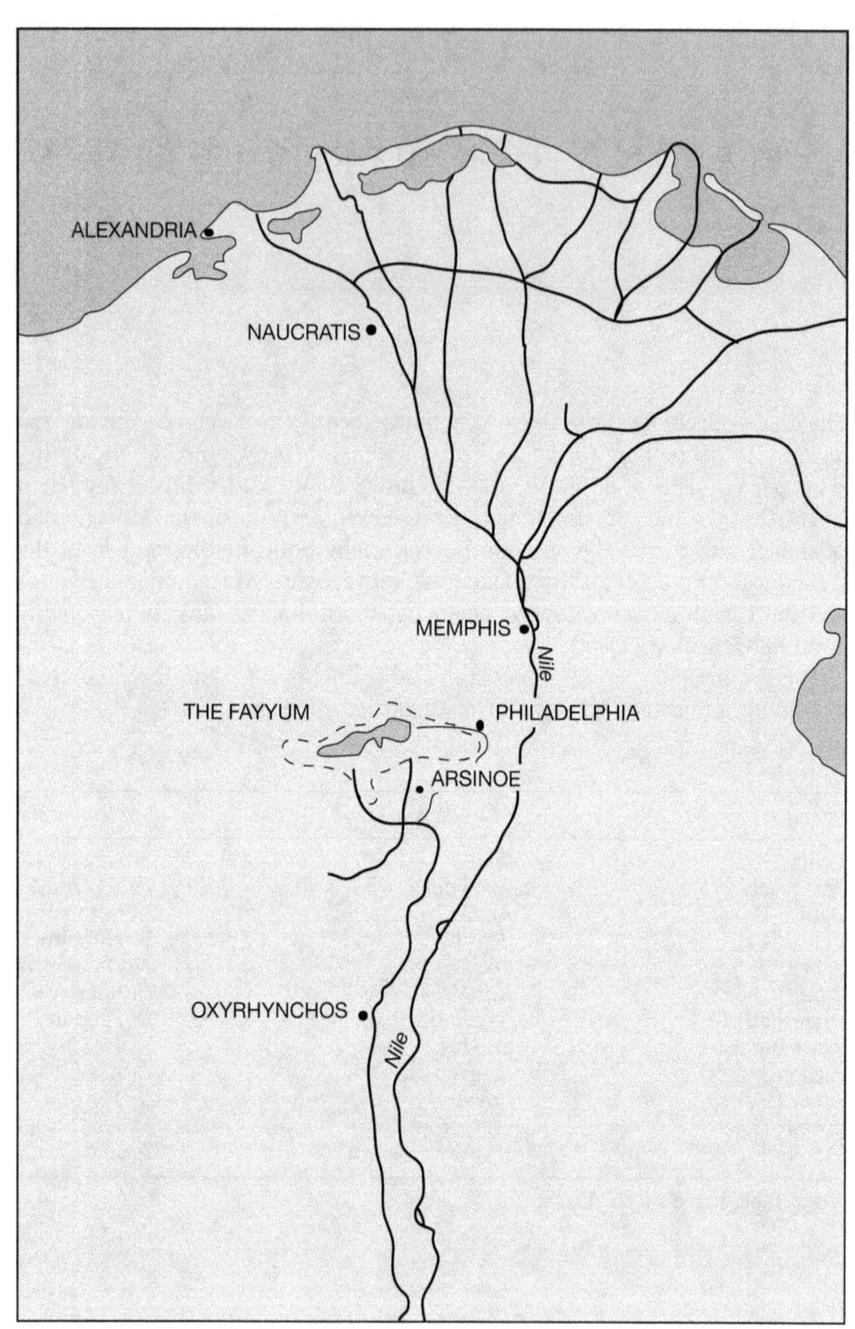

Egypt and *The Fayyum*

1

GREEK LETTERS

An introduction

The form and function of the Greek letter

In the modern world a letter is instantly recognizable by its opening formula of address and closing convention, both of which customarily contain polite expressions of friendly greeting. A recent clear-thinking anthologist of Greek and Latin letters has given a bare, rational definition with which it is hard to disagree:

> A letter is a written message from one person (or set of people) to another, requiring to be set down in a tangible medium, which itself is to be physically conveyed from sender(s) to recipient(s). Formally it is a piece of writing that is overtly addressed from sender(s) to recipient(s) by the use at the beginning and end of one of a limited set of conventional formulae of salutation (or some allusive variation on them) which specify both parties to the transaction.[1]

Most ancient Greek letters are easily recognizable too: they begin with 'A to B, greetings' (or a slight variant of that) and usually end with a single word of good wishes 'Farewell' or 'Best wishes'. The typical form, however, took time to evolve. The earliest surviving Greek letter, written on a thin sheet of lead by a Greek who was working in the region of the northern Black Sea in the fifth century BC, contains a rather impenetrable message without any opening or closing convention[2] and, though both Herodotus and Thucydides include letters in their works, the letters they quote likewise do not have the expressions at the start and finish which later became the norm.[3] Had the later pattern for the typical Greek letter been commonplace in their day, it would have been strange if Thucydides in particular had not used it. It seems therefore that the Greek letter did not begin to reach a stable form until at least the late fifth to mid-fourth century BC when the first examples are attested, and it is a reasonable guess that letter-writing only began to be a more frequent social activity from that time on. Discovery stories are common, and there was a curious tale that the habit of starting letters using the word 'Greetings' originated with the fifth century BC Athenian politician Cleon who, after an unexpected and spectacular victory during the Peloponnesian War in which a number of Spartan prisoners were taken on the island of Sphacteria in 425 BC, prefaced his written report to the Athenian Council with that word (with its connotations in Greek of rejoicing) and thereby started a fashion in letter-writing. The story is said to derive from the comic poet Euboulos[4] and is doubtless part of a joke but it does at least locate the beginnings of the typical form of the letter in the last quarter of the fifth century – perhaps not so far out. By the middle of the fourth century BC Xenophon quotes a letter allegedly written by the Persian king, Cyrus, and uses the typical later form of the Greek letter with formulaic top and tail,[5] and an actual surviving letter – also on lead – from the fourth century BC and probably originating in Attica has what is plainly quite close to the standard type of opening: 'Mnesiergos sends greetings and wishes for good health to those at home … ' And he follows this with an assurance that he too is in good health – an expression which later became pretty well formulaic. Probably a little later in the fourth century another Greek letter from Olbia in the Black Sea region (also on lead!) looks very like what became the norm:

> Articon to those at home, greetings.
>
> If Myllion throws you out of the house, go to the Atacos's, if permitted. If not, to Agatharchos. Let part of the wool be taken to Cerdon's place.[6]

Once established, the opening formula 'A to B, greetings' was sometimes expanded a little depending on the degree of warmth or familiarity desired. Relations or close friends writing to each other might add 'many' or 'very many' to their greetings; a respectful son writing to his father with a request might use a polite, formal acknowledgement of his parent's superiority ('respected sir'), and sometimes relations might casually mention their relationship 'brother' or 'sister' (though in Greek letters from Egypt, 'sister' may sometimes signify 'wife' – some care is in order).[7] More formal letters might involve other variations: when someone wrote asking a favour from someone else higher up the social or official ladder, it was usual to put the name of the more exalted person first – 'To B from A, greetings'. In Ptolemaic Egypt it was conventional politeness in official dealings to address one's letter to the king himself, even though the matter was probably dealt with by an official. So, Pappos making a complaint about his son's yobbish behaviour starts his letter: 'King Ptolemaios from Pappos, greetings'.[8] In official or business letters there were other customs: the quick letter might follow the usual pattern but it was also quite usual for the sender to make sure that he was recognized by including his patronymic and his office (or occupation) and even the place from which he was writing. So, even though he is writing to a relative,

Petesouchos begins a letter about the floods on his farm: 'Petesouchos, son of Marres, farmer in Cercesephis, to Marres, son of Petosiris … his brother, greetings'.[9] The apostle Paul went further in adapting the convention of identifying oneself (and one's addressee) at the start of a letter by introducing to the Greek business pattern a thicket of Christian missionary phraseology, thereby creating a precedent followed by other Christian leaders:

> Paul, called to be an apostle of Christ Jesus by the will of God, and our brother Sosthenes, to the church of God that is in Corinth, to those who are sanctified in Christ Jesus, called to be saints, together with all those who in every place call on the name of our Lord Jesus Christ, both their Lord and ours: Grace to you and peace from God our Father and the Lord Jesus Christ.[10]

It was not done to leave out the formalities and send a bare message when a proper letter was expected; that was the prerogative of autocrats. Alexander the Great, with his designs on the Persian empire accomplished and self-importance to match, is said to have decided to drop 'Greetings' from his correspondence, reserving the word for letters to two close associates, Antipater and Phocion, who alone, he felt, deserved the familiarity.[11]

The opening of a letter, therefore, while showing some variety was in essence consistent and formulaic. The ending was much simpler – usually a single word 'Farewell' or 'Best wishes', the latter being preferred for business or official letters. Occasionally the sentiments became a little more wordy – 'I pray that you fare well' – and sometimes the end was just left bare. One characteristic of business and official letters was the almost invariable habit of dating by the day, month and often the regnal year of the monarch – occasionally, in an emergency, even the hour.

In the body of the letter there were noticeable habits or perhaps taught patterns. In private letters some variant on 'I hope you are well' was common at the start, plus an assurance that the writer too was in good health (it is curiously rare to find a writer not in good health).[12] Another common theme near the start of the letter was the expression of thanks for the receipt of a previous letter, or sometimes rather tetchy complaints that no letters had been written recently along with a request for an explanation. Acknowledgements of goods received with the letter also tended to come near the beginning. Between relatives it was a quite common mark of affection to say that the writer was remembering the addressees before the gods or in prayers, again a custom much amplified by Christian letter-writers. The personal touch cropped up again at the end of letters: if the letter was being physically written by another party, the writer might add a phrase or two of good wishes in his or her own hand, and in family letters it was usual to send one's best wishes to named and close members of the family and friends – even occasionally to pets left behind.

As with all correspondence, letters intended for specific purposes began to acquire their own loose rules, with both writer and reader knowing what was expected. The ancient Greek world relied on personal contacts for much of its business and the letter of recommendation or introduction oiled many a wheel.[13] The form was flexible but fairly predictable. The letter started with the usual formal greeting, with or without the good wishes for health. There would then follow a description of the person recommended and the circumstances in which the sender had become acquainted with him – relative, colleague, encounter at work, etc. The recommendation itself then followed, together with a polite assurance that the writer would be much obliged if the recipient would accept the advice and find a place for the person recommended. As might be expected, such letters often seem to be written between people of roughly the same social status or official position. Letters making a complaint about a grievance from people lower down the social scale to officials (of which there are a great many) also tended to fall into a pattern and even acquired a strange name of their own – 'encounters' or 'meetings' – perhaps because in the earliest days of Ptolemaic rule in Egypt it was actually possible for the relatively small number of Macedonians and Greeks to meet the king himself and present their requests.[14] The person to whom the complaint was being made was put first in the address and there were sometimes polite and formal pleasantries; the circumstances of the complaint were then set out in detail (sometimes with vehemence), a course of action to right the claimed wrong was put forward, and the letter commonly ended with respectful thanks for an anticipated successful outcome or hopes to that effect.

Letter-writing in all periods of history has tended to adopt a particular register of style and in both private and business letters some phraseology seemed to spring to the minds of Greek correspondents repeatedly, e.g. 'you would do me a favour if … ', 'know that … ', 'give my best wishes to … ' It often approached the formulaic or the cliché but it was not a strait-jacket – simply a handy repertoire of familiar and appropriate language. There were of course nuances of tone and style which it is hard now to pick up. The respectful tone of someone writing to a superior is obvious, as is the curt instruction sent down the line by someone who did not need to be polite. There were, though, more subtle differences to which there are occasional pointers: Theophrastus in the fourth/third century BC wrote about various typical human character traits and the people who displayed them. Under the heading of 'The arrogant man' he gave the following example:

> When sending instructions by letter, he does not write 'you would oblige me', but 'I want this to happen' and 'I have sent to you so that I can pick up … ' and 'make sure it is exactly as I said' and 'soonest'.[15]

Another writer on character in the third century BC, Ariston, described the self-willed man, pleased with himself:

> When he has bought a slave, he does not bother to ask his name but just addresses him as 'slave', and when he knocks at someone else's door and is asked 'Who is it ?', he does not answer until someone comes out. And writing a letter, he neither writes 'Greetings' nor 'Farewell' at the end.[16]

In a different category altogether, the letters of state which came from the chanceries of the Hellenistic kings were important mechanisms of government and they were business-like, giving the impression of controlled efficiency. They were nearly always written in a direct, unrhetorical manner and quite punctilious in their use of proper titles. Many were responses to requests or to formal measures passed by the local governments of cities under the monarch's control, and the typical pattern was for the monarch to send his greetings (and thanks if appropriate) and then to repeat the request that had been made or the decree which had been passed. This was not necessarily a verbatim quote of what had been received; it could also be a paraphrase, albeit using much of the original phraseology. There then followed the official reply or instruction in clear diplomatic language. Such letters were nearly always well-written (kings could afford the best civil servants), and they commonly specified at the end what copies of the letter were to be displayed where.[17]

Moving on from official correspondence, when the letter began to be more obviously self-conscious – that is, when the letter-form began to be used for more sophisticated purposes than the transmission of workaday messages, personal greetings or official instructions – the patterns, themes and functions became more complicated. The letter-form became a kind of disguise or costume which was assumed for teaching or instruction or entertainment, and the use of the form might add much or little to the intended purpose. In some of these 'artificial' letters the usual formalities were preserved and the letter began like a letter; in most, however, the form was soon taken for granted and writers of imaginary or didactic letters often expected the reader to 'understand' the usual format, simply beginning 'To A' and leaving the end without any signing-off. For instance, when Epicurus wrote an epitome of part of his philosophical system, he decided to do so in the nominal form of letters to his friends Herodotus, Pythocles and Menoiceus. There are few clues as to why the letter-form was chosen other than the suggestion that it necessarily involved brevity. An epitome was clearly felt to be a less demanding, more user-friendly statement of doctrine than the full text-book treatment, and perhaps the pretence of a letter between friends therefore seemed the appropriate medium.[18]

The letters attributed to Plato (and perhaps the lost letters of Aristotle too) seem to have had rather different functions. Apart from the defensive tone of *Letter vii*, Plato's letters do expound philosophy, but there is the feeling that they have been collected and in some cases fabricated in the name of the great philosopher in order to extend the canon of surviving works, or at any rate to amplify and explain it. To an extent this is also the purpose of the many letters that surround the Stoic and Cynic traditions. You are not meant to read them as 'real' letters but you are meant to accept the form and to learn real lessons from them – so, though addressed to others, the letters are in part addressed to you. The Christian letters of the New Testament fit partly into this picture too. Many of them were written by Paul to specific communities for specific occasions, but they soon became treated as more general expositions of doctrine meant to unify and instruct the thoughts of all the faithful. And the non-Pauline letters attributed to the apostle, sometimes written with quite elaborate attempts to convince the reader of their authenticity, were clearly intended to extend and amplify the teaching of Paul himself – they were as good as the real thing, and kept communities in touch with their spiritual leaders and more or less on the doctrinal rails.

Philosophical and religious belief produced then a genre of its own; another had its origin in a combination of romantic historical imagination with literary conceit. When the fifth and fourth centuries BC had passed into Greek and Roman consciousness as a legendary period of greatness, the temptation to bring some of the great names to life again by recreating their thoughts and feelings produced collections of pretend letters. There was no connected story, but various facts known or reported about famous characters were used as pegs from which to hang letters purporting to give the reader access to particularly intriguing moments of the past. Euripides, for instance, at the end of his life left Athens for faraway Macedon and the court of King Philip; if he had written to a friend in Athens, what might he have said? A literary letter-writer obliged. Likewise Socrates' unwillingness to commit anything to writing was legendary; nevertheless an enterprising letter-writer 'discovered' some correspondence.[19] It was not a large step from the invention of single letters to the creation of sequences of imaginary letters as a story-telling device, but with that the intentions became a little more complicated and the boundaries between historical curiosity, philosophical moralizing and literary invention a little more blurred. The sequences which told of the supposed meeting between Hippocrates and the 'laughing philosopher' Democritus or those which told the story of Chion of Heraclea, for instance, had at least two main purposes. They taught lessons, but there was also a conscious attempt to engage and entertain by means of literary and imaginative devices. Philosophy of a sort, entertainment and a kind of historical imagination became indissolubly mixed.

Letters like this pretended to have reference to real people and real situations even if their substance was largely imaginary. In the period of the so-called Second Sophistic (a loose term covering the first three centuries of the Christian era) the imaginary literary letter took leave of reality altogether and entered upon an artificial world of fancy and cultivated taste – not without its charm or its moments of sharp observation, but a long way from the letters of everyday life.[20] The language was artificial too – an attempt to hark back to the Greek which was spoken in the fifth and fourth centuries BC. Such letters were written for the admiration of highly cultivated and leisured readers and not least as a display of the author's skill and his literary and cultural credentials.

To move to a more general level, below the surface-subjects of literary letters of all kinds some modern scholars have detected themes which are part and parcel of 'ordinary' letters but which seem to crop up in intensified form in more artificial creations.[21] First, there is the tendency to dwell on the distance which separates the letter-writer from the supposed addressee, a distance which may be physical but can also be emotional – this usually being the cause of pain or frustration or a longing to bring the separation to an end. Following from this is a periodic unease about the medium of the letter itself: is it capable of making an adequate bridge, does it properly represent the character and intentions of the writer, or does it still leave an unsatisfying distance between the correspondents, not saying all that needs to be said?

This can go further and raise suspicions about whether a letter may in fact be playing tricks. On the surface letters are polite conversations at a distance and the conventional form involves formulas of greeting and best wishes for health and good fortune – they therefore look to be essentially friendly things. However, the first recorded Greek letter (or message) in Book vi of the *Iliad* in which Proitos tells the king of Lycia to murder Bellerophon uses this apparently friendly medium to send a treacherous and lethal message,[22] and thereafter many letters figuring in Greek literature (history and drama especially) seem to be involved in deception and violence. In the background there is sometimes a lurking suspicion that the friendly convention may be hiding something.[23]

The themes of many ordinary correspondents were of course simpler and more direct and linked to the problems of everyday life, the needs of individuals and the family, and the processes of administration and government. To a great extent the subjects of the surviving private and public letters reflect the particular circumstances of the Greek community in Egypt in Ptolemaic and Roman times and the world of the Hellenistic states before the coming of Rome. It is worth asking whether there are any topics we should expect to find which do not seem to crop up. In the private letters two spring to mind at once. First, in a society which had by modern standards a very high mortality rate we might expect to find a fair number of letters intended to console or sympathize with the bereaved. In fact, among some two thousand surviving papyrus letters only twelve or thirteen are of this character, and of those only six can be said to have had consolation or sympathy as their main purpose. None of them is earlier than the first century AD and two are plainly Christian; it may simply be an accident that three of the letters were written by women. It looks as though letters were not a usual way of expressing condolence; or perhaps death was so common and expected an occurrence in private life that it did not occasion the depth of emotional sympathy taken for granted today.[24] The other notable absence is what might be described in modern terms as the love letter. In poetry and imaginative prose there is a fine range of lovers' sighs and complaints, but in the letters of everyday life love is a theme almost entirely unrepresented. The private letter was evidently not a natural place or vehicle for romantic feelings; Greek lovers in Egypt cannot always have destroyed their letters. Behind this remarkable absence of two apparently basic areas of human experience – and perhaps also in the odd clues in the letters to what seem to be strangely hostile relationships between children and their parents – there may be a salutary warning against assuming that the many undoubtedly recognizable feelings and situations in the letters imply that we are meeting people who shared most of our perceptions and constructions of the world and who had notions of individuality very like our own. The 'otherness' of the ancient world is sometimes easy to forget.[25]

One extremely valuable opportunity offered by the letters is the rare chance to hear uncensored women's voices from the ancient Greek world and they are often a useful antidote to over-simplified views about women's subjection. Subject they may have been in all sorts of ways, and some were desperately poor and neglected, but some carried material responsibilities outside the home and were also remarkably independent and outspoken – not at all afraid of taking on officialdom when they felt that their rights were being infringed or their livelihoods put at risk.[26]

Another value of the original surviving letters is the evidence they give for the evolution of the Greek language. No languages remain static and, although some of the correspondents make mistakes and indeed in some cases have a very shaky command of Greek, the letters do chart changes in everyday language and provide useful evidence for changing habits of spelling and pronunciation.[27]

Writing and sending

The writing of letters is obviously one indication of the extent of literacy in various parts of the Greek world at various periods and this has been the subject of constant debate. Until recently it was often assumed that literacy was much more widespread than it almost certainly was, and a thorough survey of the meagre evidence and cautious use of modern comparative statistics suggests that, even in the most favourable circumstances – which are perhaps those of the Greek cities from the fourth to the first centuries BC from which many of the letters in this book come – the literacy rate was far below 50 per cent.[28] The implications for letter-writing and its place in society are obvious, but it is a mistake to think therefore that letters were solely the preserve of the literate. As still happens in parts of the Near and Far East, people who needed to write and read letters but could not do so themselves found it quite easy to employ those with the necessary basic skills who would work for modest fees. This was especially the case in the Hellenistic kingdoms where bureaucracy flourished, and most particularly in Egypt which had by far the most complicated administrative systems in the Greek world – systems which made demands on some of the lowliest in society.

The humblest surviving letters are those written for illiterate people by 'professional' letter-writers – the sender could not even manage a signature; in these the customer's wishes are translated into writing, often with much use of clichés and conventional formulas. The skill of the letter-writer, both as scribe and composer, varied greatly, and although the best professional secretaries were extremely good with language and used small and attractively uniform script, the street-corner service available to poorer people was something else – the writing could be poor with frequent spelling and grammar mistakes and the papyrus low-grade. Surprising people could not manage their own letters; a village clerk who kept an office might have been expected to have had the skill, but is described as one 'who did not know how to write'; presumably he had the use of someone who did.[29] The next stage up from the totally illiterate sender was the letter written by a scribe but to which the sender added his own name – sometimes written with obvious difficulty – or perhaps a phrase or two. Such correspondents were often politely referred to as 'slow writers'. However, the habit of adding something personal in your own hand became quite common and was not necessarily an indication of illiteracy; nevertheless, your writing might not be as neat as that of the professional scribe. Paul writing to the Christian community in Galatia added wryly 'See what large letters I make when I write in my own hand' and at the end of his first letter to Corinth he wrote the postscript himself.[30] The scribe's role extended from mechanical copyist to quite extensive drafting and composition; the careful administrator might rough out letters on the back of old documents, leaving the formalities to be added by the scribe, and monarchs might dictate expecting their court officials to put everything in due form.[31] If a scribe was well enough known to both parties, he might occasionally add his own best wishes to those of the sender at the end of a letter.

Official letters in government and administration were normally direct and to the point; they were meant for getting things done and the pleasantries were mostly formal, even if subordinates sometimes waxed a little fulsome. Moreover, it was assumed that such letters were meant for filing and future reference, so they were nearly always dated, and it was usual for the receiving office to add a brief note or docket identifying the subject-matter, sender and date (and sometimes the place) before the letter was filed. And if action was needed and subsequently taken, that too was recorded.[32]

With the letters which were originally written by philosophers and their disciples or with those written by religious missionaries to like-minded communities, something more fundamental happened to the letter. The form might remain (only just in some cases) but the politely transactional function which the letter-form seems to imply was overwhelmed by a strong didactic and instructional purpose. The conversation was no longer potentially two-sided; everything flowed from the writer to the addressees in the form of teaching or instruction. Replies were neither sought for nor were they appropriate. This applied to many of the letters in the New Testament and even more to the letters Epicurus wrote to explain an epitome of his scientific ideas; they were composed in the study from an urgent need to instruct or correct, and although particular individuals were nominally addressed, the letters were intended for a much wider readership and for 'publication'. This indeed was true (or became true) of many of the letters written to serve the purposes of philosophy or religion.

With literary letters the letter-form again became a disguise for one-way traffic; the conventions became a matter of secondary or even cosmetic utility. Even if a two-way exchange of letters was presented, the writer had the real reader always in mind and the over-riding purpose behind the writing was the awakening of sympathy, entertainment, curiosity, and all the elements of literary response. This even enabled the writer to make deliberate play with the conventions of letter-form.[33]

With 'real' letters one obvious problem was making sure that the letter was delivered. When it had been written, a papyrus letter was usually folded lengthways into a strip with a fibre of papyrus tied round and fixed to the letter by a clay seal; the address was then written on the outside. Addresses varied considerably according to how it was thought the letter would be conveyed. Some were very simple indeed: 'To Zenon', where the writer knew that the letter was going straight to the addressee by a reliable carrier. Occasionally fast delivery is indicated: 'To Zenon – now'. If it looked as though letters were in danger of not getting through, the address might be a little more specific: Sarapion, for instance had already sent two letters to Heracleides and on the outside of the third he wrote: 'Deliver to Alexandria, to the Imperial Market to … to Heracleides from Sarapion' (unfortunately the full wording cannot be read).[34] If the location was tricky, the address could be more precise still: Theon wrote to his mother and gave the address as: 'In the Teumenous quarter in the lane opposite the well'.[35] Safe delivery was problematic in the absence of a civilian postal service and was down to whoever was entrusted with the letter, someone for instance like a merchant who happened to be going to the right place. Where shorter distances were involved, a slave could be dispatched or even a paid letter-writer. If the carrier was sufficiently close to the writer or sufficiently trusted, he could be expected to explain or amplify the news conveyed, and the writer then not infrequently asked the recipient of the letter to look after his agent suitably:

'Heracleides, who is delivering this letter to you, is my brother, so I ask you to do all that you can to keep him under your protection.'[36] Government and local authority correspondence was another matter; in some places there were distribution networks available to officials. In classical times some Greek cities made use of specially appointed 'day-runners' for swift messaging – the legendary Pheidippides being an Athenian example. In the Hellenistic world senders of official documents and letters could make use of distribution systems which had been adapted from the highly efficient system instituted by the Persian king, Cyrus, in the sixth century BC for internal communication in his empire. This was based on a network of relay stations roughly a day's journey from each other for fast riders. Herodotus had come across it and thought it was wonderful; whatever the weather, the post got through, and 'no mortal agency is swifter than these messengers'.[37] Alexander's conquests bequeathed the same system to some of the Hellenistic kingdoms, and in 302 BC Antigonos I reorganized it with a network of 'book-carriers' *(bibliophoroi)* to serve the Seleucid kingdom. The system was developed even further by the Ptolemies in Egypt, who established a regular postal service for official communications which ran north and south throughout the kingdom based on relays of riders and sub-post offices, with a further service for heavier goods based on camel transport. Postal workers even had their own regional associations which had their own secretaries and among other things acted as centres for the allocation of the corn-rations which were part of the postal workers' employment package. Two receipts sent by the secretary of the Oxyrhynchos association survive; one reads:

> Menophilos, secretary of the postmen, to Bes, on the staff of Haruotes, royal secretary, greetings.
>
> I acknowledge that the due quantity [of corn] has been allotted through you from Ptolemaios, corn-supply officer of the eastern region, to the postal workers in the Oxyrhynchos district for Tubi and Mecheir of the seventh year – seventy [*artabai*] of wheat (70 art. wh.).[38]

The official postal service was a busy one. A part of the day-book for one of the sub-post offices survives from about 255 BC in which the clerk recorded the documents received and transmitted. The entry for the nineteenth day of whatever month it was gives some indication of the traffic including a record of the relay hand-over :

> 19th – at the eleventh hour
> Nicodemos from the lower region handed over to Timocrates [x] rolls
> From the King Ptolemy to Antiochos in the Heracleopolite district, 1 roll

To Demetrios in charge of elephant supply in the Thebaid, 1 roll
To Hippoteles left in charge by Antiochos at Apollonopolis the Great, 1 roll
From the King Ptolemy to Theugenes the money-messenger, 1 roll
To Heracleodoros in the Thebaid, 1 roll
To Zoilos, banker in the Hermopolite district, 1 roll
To Dionysios, administrator in the Arsinoite district, 1 roll[39]

Doubtless some of the business letters quoted in Chapter 3 were sent via this network. Under the Roman empire a remarkable international distribution system was set up by the emperor Augustus and maintained by his successors, the *cursus publicus*. This too was based on a relay principle, though it did not depend on horses – messengers sometimes travelled on foot. It became a regular vehicle for goods and official letters, including, it seems, communications from ordinary serving soldiers, and it is a tribute to its efficiency that young Greeks from Egypt who went to Italy to join the Roman armed services could have personal letters safely delivered to their parents in small towns in the Fayyum.

There were more exotic methods of sending letters and messages. In classical times one of the best known was the Spartan *skutale*, which Plutarch describes in some detail. It was said to be used by Spartan magistrates when they needed to communicate with naval or military commanders abroad. Two identical round sticks were made, the diameters being crucial, and a strip of leather was wound slantwise around one of the sticks. The message was written along the length of the stick and, when the leather was unwound, the strip of leather was illegible. The commander who possessed the other stick only had to unroll the leather strip when he received it, wind it on to his stick, and read off the message. This may well have been a Spartan custom, but it can hardly have been a very effective secret-keeper.[40] More thorough-going are some of the secret delivery devices reported by Herodotus. Apart from a Persian using the dead body of a hare as a post-bag (i.125), Greeks, he said, made use of two devices for sending secret letters. Histiaios, tyrant of Miletus, who was being detained by the Persians in Susa, needed to get a letter to his relative Aristagoras urging him to lead a revolt of the Ionians:

> Having shaved the head of his most reliable slave, he tattooed it and waited for the hair to grow again. As soon as it had, he sent him to Miletus with orders to do nothing when he got there except tell Aristagoras to shave the hair and look at his head. The tattoo carried the message about the revolt as I explained before.[41]

The other device made use of the folded waxed tablet – the natural form for a letter when papyrus was not commonly available. Demaratos, a Spartan king detained in Persia, needed to get a message home to warn of the coming Persian invasion:

> Having taken the folded tablet, he scraped off the wax and then wrote on the wood of the tablet what the King's intentions were. Having done this he poured molten wax back over the writing so that if the tablet was being carried it would cause no trouble with guards on the roads.[42]

This trick was borrowed by a Greek military writer, probably a general, usually referred to in Latinized form as Aeneas Tacticus, who wrote a treatise in about the middle of the fourth century BC about siege warfare.[43] Section 31 of his handbook lists useful ways of sending letters secretly, and the device of writing under the wax is described with similarities of wording which leave little doubt that Aeneas took it from Herodotus. Other modes of sending secret letters described by Aeneas are closer to Cold War techniques: there is the device of lightly dotting letters in an otherwise harmless book or document so that the recipient who knows about the dots can recover the message (31.2). Then there is the trick of doctoring a messenger's sandals by unstitching the sole and inserting a message written on a thin sheet of tin (for durability) while the messenger is asleep; the messenger is then given a harmless missive. The recipient waits till the messenger is again asleep, unstitches the sole, reads the message and sends a reply by the same method, supplying of course a fake response to be taken back. Aeneas helpfully notes that you have to be careful with the stitching (31.4)! Lead makes another appearance; messages can be written on small, thin leaden sheets which are rolled up and can be worn disguised as ladies' ear-rings (31.7).

The materials of letter-writing

The oldest vehicles for letter-writing were probably wooden writing tablets in their different forms, and it is very likely that the habit of using them was imported along with the adaptation of the alphabet from the Semitic world.[44] There were two kinds in common use: the more familiar, and perhaps the more expensive, consisted of a very shallow, hollowed wooden rectangle into which molten wax was poured to form a smooth writing surface. The pen used to inscribe the wax was a short pointed rod of metal, ivory or wood, often with a broad blade at one end to scrape the wax and make corrections. Many examples of such tablets survive and they were sometimes assembled book-like in sets of up to nine, the hinges being supplied by thongs passed through holes in the margins of the tablets; the sequence of tablets in a set was sometimes indicated by the simple device of a diagonal saw-cut across the outer edges. Fairly short messages or letters could be accommodated on two tablets folded, with the two waxed surfaces which carried the writing facing inwards, and this may be what Homer refers to in what is often cited as a reference to the first Greek letter when in Book vi of the *Iliad* Proitos sent his dire message 'in a folded tablet'.[45] Large numbers of the other type of writing tablet in familiar use have quite recently come to light in the astonishing finds at Vindolanda, the fort close to Hadrian's Wall in Northumberland, some of which are letters. They consist of thin wood leaves, between 1 mm and 3 mm thick, with a smooth surface; leaves are again sometimes used in pairs face-to-face so that the writing on the inside is protected. The writing is in durable ink – carbon in a solution of gum arabic and water.[46] All these tablets are written in Latin, but the same form was used in the Greek world, and tablets of both kinds – waxed and plain wood – were commonly employed in situations like schooling or accounting where erasing and re-use were part and parcel of the process. Sometimes the surface of a plain wooden tablet was whitened to highlight the writing; on one such a tablet a hapless Greek schoolboy was made to practise copying the model sentence 'Work hard, boy or you'll be beaten.'[47] The wood used for such tablets was often local – birch, alder and oak on Hadrian's Wall, but in the Mediterranean lime was common.[48] Before papyrus became readily available in Greece, writing tablets seem to have been the natural medium for sending more formal messages and for writing letters. No examples of early letters survive, but Euripides, for instance, writing towards the end of the fifth century BC, took it for granted that his audience would expect personal, important letters written in the past to take the form of sealed or tied writing tablets rather than papyrus.[49] Although most of the surviving writing tablets of all kinds come from Egypt, none contains a formal letter – there it must always have been easier and cheaper to use papyrus.

A rather unexpected medium for early Greek letters was the thin sheet of lead. Six examples survive, the best-known being a letter which someone called Achillodoros meant to send to his son and to another person, Anaxagoras. It was written about 500 BC, probably in the region of the Milesian colony of Borysthenes near modern Berezan, a small island in a river estuary east of Odessa. The sheet is about 1 mm thick and rectangular (153 × 65 mm) and was discovered tightly rolled and sticking out of a high bank. The address is written on the outside and the text is written in neat, easily readable letters; the dialect is Ionic, the dialect of Miletus.[50] It is undoubtedly a letter, even though it does not yet show any of the usual Greek letter conventions, and in the address it is identified simply as 'Achillodoros' lead', apparently no obvious word for 'letter' coming to the writer's mind. Two other examples of Greek letters on lead sheets were found in the neighbourhood of Olbia and one has been found in Attica dating to the fourth century BC;[51] another has turned up at Emporion in Spain just north of Barcelona and appears to date from the first quarter of the fifth century BC.[52] There are also occasional mentions of letters like these in ancient authors[53] but it seems that lead sheets were an exceptional writing material. This prompts the question of why lead was used at all; thin lead sheeting, after all, cannot have been so very readily to hand. The answer probably lies in two specialized uses of lead as a vehicle for messages in the ancient world. Curse tablets on which one person ritually invoked dire ills upon another were frequently made of small rectangles of lead sheet, rolled up and sometimes stuck through with a pin. Likewise at some oracles like that at Dodona in Epirus questions were addressed to the oracle on small lead sheets, the answers being given verbally.[54] Lead 'blanks' were therefore available in some places, and it is not such a big step to think of using them for messages to human beings rather than divine powers.

Broken pieces of pottery – *ostraca* – were the scrap-paper of the ancient world and the vast majority of written messages on *ostraca* are simple receipts, short notes and messages, lists and records of the usual minutiae of everyday life.[55] They do not seem to be the obvious medium for letters, but there are examples where the formalities of the letter are used and where the correspondents do not seem to feel that they are doing anything unusual in writing on broken pot. For example, in the first century AD a certain Memnon wrote a letter to two corn-agents on a piece of pot and expected an answer on a similar medium: 'You would oblige me by giving your *ostracon* to the person who is delivering this letter.'[56] Nevertheless there usually seems to be a particular reason for choosing an *ostracon*. In a remote Roman fort to the east of the Nile surrounded by mountains, forty-eight letters written in Greek on *ostraca* were discovered, dated to a short period in Trajan's reign.[57] Many are domestic letters in which the writers are trying to keep in touch with friends and family in the Nile valley; they take it for granted that their own letters are written on *ostraca* and again expect similar replies. Maximus had quarrels with both his sister and his brother and wrote to his sister telling her that she should have tried to mend things: 'You should have told him, "Write an *ostracon* to your brother."'[58] Another set of letters on *ostraca* which also seems to come from a military context and is probably to be dated to the mid-first century AD contains similar evidence of taking the *ostracon* letter for granted.[59] Another Maximus wrote to his sister who was about to have a baby: 'the man who is bringing you this *ostracon* is returning … to me. Through him don't forget to write about the house-by-house census.'[60] Maximus wrote on an unusually large piece of broken pot (173 × 155 mm), and his letter shares a peculiarity with many of the other letters in the two collections mentioned in that it is written in Greek by someone with a straight Roman name. The correspondents may be Greeks who had joined the Roman armed forces and had therefore had to take Roman names. The military contexts may be the reason for the use of *ostraca*; perhaps soldiers could not or would not afford to buy papyrus. There are stories suggesting that *ostraca* were used when you could not afford anything else: Zeno's student, Cleanthes, was said to have taken down Zeno's lectures 'on *ostraca* and the blade-bones of oxen' because he had no money to buy papyrus.[61]

Nearly all the letters in this book were originally written on papyrus, even if some were later transcribed on to stone. Papyrus sheet was arguably Egypt's most important technological contribution to Mediterranean civilization and had a run of at least 4,000 years (the earliest extant roll dates from *c.* 3000 BC and the last surviving documents to the mid-eleventh century AD).[62] It was made from a type of papyrus plant which still grows in southern Sudan in fresh water. The stems are long and triangular in section and are formed of a tough green skin with a white pith. The top of the stem carries a splayed mass of brown leaves, and that characteristic shape and the bright green colour of the plant made the papyrus marshes the equivalent in Egyptian art of the European pastoral landscape. Papyrus came to be used as the name of both the plant and the writing material made from it. Papyrus sheets for writing were made by peeling or cutting strips of pith, putting them side by side to form a sheet and over-topping them with another layer of pith strips at right-angles. Pressure was then applied with either a mallet or a press and, provided that the pith was fresh, the two layers adhered naturally to produce, when dry, a smooth, thin writing surface which was quite supple enough to be rolled or folded. The pith contained fine fibres, and on the one side the fibres ran horizontally (the *recto* in modern parlance), on the other vertically (the *verso*). Writing with the flow of the fibres was obviously easier, so the *recto* was the normally preferred side for writing. Papyrus was distributed, bought and sold by the roll and the individual sheets were glued together with a flour paste, the joins usually being left over right (scribal convenience again). The quality of the surface and the colour mattered, and finer grades were probably bleached in the sun to produce as whitened a surface as possible which was also lightly smoothed. Quality varied greatly (some of the earlier papyri being the finest), and by the time that Pliny the Elder wrote his *Natural History* in the latter half of the first century AD there was a wide choice ranging from the top-quality hieratic (which had been tactfully rebranded as Augustan) to the emporitic (shopping-grade and only good for wrapping-paper).[63] In Egypt there was doubtless even greater choice: in the second/third century AD there even seems to have been a letter-grade.[64] Most personal letters were no longer than could be fitted on to one sheet of papyrus and perhaps the need to cut sheets from a roll was a useful discipline; one of the critic Demetrius' recommendations on style was that letters should not be over-long.

It is not certain when papyrus became a major export to the Greek world. It was certainly being distributed in the Near East in some quantity as early as the twelfth or eleventh century BC, for Zakar-Baal, the ruler of Byblos, is said then to have received 500 rolls in exchange for timber.[65] Byblos may have been a distribution point for places further away, for the Greeks adopted the place-name to denote both the papyrus plant and the papyrus roll. Guesses put the early use of papyrus in Greece around the seventh century BC, and the establishment of a regular Greek trading station at Naucratis in the

Nile delta during the reign of Psammetichos I (664–610 BC) must have given the opportunity for an increased supply.[66] By the fifth century BC papyrus was clearly a regularly available writing material in Greece (for Herodotus it was outlandish *not* to use it – v.58), though it was probably never cheap and may not have been in common use for purposes like writing letters until the following century. The actual cost of papyrus in the ancient Greek world is notoriously hard to estimate and must have varied hugely.[67] However, by the time most of the letters in this book were composed, writers would not have considered any other medium unless there special circumstances like military service in a remote posting.

The ink used for writing on papyrus was a combination of a simple pigment, usually carbon for black ink, with a binding agent like gum arabic. Egyptian scribes also used red ink with ground haematite as the pigment, and this was used to highlight important features like accounting totals or dates (hence the tradition of red-letter dates). Pens were mostly reed pens with split nibs, though there are examples of brush-writing.[68] People probably wrote with work on their knees or on a table; the classic position of the Egyptian scribe with a papyrus resting on a garment or cloth tightly stretched across the lap was appropriate for writing with a brush but not at all convenient for pen-work.[69]

One writing material which crops up intermittently in the historical record but was rarely used by Greeks for letters is leather or parchment; its use seems to be associated with difficulties in the supply of papyrus.[70] Herodotus reported, for instance, that the Ionian Greeks used the skins of goats or sheep (i.e. conventionally 'parchment') because they could not easily get papyrus, and a well-known story attributed by Pliny to Varro assigned the 'invention' of parchment to the city of Pergamum at a time when rivalry with Egypt over libraries cut off imports of papyrus (probably in the reign of Eumenes II – 197–159 BC). The story is plainly false (along with the supposed invention of papyrus at the time of Alexander the Great!), but until the Christian era, when parchment became an element in the development of the *codex* or book-form, leather and parchment seem to have been reserved for special purposes like the keeping of sacred or canonic texts (Euripides talks of the prophecies of Apollo recorded on leather, Hippocrates' son is said to have come across his father's memoirs written on leather, and the writer of the second New Testament letter to Timothy tells him 'to bring the papyrus books and especially the leathers').[71] The medium was sometimes used for official transactions and records; the kings of Persia had their deeds recorded on leather, and much diplomatic and military correspondence in the Persian empire seems to have used this material. Early in the first century BC the Council and people of Priene recorded their official thanks to their secretary, Zosimos, 'because he had given security to a faithful record of the documents entrusted to him by making a double transcript of them in the medium of both leather and papyrus'.[72] It would not be improbable that some Greek letters were written on parchment, but the likelihood is that they would have been official or even ceremonial documents; none have survived.[73]

The letters which have survived on stone inscriptions are nearly all transcripts of texts originally written on papyrus. They were official publications which made the intentions of the sovereign or the governing bodies clear both to executives and to the people governed. They were cut by professional stonecutters and were set up in places usually specified in the document itself – mostly central and obvious public spaces like the agora or temple precincts.

Ancient theory and practice – teaching and learning

Quite apart from casual mentions of the uses and delights of letters in ancient authors, a number of works, or sections of works, survive from the ancient Greek world which seem consciously to stand back from the everyday process of letter-writing and try to describe it, analyse it and teach it. All are concerned with 'real' letter-writing rather than letters conceived as literature, for ancient literary critics seem largely to have ignored letters composed with avowed literary intent. In a society in which the manner as well as the matter of what was said became steadily more important, particularly under the growing influence of rhetoric, personal presentation through an intimate means of communication like the letter began to attract attention too. Guidance came in two main forms: style and substance. Style seemed to reveal the character of the writer with particular honesty, so proper writing went with proper character and perhaps helped to form it – *le style, c'est l'homme même.* Along with this went a passion – almost an academic passion – for the classification and categorization of substance which marked many ancient attempts to produce practical handbooks. So letters were divided into one-purpose categories – e.g. the letter of blame, the letter of commendation, the letter of apology – and definitions were given followed by typical sample passages to offer skeleton content and a flavour of style appropriate to the topic. It is very uncertain how much such handbooks were used; certain obvious letter-types can be identified, but on the whole much actual correspondence displays a variety and mixture which does not fall easily into neat categories.

The earliest Greek critic to deal with letter-writing at all analytically was Demetrius, who was probably active in the middle of the second century BC.[74] He wrote an essay *On Style* and a short section of it (223–35) was devoted to the appropriate style for a letter – not, however, the proper formalities of the letter. The examples he used included Plato and Aristotle (including Plato's *Letter vii*) and he began with an observation attributed to Artemon, the editor of Aristotle's letters. The style of a letter, he said, should be plain, and it should be written in the same way as a dialogue – that is, a conversation – for a letter is one side of a conversation. Demetrius only partly agreed:

> Perhaps he has a point, but not the whole story; for a letter needs rather more care than a conversation, since a conversation presents someone speaking *extempore* whereas the letter is written down and is sent as a kind of gift.

The style of letters, according to Demetrius, should not come over as self-consciously oratorical or be punctuated with short breaks such as one finds in a script meant for acting (the opening of Plato's *Euthydemus* is interestingly taken as an example of a dramatic scene). Letters should be characterful for 'everyone draws a picture of his soul' in his letters, and, although other kinds of writing reveal an author's true nature, none does this so well as a letter. Letters should not become too long or they risk becoming tracts (many of Plato's letters are given as examples and 'the letter of Thucydides' – almost certainly Nicias' long dispatch to the Athenians in Book ii). Another trap is stylistic – the kind of artful, patterned composition to be found in courtroom speeches is not suitable for friends who are used to 'brass tacks'. One point made with tantalizing brevity is that there are some subjects suitable for letters and, by implication, some that are not. Aristotle – by repute a very good letter-writer – is quoted in support, and Demetrius goes on to outlaw learned arguments and natural science, so perhaps it is academic subjects of an Aristotelian kind which are thought not to belong; he does not appear to be thinking of the kind of 'epistolary topics' which have preoccupied some modern theorists. A letter, he continues, is a concise expression of goodwill – simple subjects in simple words. Proverbs and friendly expressions rather than cleverness go to create a feeling of togetherness; sententious people teaching lessons communicate artificially in letters, not naturally. Official letters between cities and monarchs need a rather more elevated style but they should not become tracts (Plato and Aristotle again). Demetrius concludes with a summary: 'A letter, so far as style is concerned, should be a mingling of two characteristics – the graceful and the plain.'

Of all the ancient writers on the 'theory' of letters Demetrius is much the most interesting and perceptive, as well as the earliest. If the second century BC is the correct context, he wrote when letter-writing was becoming an accepted part of life in educated Greek circles but had probably not been much theorized, for, though he quotes a particularly happy observation from Artemon, he does so almost as mentioning a colleague rather than an authority. He clearly had access to Aristotle's letters – perhaps Artemon had written an introduction. Along with his sensitive and civilized feelings about ordinary letters, Demetrius is also aware and not entirely approving of the letter when it breaks its 'natural' bounds and risks becoming formally something else, either because it is too long or because its stylistic tone and subject-matter are inappropriate; he sees Plato and Thucydides sometimes heading in the wrong direction and warns others off. He is not, however, as the title of his work *On Style* shows, chiefly concerned with form but with the 'feel' of a good letter and what kind of writing contributes to it.

The other surviving pieces of Greek epistolary theory are very much concerned with form, and, though the two major works start from an analytical overview of different types of letter, the avowed purpose of both is to instruct the reader in how to write particular letters properly, and they can justly be described as handbooks rather than works of criticism. The lesser-known is the work entitled *The Types of Letter* by an unknown author and wrongly attributed to Theophrastus' pupil, Demetrius of Phaleron (the author is usually referred to as Pseudo-Demetrius). The date at which it was written is quite uncertain and it may well have been through several revisions; the wide limits suggested lie between 200 BC and 300 AD.[75]

The work is addressed to one Heracleides and the declared purpose is to give him the means to train as a professional letter-writer, 'one of those who undertake such work for those who are in management'. Heracleides appears to be older than the usual trainee for such work and the author therefore feels it necessary to enter a special plea for adult education. He then lists twenty-one types of letter (while admitting that more might be included if one had the time to think about it): the friendly, the commendatory, the blaming, the reproachful, the consolatory, the censorious, the admonitory, the threatening, the vituperative, the laudatory, the advisory, the supplicatory, the questioning, the responsive, the allegorical, the explanatory, the accusatory, the apologetic, the congratulatory, the ironic and the letter of thanks. This list is followed by twenty-one definitions and examples; the examples are not complete letters but a handy guide to the kind of phraseology which might be useful, including, where appropriate, a skeleton structure. So in Section 2 the commendatory letter is treated thus:

> The commendatory type is one in which we write to someone on behalf of someone else, interweaving praise with talking as though people previously unknown to each other have actually been acquainted – like this:
>
> *x* who is bringing you this letter has been selected by us and, because of the trust we have in him, is warmly regarded; you will oblige me if you think it worth accepting him – both for my sake and for his, and for your own. For you will not be sorry if, in any matters you choose, you ask him to say or do anything which is private. Indeed you will praise him to others when you realize what service he can provide.

The advisory letter in Section 11 seems to envisage Heracleides punching well above his weight, for the author clearly imagines him now to be writing on behalf of one king to another:[76]

> I have given you a summary of the reasons why I am held in high regard by the people over whom I rule. Therefore I know that you too by following this course can win the goodwill of your obedient subjects, and, while you cannot make a large number of friends, you can treat everyone with moderation and humanity. If you are someone of this character, you will have a good reputation among the masses and your power will be unassailable.

Some sections are absurdly trite, e.g. the responsive letter in Section 14: 'You wrote to find out if *x* is still with us; he still is and says he will stay and wait for you.'

The other major work on letter-writing, *On the Form of Letters*, exists in two versions, one allegedly by the fourth century AD rhetorician and formidable letter-writer Libanius, the other by the fifth century AD neo-Platonist, Proclus. Both versions almost certainly derive from a common source but there is no way of knowing at what date that was written.[77] It claims to teach better letter-writing and at the outset lays out an academic agenda: letters should not be written simply as the moment takes the writer but with stylistic precision (*akribeia*) and art (*techne*) – two words with all kinds of rhetorical resonance. To do this one has to know what a letter is. A brief definition of a letter as a written conversation is followed by a list of no fewer than forty-one letter-types, some of them corresponding to those in the handbook addressed to Heracleides, and, after the list there is a series of very short definitions of each of the letter-types. The definitions are not very revealing:

> The blaming type is one in which we blame someone. (6)
> The insulting type is one in which we insult someone for something. (26)

The arid and unhelpful taxonomy is only slightly relieved by Sections 46–51 in which there are some general remarks about style. One topic of the moment was plainly how far to go in using archaizing Greek imitative of fifth century BC usage (Atticism) in a well-composed letter. Moderation is recommended, as well as choosing a middle way between wordiness and terseness – the favourite rhetorical figure of the archer aiming at a target being introduced. The final section offers some brief examples of phraseology for the different types of letter, but they are dryly academic and one can hardly imagine a real letter-writer getting much help from them – far less practical than those written for Heracleides:

> The commendatory type: 'When you have received this most respected and sought-after man, do not hesitate to give him hospitality; you will be doing what is fitting for you and pleasing to me.' (55)

Works like those of pseudo-Demetrius and Libanius/Proclus prompt questions about the teaching and acquisition of elementary letter-writing skills in the Greek world. It has been very plausibly suggested that, once established, the long-lasting form and conventions of the Greek letter imply that learning to compose one became a normal part of elementary education.[78] If so, instruction would have been given by the *grammatistes* or the *grammatikos*, for letter-writing never seems to have figured as a regular part of more advanced rhetorical training, even though there are obvious links between aspects of rhetorical education like *prosopopoieia* (creation of character) and some of the more sophisticated imaginary letter-writing. The evidence for this special kind of elementary instruction is unfortunately very sparse. Four model letters dated to 164–3 BC survive, and it is a fair guess that copying such models followed by close imitation was the normal mode of learning.[79] This certainly seems to be the case with the much later fourth or fifth century AD papyrus acquired from an Egyptian dealer in 1930 by the University of Bologna. Here there are parts of eleven model letters. The second full letter is a good example:

> I learned that Licinius, a true friend of yours, had died. I am sorry that he was so little mindful of your loyalty but I urge you to bear it resolutely. For men make wills about their final legacies but it is the Fates who distribute them.[80]

The text is in both Greek and Latin, with an almost word-for-word translation, and is written with word-division in the Latin but not in the Greek, perhaps suggesting that the author thought Latin the less familiar language. The letters are set out in narrow columns with words or phrases aligned so that the language parallels are clear. It may therefore have been intended for Greek-speakers who needed Latin or for Egyptian-speakers who needed both. The quoted letter is one of three classified as 'letters giving counsel on very small legacies' and the subject-matter of the whole set gives an indication of the intended users. Nine of the eleven letters are about wills and legacies and the document looks very like a part of a training manual for para-legal secretaries.

Something like a credible pattern therefore begins to emerge. The outline of the basic family letter with its regular constituents of wishes for good health, thanks for letters or gifts received, assurances of remembrance in prayers and final greetings to friends and relations was probably taught as a part of elementary education, and preserved and consolidated by that social expectation which still shapes such letters today. For those whose education did not stretch that far or who had for other reasons to leave it to others, professional letter-writers were employed who with varying degrees of skill put verbal messages into epistolary form. In middle management literacy was nearly always taken for granted, and administrators and officials relied heavily on trained secretarial and office staff: letters were drafted or dictated to secretaries, and correspondence was docketed and filed, with any action taken recorded. In the upper reaches of administration – the chanceries of the Hellenistic kings, for instance – standards of drafting were high. We possess only the end-products of such secretaries' work in letter-inscriptions displayed for the public but they imply an efficient and sophisticated bureaucracy. Responsible secretaries must have received formal training for specialized work and this was probably delivered by a system of apprenticeship; a contractual letter from Roman times (AD 155) gives an indication of how specialized such training could be:

> Panechotes, also known as Panares, ex-*cosmetes* of the city of Oxyrhynchos, by his friend Gemellus to Apollonios, the shorthand writer, greetings.
>
> I have placed my slave, Chairammon, with you with a view to learning the signs which your son Dionysios knows. This is for a period of two years from the present month, Phamenoth, in the eighteenth year of Lord Caesar Antoninus. The due fee agreed between us is 120 silver drachmas (feast-days excepted) of which you have had the first 40 drachmas and will get the second of 40 drachmas when the slave has mastered the manual; the third – the remaining 40 drachmas – you will get at the end of the period, when the boy can write and read from any kind of prose with no mistakes. If you get him ready within the time, I will not wait for the agreed termination date (though I have the right to take the slave away within the agreed period), and he will stay with you after the agreed period for as many days or months as he has been off work.
>
> The eighteenth year of the Emperor Caesar Titus Aelius Hadrianus Antoninus Augustus Pius. The 5th of Phamenoth.[81]

A system of Greek shorthand had become quite highly developed by the second century AD and a two-year apprenticeship is not surprising. The manual which was one of the chief landmarks in Chairammon's training was a long list of word-groups, four or sometimes eight words to a group, each group being represented by a single sign.[82] This apprenticeship was obviously a big investment for Pachotes; ordinary writing apprenticeships were undoubtedly less costly and demanding.

The handbook of Pseudo-Demetrius addressed to Heracleides fits into this pattern of training quite well. The classification of letter-types is a predictable component of a training regime, and an apprentice letter-writer would have found the sample passages which comprise the bulk of the work a useful workaday thesaurus of phraseology and vocabulary for different kinds of letter. The handbook of Libanius/Proclus is another matter; it smacks very much of an academic approach for its own sake, and it may even indicate that the subject of letters had become an option in some courses of rhetorical education. It would have been of little help to the practising scribe.

The sources of the letters

All the letters in this book composed for literary, philosophical or religious purposes have survived in the way that most ancient literature has come down to us; that is, through a network of manuscript copies, copied and copied again since the end of antiquity, with all the consequent difficulties for the establishment of a reliable text.[83] The coming of the printing press enforced a degree of uniformity and gave editors a new set of responsibilities, but it by no means prevented the dissemination of seriously faulty texts and, if anything, tended to emphasize the gap between the original author and the reader.

The same does not apply to the business and private letters on papyrus included in this book; in nearly every case it is possible to hold in the hand the actual letters which traders, young soldiers, cross parents, angry victims of violence or somewhat stressed administrators wrote. The discovery of these original letters is an important part of the story of the recovery of a vast quantity of evidence about the working of one part of the ancient world which happened for the most part from the 1880s onwards. The sudden uncovering of large numbers of authentic papyrus documents led to high hopes; the great Theodore Mommsen declared that the nineteenth century had been the age of inscriptions, and the twentieth would be the age of papyri. Initial dramatic advances in the recovery of some ancient texts and the revelations of a bureaucracy at work have not been followed by quite the same order of success, but the flow goes on and what has been discovered has already added enormously to the understanding of the personal, economic and political world of Greek communities, particularly of course in Egypt.[84]

Papyri made their first big impression on the modern world with the discovery of hundreds of papyrus rolls in excavations at Herculaneum in 1752. Unfortunately the rolls were carbonized and brittle, but diligent modern attempts to unfold the rolls and read the texts have identified many of them as books of Epicurean philosophy, in particular the works of Philodemos, who settled at Herculaneum and was a contemporary of Cicero and Horace, both of whom mention him.[85] The discovery did not, however, produce a scholarly revolution; it was very much a part of the pleasure taken by eighteenth-century travellers in exotic relics of the past which filled many English country houses with antiquities. Odd papyrus rolls turned up elsewhere and there were even stories of bundles of forty or fifty rolls offered for sale in Egypt. Some consular staff in Egypt from Britain, France and Scandinavia became genuinely interested in ancient relics and began building up collections which included papyri; some of these attracted the attention of scholars and were published. It was not, however, until the late 1870s that there was anything like a full realization of what was waiting to be discovered in Egypt. In 1877 literally thousands of papyri came to light from Arsinoe, capital of the Fayyum, where conditions for the survival of papyri at certain levels were excellent; nearby sites like Heracleopolis and Hermopolis were also prolific sources. These papyri were realized for what they were and found their way to Vienna, where they formed the bulk of the collection of Archduke Rainer, steadily becoming the objects of scholarly attention and systematic publication. The flood-gates were opening and in the 1880s local Egyptian dealers and anyone there, great or small, with an eye to making money out of apparent rubbish began searching and digging. Great museums and national libraries commissioned and dispatched scholars or agents on buying expeditions; Sir Wallis Budge, acting for the British Museum in 1888, came back with a spectacular haul which proved to contain Aristotle's lost *Constitution of Athens*, speeches of Isocrates and Hypereides, a letter of Demosthenes and the *Mimes* of Herodas. Not all buying expeditions were so successful. The vast majority of documents recovered were neither manuscripts of great authors nor New Testament/ apocryphal fragments but the small change of ordinary life – receipts, notes, orders, lists, requests, requisitions, etc., and of course private and business letters. From the start there was always a certain bias of interest in scholarly papyrologists towards literary or biblical finds, and it is really only in recent times that the value and interest of the more humdrum documents has been realized.[86]

In the 1880s the British archaeologist W. Flinders Petrie discovered a new source of papyrus documents, particularly important for the Ptolemaic era. Mummy-cases had often been made from a kind of papier-mâché composed of layers of papyrus – cartonnage. The layers were relatively easy to separate and in 1891 he published a series of documents recovered in this way. The technique continues to be an important source of new material, though there are now more scruples about the destruction of ancient burial cases.

By the 1890s there is the impression of an almost uncontrollable free-for-all in the papyrus market. Egyptian inspectors of antiquities were no more successful than their modern Italian counterparts in Etruria and, when so much depended on chance finds in the country and often illicit digging and dealing, the situation easily got out of hand. The British were the first to realize the possibilities of properly focused, professional excavation with papyri as the main objective. In 1895 the Egypt Exploration Fund was launched (later to become the still-thriving Egypt Exploration Society), and the following year three first-rate scholars were commissioned to lead an expedition – D.G. Hogarth, B.P. Grenfell and A.S. Hunt.[87] In the winter of 1896 they moved to the site of ancient Oxyrhynchos – the City of the Sharp-Nosed Fish[88] – partly in the hope of making some religious finds. After a slow and disappointing start, in January 1897 they dug a low mound of what looked like rubbish. The results were astounding. As the excavations were extended to similar mounds, papyri came to light in huge quantities, and though the dates of the papyri and their state of preservation varied considerably, the excavators had discovered a treasure-house. In the report on the first season's work which Grenfell wrote for his sponsors, the Egypt Exploration Fund, the language is measured and careful, but even so, when he describes two bumper days in March the infectious excitement the excavators must have felt comes through:

> The third and by far the greatest find, that of the Byzantine archives, took place on March 18th and 19th, and was, I suppose, a 'record' in point of quantity. On the first of these two days we came upon a mound which had a thick layer consisting almost entirely of papyrus rolls. There was room for six pairs of men and boys to be working simultaneously at this storehouse, and the difficulty was to find enough baskets in all Behneseh to contain the papyri. At the end of the day's work no less than thirty-six good-sized baskets were brought in from this place, several of them stuffed with fine rolls three to ten feet long, including some of the largest Greek rolls I have ever seen. As the baskets were required for the next day's work, Mr Hunt and I started at 9 p.m. after dinner to stow away the papyri in some empty packing-cases which we fortunately had at hand. The task was only finished at three in the morning and on the following night we had a repetition of it.[89]

The first volume of a series still running, *The Oxyrhynchus Papyri*, appeared the following year in 1898 – a remarkable feat of scholarship and hard work.

Other countries swiftly realized the opportunities there could be, and expeditions from Germany, France and Italy followed with some notable successes, though not on the same scale. Private sales by dealers continued and, since the prices were rocketing, national syndicates of academic and other institutions began to be formed. In 1907 Grenfell and Hunt left Oxyrhynchos, and the concession they had from the Egyptian Department of Antiquities lapsed. The flood had abated somewhat, but from time to time some spectacular finds still came to light. One of these is particularly relevant to a number of letters in this book, for in 1915 on the site of ancient Philadelphia in the Fayyum some Egyptian farmers came across the discarded office papers of Zenon, chief administrator to Apollonios, Ptolemy II's Minister of Finance. It was a huge collection, the largest Greek archive which had been discovered, and it was made up of letters, copies of letters, drafts of letters, memos, receipts, etc. – all the usual contents of an office filing-system belonging to a responsible executive and covering a period of twenty years (from 260 to 240 BC). Other important archives have survived too, but none is so comprehensive as Zenon's. If ever there was a case for keeping documents that belong together in the same place, Zenon's office correspondence must surely qualify. But the wild free market in papyri had disastrous results; the majority of documents very properly went eventually to the Cairo Museum and were published from there. However, agents on the spot also bought up quite sizeable numbers, and the office-archive which had remained intact from 240 BC until AD 1915 is now split up among many owners. The British Museum acquired a good selection and these documents have only recently been edited – albeit in exemplary fashion.[90] Some indication of the gargantuan problems of co-ordination, indexing and cataloguing which have resulted from this fragmentation can be seen in the modestly titled guide to the Zenon archive compiled by a Dutch scholar, Professor P.W. Pestman and his team of collaborators.[91] Since the Golden Age of discovery there has been a steady stream of new finds (and old ones edited), including numbers of letters, and it is always possible that new collections will be unearthed.

The letters from kings to their subjects which occupy the bulk of Chapter 4 also began life as papyrus documents, but the originals, which were doubtless recorded in a filing system much more comprehensive than Zenon's, have perished and what remains are the ancient copies on inscriptions – the authorization and funding for which is often detailed in the documents themselves. The evidence is therefore straight from the ancient world, but it is what the subjects of the Hellenistic kings saw in their towns – the conclusion of royal bureaucracy rather than the stuff of its operation. Most of the inscriptions were discovered as a result of the remarkable series of large-scale excavations launched from Germany at the end of the nineteenth century. The best known is probably the thorough exploration of the Hellenistic city of Pergamum, which resulted in handsome volumes recording the results and the building of the famous Pergamon-Museum in Berlin. Other expeditions were sent to Miletus, Priene and Magnesia-on-the-Maeander and also yielded rich finds.[92]

2

PERSONAL AND FAMILY LETTERS

Reading other people's letters has always been a tempting prospect. Private letters seem to give unique clues to the way people think and feel, or, at the very least, to the way they want to present themselves to their addressees. Private letter-writers certainly use conventions of both form and style, but even ancient letters are not all formulaic and readers must have expected that the voice they heard through the words was a fair reflection of personality. Letters do seem to get near to the heart of a person and, if we cannot still talk with them, the chance to hear 'one side of a conversation' may be the next best thing.

Nearly all the letters in this chapter were written with no self-conscious eye on the future and with no attempt to win admiration for their cleverness or learning. They were written by ordinary people in ordinary situations for ordinary purposes, and the writers would have been surprised to learn that their letters had survived and were still the subjects of attention. They capture flashes of real life in the ancient Greek world, moments of pleasure, panic, stress, joy, frustration, anxiety and so on. These feelings often strike a chord of familiarity – young men are still proud of their first career successes and parents are still anxious when their children leave home and go on risky journeys – and this sense of being in touch with long-gone emotions makes an immediate contact with the past which is rare. However, the temptation to assume that we are therefore in touch with a world not so very different from our own is soon dispelled. The material circumstances are obviously different and the attitudes implied or stated are sometimes startlingly alien.

At this point it is only fair to come clean and say that the nature of the material in this chapter involves severe limitations, both geographical and temporal. The fact that the originals of the letters survive has to be set beside an awareness that they all come from Greek communities in Egypt – and a small part of Egypt too – a society which was initially imposed on a native population and which increasingly accommodated itself to an ancient and very different culture in a way that the population of mainland Greece did not. Moreover, there is a time-shift as compared with Hellenistic royal communications or business letters; many of these private letters were written in the first centuries AD when Egypt was a Roman province and it was – as an essential contributor to the corn-supply of the city of Rome – carefully watched over and managed by Roman garrisons and at the highest levels supervised by Roman administrators.[1] The effects can be seen in the correspondence: Greek, Roman, Egyptian and occasionally Jewish names begin to intermingle. Greek continues to be the language of business and administration, and Greek language and culture, the path to career and social success, is sought after by people with an increasingly wide range of ethnic backgrounds. Surprisingly, Rome does not occur in the letters as a particularly resented or oppressive power so much as one which offered career prospects, particularly in the armed forces. The more attractive parts of Egypt, such as the Fayyum,[2] became favourite places to which those who had served their time in the Roman army retired, and the evident relative prosperity of such veterans (plus doubtless some old soldiers' tales) probably helped to inspire lively young Greeks to follow suit and see the world. However, although Greeks, Egyptians and Romans began to extend their mutual contacts and family connections and although Rome maintained an iron grip and constant military presence, the impression remains that ordinary Greek family life continued in recognizable, if modified form, and that some of the people we meet in the letters would not have seemed utterly foreign to the characters portrayed in the cameos of Aristophanes or the New Comedy. They enthusiastically maintained some of the typical institutions of Greek city life like the gymnasium and the *ephebeia*, and, as 'colonials' do, used them as a carefully watched means of entry to their own circle. In Alexandria too there was the foremost research institute and library of the ancient Greek world, and, though the eternal character of academics led to it being wryly described as the 'bird-cage of the Muses',[3] its scholars were working to preserve and explain the heritage of classical Greek culture. Ordinary Greeks working in ordinary jobs probably never went there but its presence and mission mattered.

A letter probably from the third century AD well illustrates the mix of cultures that could be involved in family life in Graeco-Roman Egypt. A lady called Diogenis was writing to her brother, whose name had both Greek and Roman components – Aurelius Alexandros – on a number of domestic points. She had been looking for a new house and had found one which had taken her eye when she was last house-hunting. Her brother had been instructing someone with an Egyptian name on her behalf – perhaps a kind of estate agent. She gave the location of the house in the usual ancient way – adjacent to a landmark and near someone else's house (again a Latin name) – and an approximate moving date. One or two domestic details settled, there followed a touching and mildly intriguing sending of good wishes to 'little Theon' – presumably Alexandros' small son. The eight toys as presents for him had been given to Alexandros' sister, who was not only the deliverer of the toys but also the channel of greetings from Alexander to 'the lady'. It is a pity that the rest of the letter is lost.

> Diogenis to her brother Alexandros, greetings.
>
> Following your instructions to Taamois about a house for us to move to, we have found the one we gave up before moving in next to Agathinos. This house is near the precinct of Isis, close to the house of Claudianus … We move there in Phamenoth. I want you to know that I had 120 drachmas from Bottos. I have sent you a [flask?] … of purple dye by means of Sarapiacos. The letter you sent me to give to Bolphios I have delivered. Give little Theon many greetings; eight toys have been brought here by the lady to whom you indicated I should send greetings on your behalf and these I have sent on to you …
>
> [Address on the outside]
> To Aurelius Alexandros.[4]

This family domesticity may seem familiar but is in sharp contrast to the circumstances and attitudes expressed in the next letter from the first century BC. The writer, Hilarion from Oxyrhynchos, was in a situation familiar to many Greek men; he needed to go where the work could be found and to send money home from the big city. He evidently had a son already and his mother, Berous, was living with his wife at home. He addresses his wife, who is pregnant, as 'sister'; this may either be a conventional term of endearment or be quite literally true, for by this time the Egyptian habit of brother/sister marriage was not unknown. The sentence about the forthcoming baby is breathtakingly brutal, the more so since it seems so matter-of-fact and is followed immediately by expressions of concern and affection.

> Hilarion to his sister Alis, very many greetings – and to my respected Berous and to Apollonarion.
>
> Know that we are still at this moment in Alexandria. Don't be anxious if all of them return and I stay in Alexandria. I ask you and urge you, look after the child, and, as soon as I receive my pay, I will send it up to you. If by any chance you give birth and if it is male, let it live; if it is female, get rid of it. You said to Aphrodisias, 'Don't forget me.' How can I forget you? I ask you therefore not to be anxious.
>
> 29th year of Caesar. The 23rd of Pauni.
> [Address on the outside]
> Hilarion. Deliver to Alis.[5]

Once in the family, however, and particularly the Greek family, girls are the recipients of motherly concern just as naturally as boys. In the following letter from the second or third century AD Serapias is clearly missing her family.

> Serapias to her children, Ptolemaios, Apollinaria and Ptolemaios, very many greetings.
>
> Most of all I pray that you are in good health, which is for me the most important thing of all. I make a prayer for you to Lord Serapis, praying that I find you meeting with good health – that is what I pray. I was delighted to get your letters saying that you were safe and well. Greet Ammonous and her children and her husband and your friends. Cyrilla greets you and her daughter, Hermias, Hermanoubis, your nurse, Athenais, your teacher, Cyrilla, Casia … Empis and everybody here. So I ask you, write to me about what you are doing since you know that, if I get a letter from you, I am overjoyed to know that you are safe and well.
>
> I pray that you fare well.
>
> [Address on the outside]
>
> Deliver to Ptolemaios, brother of Apollinaria.[6]

And older sisters lecture younger ones, adding a badgering postscript to their reassurances about their mother's health:

> Apollonia and Eupous to their sisters Rasion and Demarion, greetings.
>
> If you are in good health, that is well. We ourselves are in good health too. You would do us a favour by lighting the lamp in the shrine and shaking out the cushions. Keep studying and do not worry about Mother. For she already is enjoying good health. Expect our arrival.
>
> Farewell
>
> And don't play in the courtyard but behave yourselves inside. Take care of Titoas and Sphairos.[7]

Children sent away for their schooling were also a source of parental anxiety. There was nothing like the boarding school of today and children were usually sent to a particular private teacher along with their attendant (the *paidagogos* – normally a slave) who often sat in on instruction and kept a watchful eye open for doubtful influences, especially in the gymnasium, as well as reporting to parents on the progress and quality of teaching. The beginning and end of the following letter are unfortunately missing but the situation is clear: young Ptolemaios had been sent away to be taught by Diogenes and his mother believed she had made a good choice of teacher. She had asked for a report and had been assured by Diogenes that all was well and that Ptolemaios was reading Book vi; there was no need to specify further to a Greek mother. Homer and the *Iliad* were still – even in the second or third century AD – at the heart of Greek education, and Book vi of the *Iliad* with its famous episodes of Hector meeting with Paris and Helen and then looking out from the Trojan walls with Andromache and their baby son, who was frightened by Hector's battle-helmet, was a favourite set book, then as now. All seemed to be well until news came that Ptolemaios was suddenly teacherless; he seems to be responsible for finding another teacher himself and it is a little odd that such a concerned mother did not take a personal hand in such a situation.

> … do not hesitate to write to me about anything you may need from here. I was distressed to learn from the daughter of Diogenes, that teacher of ours, that he had sailed down-river. For I had no worries about him, knowing that he was going to attend to you to the best of his ability. I took the trouble to send to him, ask about your health, and enquire what you were reading. He said 'Book vi' and gave me a full report on your attendant. So, my child, take care – you and your attendant – that you put yourself in the hands of a suitable teacher. Your sisters send you many greetings and so do Theonis' children (safe from the evil eye) and all of us – by name. Greet your valued attendant Eros … Fare … Athyr …
>
> [Address on the back]
>
> … to Ptolemaios, her son.[8]

Hiring teachers was plainly a tricky business, and parents were not always without their faults. In the next letter, from the early third century AD, an aggrieved son hectors his father for not taking the trouble to write and for not coming in person to sign up a teacher whom the young man had already approached. Thonis observes the proprieties – just – by sending his father customary wishes for health and well-being at the start, but then unceremoniously fires the first salvo. He signs off conventionally and politely – and at the last minute remembers the pets at home, perhaps left over from boyhood.

> To my respected father, Arion, Thonis sends greetings.
>
> Most of all I say a prayer every day, praying to the ancestral gods of this land in which I am staying that I find you and all our family flourishing. Now look, this is the fifth letter I have written and, except for one, you have not written to me, even about your being well, nor have you come to see me. Having promised me 'I am coming', you didn't come so that you could find out whether the teacher was attending to me or not. So, practically every day he asks about you, 'Isn't he coming yet?', and I say just the one word 'Yes' … So make the effort to come to me quickly so that he can teach me – as he is keen to do. If you had come up here with me, I should have been taught long before. And when you do come,

remember what I have written to you many times. Come quickly to me before he leaves for the upper territories. I send many greetings to all our family by name and to my friends. Goodbye, my respected father, and I pray that you may fare well for many years along with my brothers (safe from the evil eye).

Remember my pigeons.

[Address]

To Arion, my father, from ... [9]

At roughly the same period another even more petulant son sent an untidy, misspelt and ungrammatical letter to his father when he discovered that his father had gone off to Alexandria without him. He obviously wrote as the words came in the considerable heat of the moment, and we can only imagine the family row which ensued when his father returned. Did Father succumb to the onslaught and bring the lyre as a peace-offering?

Theon to his father, Theon, greetings.

A fine thing you did in not taking me to the city with you. If you are not going to take me with you to Alexandria, I won't write you a letter, I won't speak to you, and I won't wish you well. If you go to Alexandria, I won't take your hand or greet you ever again. If you are not going to take me, this is what will happen. My mother told Archelaus that it gets me into a state when I am left out. It was a good thing you sent me some big presents (and some clothes?) on the 12th, the day that you sailed. I'm asking you to send me a lyre. If you don't send one, I won't eat, I won't drink. So there. I pray that you are well.

The 17th of Tubi.

[Address on the back]

Deliver to Theon from Theon, his son.[10]

Young people get into financial difficulties, and in the next letter Antonius Longus, who in spite of his Roman name seems to belong to a Greek family, writes to his mother about his sorry plight; his spelling is pretty awful. The formal beginning of the letter invokes the popular god Serapis or Sarapis; he was originally an Egyptian deity but by the time this letter was written in the second century AD his cult had spread all over the Roman world. The letter seems to refer to a misunderstanding about a meeting between Antonius and his mother in Arsinoe ('the capital') and Antonius confesses he has been ashamed to return to his home, Karanis, because of his abject poverty. The problem which his mother's informant seems to have explained was probably debt, as the pathetic little sentence at the end, struggling for a little dignity, implies. We do not know what else Antonius said in his letter or how his mother reacted.

Antonius Longus to his mother Neilous, very many greetings.

I pray constantly that you are in good health. Every day I say a prayer before the Lord Serapis on your behalf. I want you to know that I didn't expect that you were going up to the capital. For this reason I didn't go to the city myself. I was ashamed to come to Karanis because I am walking around in a disgusting state. I wrote to you that I have no clothes. I beg you, Mother, make it up with me. In the end I know what I have done to myself. I have been taught a lesson which fits the case. I know that I have done wrong. I heard from … ymos who found you in the Arsinoe district and with bad timing has explained everything. Don't you know that I would rather be disabled than know that I still owe anyone an obol … [eight lines missing]

[Address on the back]

To his mother Neilous from Antonius Longus, her son.[11]

One element in the mixed-race population of Egypt was Jewish, and Jews sometimes crop up quite casually in the correspondence. The following letter was written mainly to let Thermouthion, the mother of Isis, know that her daughter had made the journey safely from Philadelphia in the Fayyum to Alexandria. The family good wishes intriguingly include two undoubtedly Semitic names – Elouath and Sanpat. Greek and Jewish families were evidently living side by side on equal social terms. A small hint of the Roman world comes in at the end: careers in the Roman armed forces were attractive, and Isis is all for encouraging Aion to join up – 'everyone is joining the army'.

Isis to her mother, Thermouthion, very many greetings.

I say a prayer for you every day before the Lord Sarapis and the gods who share his temple. I want you to know that I reached Alexandria safe and well in four days. I greet my sister and the children, Elouath and his wife, Dioscorous, her husband and son, Heron, Ammonarion, her children and her husband, and Sanpat with her children. If Aion wants to join the army, let him go; for everyone is joining the army. I pray that you and all the household fare well.

[Address on the back]

… from Isis, her daughter.[12]

Philadelphia was also the home of one young Greek, Apion, who signed on for a career in the Roman armed forces in the second century AD, and the two letters he wrote back to his family in Egypt offer one of the most fascinating and personal glimpses of what it meant for a young man to leave home and become part of the Roman military machine as a raw recruit. He had brothers and sisters, one of whom, as we later learn, was called Sabina, and his father's name was Epimachos; there is no mention of his mother so she may have died before Apion grew up. What persuaded him to follow a military career we do not know, but he came from an area in which many retired soldiers lived in some style and that may have influenced his decision. As a young Greek he would not have been eligible to join the legions but would have expected to join an auxiliary unit. After signing up, he was posted to Misenum, the headquarters of the Roman fleet on the bay of Naples and a large basic training camp for recruits. The journey from Philadelphia to Alexandria would have taken three or four days and the voyage to Italy would have been a great and hazardous adventure. Apion's letter shows that the voyage (almost certainly his first) had some anxious moments, but Sarapis heard his prayers and all was well. He had had to spend money on his journey, but when he got to Misenum he received the official allowance for his travel expenses, and he reports this with all the glee of the student getting his first grant cheque. He was plainly excited by the new life and thanks his father fulsomely for giving him the education which he hopes will ensure his promotion. Perhaps there is a touch of homesickness too in the request for a letter from home – more than a formality on this occasion? The good wishes to friends and relations again testify to the intermingling of Roman and Greek elements in Apion's background. The pride of the fledgling soldier comes out unmistakeably at the end: he sends his father a picture of himself – and it is not too fanciful to suppose that it is a picture of the recruit in his new uniform. There were presumably enterprising portraitists waiting for the recruits at the base. He also gives his father his new name – Antonius Maximus – for the Roman army insisted on a Roman, not a Greek, identity. Finally he signs off with the name of the unit, which he translates into Greek for his father's benefit – it was presumably the Centuria Minerva Victrix. The address on the back can only be partly read but it is intriguing in that it was written for the remarkably efficient official Roman army postal service. It was no small achievement to take a letter written by a young soldier near Naples and deliver it to his father in a small Egyptian town some days' journey from the coast. Why has this particular letter survived? Perhaps pure accident, but it was Apion's first letter home at the start of his new life, and parents do tend to keep letters like this from their children.

Apion to Epimachos, his respected father, very many greetings.

Most of all I pray that you are in good health and doing well in every way along with my sister and her daughter and my brother. I give thanks to the Lord Sarapis because, when I was in danger at sea, he saved me straight away. When I reached Misenum, I got my travelling grant from Caesar – three *aurei* – and I feel fine. So, I ask you, respected Father, write me a letter, first, to say that you are safe and well, second, that my brothers and sisters are too, and third, so that I may kiss your hand because you gave me a good education and as a result I hope to get on quickly, if the Gods are willing. Give Capito my best wishes and my brother and sister and Serenilla and my friends. I have sent you a picture of myself via Euctemon. My name is Antonius Maximus. I pray that you fare well.

The Century Athenonike.

[Postscript in left-hand margin]

Serenos, son of Agathodaimon, greets you and … son of … and Tourbon, son of Gallonios, and … son of …

[Address on the back]

To Philadelphia to Epimachos from Apion, his son.

Deliver to the first cohort of Apamenians, Julianus being in charge, to the under-secretary from Apion to be sent to Epimachos, his father.[13]

In one of the minor miracles of historical survival we hear from Apion again a few years later. By this time he is thoroughly house-trained and writes to his sister, Sabina (his father, Epimachos, has presumably died), under his military name of Antonius Maximus. The Greek education which enabled him to write a copy-book letter to his father, compliments and all, is now some way in the past and this second letter is in the terse, no-nonsense style of the soldier – even a little awkward. Perhaps he does not now use Greek that much – however, his hand-writing is still recognizable. He is now married to a girl with an Italian name, Aufidia, and they have a little son named after his father, Antonius Maximus – we even learn his birthday. The letter was found at Philadelphia so it must have reached Sabina, but unfortunately there is no clue as to where it was written; it would have been interesting to know where Apion/Antonius was then stationed.

Antonius Maximus to his sister, Sabina, very many greetings.

Most of all I pray that you are in good health; I am in good health myself. While I was remembering you before the gods here, I received a letter from our fellow-citizen, Antoninus, and learning that you are doing well, I was very delighted. I don't hesitate to write to you at every opportunity about my being safe and well and my family. Give Maximus my best wishes and my respected Copres. My wife, Aufidia, and Maximus, my son, greet you (his birthday is the thirtieth of Epeiph on Greek reckoning) – so do Elpis and Fortunata. Greet my respected … [six lines missing]

I pray that you fare well.

[Address on the back]

To Sabina from Antonius Maximus, her brother.[14]

Letters home like this were not uncommon. At about the same period another young man, Apollinaris, joined up and wrote two letters to his mother, who lived in Karanis, quite close to Philadelphia, to tell her that he too was safely arrived in Italy; he, though, had managed to send her a note from Cyrene on the way:

> Apollinaris to Taesion, greetings.
>
> Most of all fare well in good health – I make this prayer for you before all the gods. Finding someone coming in your direction from Cyrene, I of course had to write to you to say I was safe. And you, write to me very soon to tell me that you and my brothers and sisters have no problems. I am now writing this to you from the Port [Ostia] for I have not yet gone up to Rome and been posted. When I have been posted and know the details, I will write to you straight away. Do not hesitate to write to say that you and my brothers and sisters are safe. If you do not find anyone coming in my direction, write to Socrates and he will convey it to me. I send many greetings to my little brothers and to Apollinaris and his children, and to Calalas and his children, and to all your friends. Asclepiades sends greetings to you.
>
> Farewell and be in good health.
>
> I got to the Port on the 25th of Pachon.
>
> [Another hand] Know that I have been posted to Misenum – I found this out later.
>
> [Address on the back]
>
> Deliver to Karanis for Taesion from Apollinaris, her son.[15]

Apollinaris was a dutiful – and perhaps a homesick – son, for very soon after writing the postscript above, he found another scribe and dictated another letter home in much the same terms as the first. He had not yet discovered the name of his unit (century) as Apion had done before he wrote home:

> Apollinaris to his respected mother Taesion, many greetings.
>
> Most of all I pray that you are in good health. I too am in good health and I make this prayer for you before all the gods here. I want you to know, Mother, that I got to Rome safely on the 25th of Pachon and I was allotted to Misenum. I don't know my century yet for I hadn't reached Misenum when I wrote you this letter. So, Mother, I ask you, look after yourself and don't worry about me. For I have come to a splendid place. You would do me a favour by writing a letter to say you, my brothers and sisters and all of you are well. If I can find someone, I will write to you – I won't hesitate to write. I send many greetings to my brothers and to Apollinaris and

his children and to Calalas and his children. I send greetings to Ptolemaios, Ptolemais and her children, and to Heraklous and her children. I send greetings to all your friends by name.

I pray that you fare well.

[Address on the back]

Deliver to Karanis to Taesion from Apollinaris, her son, who is at Misenum.[16]

Both letters were discovered in the same house in Karanis, so Apollinaris' family, like Apion's, must have kept them originally as family history.

New recruits were likely to send news home in the excitement of a fresh career, but serving soldiers also sometimes took the trouble to reassure mothers about their welfare. In the following letter, written in the second century AD, contacts between home and a son in the army seem to be quite frequent:

> Theonas to his respected mother, Tetheus, very many greetings.
>
> I want you to know that I haven't sent you a letter for such a long time because I am in camp and not because I am ill – so don't worry. I was very grieved to hear that you had heard about me, for I was not terribly ill; I blame the person who told you. Don't trouble yourself to send me anything. I had the presents from Heracleides; Dionytas, my brother, brought that present and I received your letter. I thank the Gods always …
>
> [written in the side margin]
>
> Don't burden yourself with sending me anything.
>
> [Address on the back]
>
> From Theonas to Tetheus.[17]

And sometimes the traffic is reversed. In the following case a soldier surprisingly has a smallholding of his own which he has left behind to follow a military career. His brother is his tenant farmer, and his wife, Apollonous, is managing the farm as well as the family. Although her husband is referred to in the letter as 'brother', Apollonous is very likely using a commonly ambiguous form of address. The mixture of cultures at this date is again obvious: the names are Greek, Roman and Egyptian, and the date is given with explicit reference to the full titles of the emperor Trajan as well as the Egyptian month. We do not know where Terentianus was serving when Apollonous wrote to him.

> Apollonous to her brother, Terentianus, greetings and most of all good health.
>
> I want you to know that, when I wrote to you before about the situation, now therefore … that all the rents and the seeds will come

out satisfactorily. And don't be anxious about the children; they are fine and fixed up with a teacher. About your fields, I have let your brother off two *artabs* of his rent, so in future I shall get eight *artabs* of wheat and six *artabs* of vegetable seed from him. Don't be anxious about us and look after yourself. I heard from Thermothoutas that you had got a pair of belts for yourself and I was very glad. About the olive groves, they are fruiting well up to the present. Gods willing, if you can, come to us. Very best wishes – the children send greetings and all your folk.

Farewell.

[Year] 2 of the Emperor Caesar Nerva Traianus Augustus Germanicus.

The 20th of Phamenoth.

[Address on the back]

Deliver to Julius Terentianus, soldier.[18]

Officers in the Roman army, like those in any army, were sometimes called upon to adjudicate disputes between subordinates, and the opening of the following letter (unfortunately not complete) indicates one such. A veteran soldier has a complaint against one of his fellows, who bears an Egyptian name, Petesouchos. It looks as though what was thought to be a safe, temporary deposit with a fellow-soldier had been misused, and the centurion was probably asked in the second half of the letter to investigate and adjudicate.

To Severus Iustus, centurion from Aurelius Abus, veteran.

When I was still serving, sir, in Pelusium, I deposited with one Petesouchos, my fellow-soldier and friend, goods to the value of eight hundred drachmas. When I transferred to the *ala Vocontiorum* and when I sought for an accounting on these matters with a view to a settlement between us both, no account was produced. Therefore I think that, since I have Syrion, son of Isidoros, as a go-between … [end lost][19]

One of the main reasons for Egypt being so closely supervised by the Romans for centuries after the defeat of Antony and Cleopatra and the annexation of Egypt as a Roman province was the fact that it was essential to the food-supply of the city of Rome. It has been estimated that a third of the corn needed to feed its citizens was imported from Egypt, and Egypt paid a huge tribute in kind. This annual tribute of corn was brought in convoy to Italy and the next letter is from one of the sailors in the corn convoy to his brother in Egypt announcing his safe arrival. Eirenaios has travelled from the coast to Rome, and, after he is discharged and paid, will doubtless be sampling the sights and delights of the capital.

Eirenaios to Apollinarios, his dearest brother, many greetings.

I pray constantly that you are in good health; I am in good health myself too. I want you to know that I landed on the sixth of the month, Epeiph, and we finished unloading the cargo on the eighteenth of the same month. I went up to Rome on the twenty-fifth of the same month and the place received us as God willed. Every day we are expecting to be paid off since up to today no-one from the corn-convoy has been discharged. I send many greetings to your wife and to Serenus and to all your friends – by name.

Farewell. The 9th of Mesore.

[Address on the back]

To Apollinarios from Eirenaios, his brother.[20]

As was mentioned in the introduction, one category strangely under-represented in the surviving correspondence is the love letter. In the following letter from the second century AD Taus, who is probably Egyptian, is plainly deeply attached to Apollonios, but they do not seem to be social equals and, although she writes with passion, her letter reads as a kind of petition:

Taus to her respected Apollonios, very many greetings.

Before absolutely everything I greet you, my lord, and I am always praying for your health. I was, sir, suffering more than somewhat when I heard that you were ill, but thanks be to all the Gods that they are keeping you from harm. Sir, I ask you to send for me if you think it right, for, if you don't, I die if I do not see you every day. I wish I could fly and come to you and throw myself at your feet. For I suffer when I do not see you. So be in touch with me and send for me.

Farewell, sir … and we have everything …

The 24th of Epeiph.[21]

[Address on the back]

To Apollonios, the *strategos*.

Weddings, however, and invitations to them are much more common topics. In 154 BC Sarapion happily wrote to his brothers to announce that he had signed a nuptial agreement and named the day. Why Ptolemaios too was not urged to come is a mystery.

Sarapion to his brothers Ptolemaios and Apollonios, greetings.

If you are doing well, I am doing well too. I have signed an agreement with the daughter of Hesperos and I intend to get married to her in the month of Mesore. I'd be obliged if you would send me a half-measure of olive oil. I have written to you so that you may know.

Farewell [Year] 28. The 21st of Epeiph.
[left-hand margin]
Be with us on the day, Apollonios.
[Address on the back]
To Ptolemaios. To Apollonios.[22]

One slightly odd thing about some ancient Greek wedding invitations is the very short notice given to the invitees:

> Dionysios asks you to dinner on the occasion of his children's marriage in the house of Ischyrion – tomorrow, which is the 30th from the ninth hour.
>
> Theon, son of Origenes, invites you to the wedding of his sister – tomorrow, which is the 9th of Tubi from the eighth hour.[23]

Some things seem never to change. Flowers and wedding celebrations go together and the Egyptian soil and climate could supply blooms in abundance – at the right time of year. Apollonios and Sarapias at some time in the second century AD were invited to the wedding of Alexandros and Dionysia's son, Sarapion, and were asked to supply a prodigious quantity of roses and narcissi. Unfortunately this led to complications: Apollonios and Sarapias were unable to come themselves to the wedding, pleading official commitments and illness, and the roses were not fully in bloom so the required quantity was not available. The letter was probably written in late January since, in at least one of the nearby villages, there was in early February a Greek festival picturesquely named 'The Rosebearing' and presumably roses were expected to be in good supply by then. On this occasion narcissi were substituted, but there was also clearly a nasty misunderstanding about payment for the flowers; Apollonios and Sarapias had taken offence since they regarded the two families as close friends. There is perhaps an edge to the last sentence – if you don't believe us, ask Sarapas (who has brought the roses and narcissi, and the letter too). Bruised sensibilities are not unknown in wedding preparations.

> Apollonios and Sarapias to Dionysia, greetings.
>
> You filled us with great joy at the good news of the wedding of the excellent Sarapion, and we would have come directly to support him and share his pleasure on a day we have longed to see, but, because of the circuit review and because we are recovering from illness, we could not come.
>
> There are not yet many roses here – rather a shortage – and from all the farms and all the garland-makers we had difficulty in putting together the thousand which we sent you via Sarapas, even by

picking the ones which should have been picked tomorrow. We had as many narcissi as you wanted so we sent you four thousand instead of the two thousand you ordered. We wish you had not put us down as petty-minded by mocking and writing that you had sent the money, when we regard your children as if they were ours and we respect and love them more than our own, and therefore we are as pleased as you and their father. If you want anything else, write to us. Greet the excellent Alexandros and Sarapion and Theon (no evil eye) and Aristocleia and her children. Sarapas will confirm what I said about the roses, that I have done all I could to send you the number you wanted but couldn't find them.

Respected lady, I pray you fare well.

[Address on the back]

To Dionysia, wife of Alexandros.[24]

Sensible bridegrooms have always paid attention to their future mothers-in-law. Papais who was getting married – probably in the fourth century AD – was very anxious to be tactful towards Nonna, the mother of his bride-to-be. He obviously wasn't quite sure whether Nonna wanted the couple to live near her or not after the wedding, so he keeps the options open for her to choose. It looks as though he is sending the last things on the list for the wedding, and the hasty postscript seems to imply that Papais doesn't want any of the goods already assembled to be touched.

Papais to his most respected Nonna, greetings.

Most of all I salute you and the lady, my bride. I indicated to your goodness and through Serenos, the reader, that you should make efforts to look out for a house for me – only, near your place. For it is proper that we should not be separated from each other. For, after God, I hold you as my mother and sister and all, provided that my bride is well. But if you do not want to do this and you do not like us staying very close to your house, indicate that to me so that I can write to my brother, Cronios, and he may fix up a house for me … or take a house … [ten lines lost, obviously still about the house].

I am sending you the seven-bottle container full of ordinary oil and the pillows and anything else I find. Let me know whether you have received the gold ring from Dorotheos, Anysios' assistant, with the pearl of the teacher, Arethousios, so that you can buy perfumes. When I come I shall bring the sandals of P … ias too. And if you have thought up anything which will be useful for the marriage, write to me so that I can bring it when I come; for there is no quarrel between her and the bride.

Farewell to you, I pray for many years.

[Left-hand margin]
I salute all those in your house and your friends. The 22nd of Mesore.
[Address on the back]
Deliver to the house of Antinous Marcus.
[Upside down near the address]
Take nothing from the store … [25]

Celebrations and parties need entertainments as well as food and drink, and it is handy for a boss to be able to delegate to a reliable underling. In the third century BC Demophon, a government official, was arranging a party of some kind and it is clear that women were involved and making their needs clear too. Demophon's subordinate in the government service, Ptolemaios, received the following slightly hectic instructions and it is curious to see in the postscript that he is charged with also making security arrangements for the transport of both entertainers and goods. A hapless runaway slave is referred to as 'the body' and is therefore in the neuter gender – quite a common usage.

Demophon to Ptolemaios, greetings.

Whatever you do, send me Petous, the *aulos*-player, with the Phrygian instruments and the others, and, if you have to spend anything, you will get it back from me. Also, send Zenobios, the drag-artist, along with drums, cymbals and castanets – the women need him for the sacrifice. And let him have a really fashionable costume. Get the kid too from Aristion and send it to me. If you have captured the body, hand it over to Semphtheus so that he can send it to me. Send me also as many cheeses as you can, an empty pot, a variety of vegetables and any special treats you have.

Farewell

Put these things on board and security people who will travel with the boat and guard it.

[Address on the back]
To Ptolemaios.[26]

The letters contain many of the odds and ends of ordinary life. In the third century AD, another Apion sends an urgent note from the village of Theogenis in the Fayyum to a friend or relation, Didymos, to say that Didymos' sister is seriously ill and that he should come at once. Apion seems in something of a state – hence the apparently contradictory instructions about the white tunic:

Apion to Didymos, greetings.

As soon as you get this letter of mine, straight away put off everything and come to me here since your sister is ill. And bring her white tunic when you come – the one you have there – and don't bring the bluey-green one. If you want to sell it, then sell it; if you want to let it go to your daughter, let it go. Don't neglect her in any way and don't let your wife and the children get worried. When you come, come to Theogenis.

I pray that you fare well.

[No address]

Housewives write to each other to make sure that things for the kitchen have arrived – and add some family greetings. The names of the writer and recipient here look a little odd – Thaeisous is certainly an Egyptian name. Indice is presumably the wife or partner of the oil-massage man at the gymnasium; he seems to have good Greek credentials. The date unusually has a Roman name for the month; occasionally Egyptian or Macedonian months were temporarily renamed *honoris causa*, and at the time of this letter the Roman emperor Domitian had re-designated the month of Thoth as 'Germanicus' (one of the imperial titles). In the same way Augustus had earlier and more permanently re-named one of the Roman summer months after himself.

Indice to her respected Thaeisous, greetings.

I sent you the bread-basket by Taureinos, the camel-man, and you would do me a favour by letting me know that you received it. Greet my respected Theon, Nicoboulos, Dioscoros, Theon and Hermocles (no evil eye). Longinus greets you.

Farewell. The 2nd of Germanic …

[Address on the back]

To the gymnasium, to Theon, son of Nicoboulos, the oil-massage man.[27]

Bookish and serious-minded intellectuals – perhaps within the orbit of the famous library in Alexandria – sometimes write to each other with recommended reading-lists. In this case another Theon writes to his friend, the philosopher, Heracleides, in the second century AD to send some books of Stoic philosophy; he seems a little concerned, however, that Heracleides does not actually read all the books which Theon gets for him. Of the titles of books listed, only the third and the last are known from elsewhere in ancient sources:

Theon to Heracleides, greetings.

Since I bring all my enthusiasm to looking out books that are useful and specially relevant to life, I think it is therefore right for you not to neglect reading them – the benefit that they confer on those keen to be helped is no ordinary one. The appended items are what I have sent by Achillas. Farewell; I too am well myself. Give my greetings to those who should have them.

Written in Alexandria

Boethos, *On training* 3 and 4
Diogenes, *On marriage*
Diogenes, *On being free from pain*
Antipatros, *On the treatment of house-slaves* 1 and 2
Poseidonios, *On exhortation*
[Address on the back]
From Theon to Heracleides, the philosopher.[28]

On a more mundane level, delays to building works in private houses are a perpetual source of anxiety. On 29 August AD 118 a builder, Herodes, wrote a formal, respectful letter to his client to explain some anticipated difficulties in the progress of a building contract and to ask that a delay enforced by the owner's house-steward's recent bereavement should make it possible for Herodes to pay a visit to his brother. Herodes is perhaps a little anxious about this request, for builders did not commonly say prayers for their employers, and a two-day journey each way could well make Apollonios a little cautious.

Herodes to the respected Apollonios, greetings.

You are not altogether unaware of the urgent carpentry-work for the shrine and the guest-room. Because of this we were hard put to it to set in place the doors of the bedroom in the hall as per the agreement on the second of the intercalary days. And at my suggestion your steward is minded to agree to the two doors of the dining-room and the porch so that the work can be done without difficulty and not on the daily invoices. For the beam has been sawn for this.

Because of his daughter's death, he has halted the work until the mourning is over and also to reduce his public commitments. So, sir, I ask you to let me go to visit my brother on Hieracion's boat for these workless days, since I shall not be able to go on foot to those parts … because those parts have been devastated and the lack of..... businessmen invited to go to Memphis for an assessment, so that, having seized this good opportunity, I may find out what Hieracion is doing. The journey takes two days. I said a prayer for you at the festival of Isis on her birthday-night and I further prayed that you should enjoy most prosperous success.

Farewell, sir. The 1st of Thoth.
[Address on the back]
To the respected Apollonios.[29]

Farming was one of the main pursuits in Egypt and the ultra-fertile land maintained by the annual inundation of the Nile was carefully husbanded. Sometimes the owner of a farm might be an absentee landlord, but this did not mean that he did not keep a close eye on what his farm manager was doing. In the next two letters – written respectively in AD 38 and AD 40 – Ammonios was clearly very concerned about the details of farm life and the activities of his manager as well as his own creature comforts.

Ammonios to his best Aphrodisios, greetings.

I wrote a letter to Heracleos, the herdsman, so that he should give you an ass, and I told Ophelion that he should himself give you another and send me the loaves. So, since you have sent me three, I ask you to send me straight away by any means the other three and the pickled fish, since I am on a boat. About the pig-food and the rest of the payment for the hay, settle in advance until I come; for I think I shall go through the accounts with you. I have handed everything over to you; so, on my authority ask your wife to take care of the pigs – take care of the calf too. In any case, Aphrodisios, send me the loaves and the pickled fish. Be good enough to write to me and say to whom I should pay the further twenty [drachmas] for the hay and the feed.

Farewell.

[Year] 2 of Gaius Caesar Augustus Germanicus. The 26th of Mecheir.

[Address on the back]

To Aphrodisios, the manager.[30]

As the content suggests, the letter was probably written in some haste for Ammonios (or his scribe) ran out of space on the papyrus sheet and the last two lines were squeezed into the space at the top. Two years later Ammonios was even more pushed for time but was writing in very much the same vein:

Ammonios to his best Aphrodisios, greetings.

You would oblige me by ordering the loaves to be made and by pickling the olives and sending me word so that I can send for them. As for the corn in the storehouse, shift it because of the Nile flood – all of it.

Farewell. Greetings to Thermion and your children.

Year 5. The 21st of Soter.

I wrote to you in a hurry.[31]

Such fussy letters about looking after the farm are not at all uncommon. Apollonios, for instance, writes to his son of the same name with reminders of what to do before the really hot weather arrives:

Apollonios to Apollonios, his son, greetings.

Do not water the vine with more than two [measures] of water and for the rest of the jobs make your own decisions. For I shall not be myself unless this business is completed … Shift the corn containers in the store and the barley containers outside, the ones with five *artabs* of corn inside where Sarapammon's barley stocks are. Keep the wine stocks cool (in the shade) if hot weather comes, not in the store-house but in another place wherever you like. Greet your sister and your brother and the little girl and all at home. Write to me about everything. Reply by Diosporos, son of Chairemon, or by whoever you come across.

Farewell. The 15th of Mesore.

[Address on the back]

To Apollonios, his son.[32]

The following letter throws an additional sidelight on the nature of Egyptian farming and how essential the irrigation systems were to the success of farms. Demetrios was clearly losing patience with his father, but it was not the danger of losing the cattle which worried Demetrios so much as the fact that they supplied the motive power for the irrigation machinery. Senao was a village in the Fayyum near Oxyrhynchos.

Demetrios to his father, Heracleides, greetings.

You have not acted properly in waylaying the food for the oxen at Senao when you were told long ago to send twelve baskets of hay there. Because you haven't sent them, the animals are in danger of dying. So, because the oxen are in a bad way and therefore the land is not being irrigated, I am rushing to write to you now so that you can straight away get the baskets properly loaded up and dispatch them. For you seem to think my hard work is a joke.

I pray that you fare well for many years.[33]

Water and the Nile floods were not always easy to manage, however, and in the next letter a farmer from another village in the Fayyum, Cercesephis, made a desperate appeal for survival because of floods out of control:

Petesouchos, son of Marres, a farmer from Cercesephis, to Marres, son of Petoseiris … [line missing] and his brother, greetings.

Know that our flat land has been flooded and we do not have so much as fodder for our cattle. So you would be doing us a favour if you would first make a thank-offering to the Gods, and second save many souls by seeking for me five *arourai* of land near your village to keep us going so that we can get a living from it. If you do this, you will have my eternal gratitude.

Farewell.[34]

The annual inundation of the Nile upon which so much Egyptian agriculture depended can be seen to have brought considerable temporary inconveniences as well as the small disasters mentioned above. Many roads were under water, and even when the water receded they remained soggy and impassable for a time. The next letter refers to this in passing, and it is of particular interest because it again shows a Greek woman, Arsinoe, and her sister, Sarapias, in what is evidently a managerial role. Sarapias owns a farm and Arsinoe is going to collect the rent for her as soon as the road is firm enough. However, Arsinoe is anxious that the farmer will not hand over the rent (to a woman?) without written instruction from her sister, and she tries to ensure that she will not have a wasted journey. Brother Achillas had obviously brought Sarapias a jar of pickle as well as her sister's letter.

> Arsinoe to her sister, Sarapias, greetings.
>
> Since Achillas was sailing downstream, I thought I had to greet you by writing. For the business which you wrote to say had been completed, do me the favour of giving it to my brother, Achillas, so that he can bring it to me. Please accept a jar of pickles from the same Achillas. If the roads are firm, I shall go straight away to your farmer and ask him for your rent – if indeed he gives it to me. For you should have sent me a letter for him. However, if you have written ahead for him to give it to me, I will go and collect it. Greet Polycrates and all your folk. Poleta and Demetrous greet you. If you want anything sent to you, write to me and I will send it straight away. I topped up the jar of pickles because they had sunk – the bottom bits are better than the top.
>
> Farewell. The 27th of Choiak.
>
> [Address on the back]
>
> From Arsinoe, wife of Polycrates.[35]

There were many vineyards in Egypt as well as farms and they had their own crop problems. When the grapes were ripening, mice could seriously damage the crop, and at this time of year the rodent operative was in some demand:

> Horos to his most respected Apion, greetings.
>
> On your behalf I paid Lampon, the mouse-catcher, eight drachmas on account so that he would catch mice in Toka. You would oblige me by sending me this sum. And I have lent eight drachmas to Dionysios, the *prostates* of Nemerai, and he has not returned them – so that you may know.
>
> Farewell. The 24th of Pauni.[36]

The genial god Serapis, or Sarapis, crops up in the letters quite often and he was the result first of an Egyptian cult-fusion in the days of the Pharaohs, and then of a politically inspired initiative by Ptolemy I in the early years of the third century BC which created an Egypto-Hellenic cult – a cult eventually so popular that it spread throughout the Roman empire. The original cult-centre was the old capital of Lower Egypt, Memphis, some thirty kilometres south of Cairo. Here the first object of worship in earliest times had been the sacred bull, Apis, which in turn became associated with worship of Osiris – the resultant deity being Osiris-Apis, or Oserapis, which was the obvious source for the Hellenistic god's name.[37] The great complex of the shrine, the Sarapieion or, as it is usually called, the Serapeum, lay some three kilometres to the west of the city of Memphis and close to the edge of the desert. Both Greek and Egyptian deities shared the shrine with Serapis: Isis who helped in times of trouble, Imhotep whom the Greeks called Asclepius and who offered healing powers which made the place legendary. There were the usual commercial adjuncts to a pilgrimage centre – shops for food, souvenirs, holy objects, etc. – all of which helped the income of the shrine. After purification the worshippers would often spend the night in the sanctuary, hoping to sleep and have a revelatory dream from the god. This in turn would have to be interpreted and explained – a sign turned up in the modern excavations saying 'Cretan dream-interpreter here'. In addition to the visiting worshippers there seem to have been groups who felt the need of a longer stay, though whether the need was defined by the god or by the individuals themselves is not altogether clear; the language in the following letter seems to imply an element of compulsion on the part of the god. Whatever the situation in the shrine at Memphis, Isias was plainly pretty annoyed with her husband, Hephaistion, who she thought was having an easy time and was in none too much of a hurry to return to the cares of family life. From the last sentence it may be that Hephaistion had originally gone to Memphis in search of a cure.

> Isias to her brother Hephaistion, greetings.
>
> If the circumstances find you doing well and in good order, that would be in accordance with my constant prayer to the gods. I myself and the child and everyone at home are in good health – remembering you always. When I got the letter you sent by Horos in which you revealed you were in retreat in the Sarapieion at Memphis, I straightaway gave thanks to the gods for your well-being. But about your not returning when all those who were on retreat there had returned, I was not pleased because I have steered myself and your child through such a crisis, and I have had the lot because of the price of corn, and I was now expecting to get some relief when you returned. But you haven't even thought of returning and haven't spared a glance at our situation – how I was need of everything even while you were still here – not to mention the length of time and such crises, with you sending us nothing. Also, since

Horos, who brought your letter, has reported that you have been allowed out of your retreat, I am absolutely fed up. All the same, since your mother too takes a dim view of this, you had better, both for her sake and mine, return to the city – unless some more urgent business detains you. Please look after that body of yours and keep healthy.

Farewell. Year 2. The 30th of Epeiph.

[Address on the back]

To Hephaistion.[38]

For the real enthusiasts in the sanctuary of Serapis, dream-time was very important. In the year 172 BC a man called Ptolemaios decided to enter the sanctuary as a kind of secluded monk and stayed in the service of the god for the next twenty years. He lived in the temple of Astarte close to the Sarapieion and received a small allowance from the shrine (though he also needed support from his brothers). Ptolemaios seems to have been a weird man and dreams (and probably the interpretation of them) were his speciality; a number are recorded. In the following letter he tells some of his bizarre, fantasy dreams in considerable detail. The Twins mentioned are the female twins appointed as the symbols of Isis and Nephthys to be attendants on the sacred Apis bull (they changed on the death of each bull).

Ptolemaios to Damoxenos, greetings.

[In the year] 23 on the 12th of Tubi I thought I was walking in Memphis from west to east and I fall over some chaff, and a man coming towards me from the west falls over too, and, as my eyes were closed, I open my eyes and see the Twins in Tothes' schoolroom. They called me. I said, 'See that you are not timid. Tothes should not grow tired of finding his way to me because I have shifted my bed.' I heard Tothes saying, 'Go away. Why do you say this? I will bring the Twins to you.' I see you yourself bringing them and I make my way towards them until I meet them and go into an alley with them. I said to them, 'I have a short time in the upper air and tomorrow … will be what I was.' Straightway I saw one of them going to someone's house in a dark place and she sits down peeing. Straightway I saw one of them sitting apart. I said to Harmaeis … he should come. And I saw many other things and I again asked Sarapis and Isis saying, 'Come to me, goddess of goddesses, be kind and hear me – have pity on the Twins. Release me – look, with my grey hairs – but I know that soon I shall die and they will be women. If they are defiled, they will never become pure.'

On the 14th I thought I was in Alexandria on top of a great tower. I had a lovely face and I didn't want to show my face to anyone because it was lovely. An old lady sat down beside me and a crowd came from the north and from the east. They shriek that a man has been burnt to ashes with many … and he says to me, 'Wait here for a short time and I will bring you to the god, Cnephis, so that you may worship him.' And I thought I was speaking to an old man, 'Father, don't you see this vision which I gaze upon?' I explained it to him. He gave me two reed-sticks. I looked and swiftly saw Cnephis. Be glad, my companions, I shall soon have my release. I have gazed upon other things, but these are altogether lovelier. You know that I am anxious for the Twins to find a safe resting-place; I care for nothing else. I saw these things up to the month of Phamenoth. Finally, ask the Twins to come … and say that I am going away. Amosis has come to me, he has shown me the road and my cell lies open before me.

Good wishes.[39]

Poor, mixed-up Ptolemaios and his obsession with the Twins! He must have become one of the odd and familiar characters around the Sarapieion. Dreams may be times when a god speaks, but Ptolemaios' relatives were not so enamoured of an absentee religious eccentric in the family, and some of his (inspired) advice seems to have landed the family in deep trouble. In the following letter Ptolemaios' younger brother, Apollonios (who calls his elder brother 'father' in that curious looseness of family expression which occurs elsewhere) gives vent to some pretty heartfelt frustration. The alcoholic *strategos* seems likely to compound the problem.

Apollonios to Ptolemaios, his father, greetings.

I swear by Sarapis that, if I hadn't had something of a conscience, you would never have seen my face again; for you lie about everything and those Gods of yours do too. They have thrown us into a great mess in which we may perish, and, when you are having visions of our salvation, we are then submerged again and again. Know that the man who has gone off will do his best not to allow us to remain in this place, for, because of us, he has lost getting on for fifteen talents. The *strategos* is coming up to the Sarapieion tomorrow and will spend two days in the temple of Anubis drinking. For the shame of it I can't ever hold my head up in Tricomia again if we have surrendered ourselves and gone over the edge because we have been led astray by the Gods and trusted in dreams.

Farewell.

[In small writing on the left-hand margin]

Addressed to those who speak the truth.

[Address on the back]

To Ptolemaios, greetings.[40]

The old religions in the end began a slow and complicated retreat before the growth of Christianity, but ordinary people who became Christians kept to the old Greek letter-forms, simply substituting the Christian God for Serapis or one of the other favourite deities. Here is Thonis in the third or fourth century AD writing to his brother, Heracleos, to say that Heracleos' son is safely arrived and is going to be well looked after. Unfortunately the end of the letter is missing.

> Thonis to his best Heracleos, very many greetings.
>
> Most of all I pray that you are in good form and good health before the Lord God. I want you to know, brother, that on the 10th of the present month of Thoth, I received your son well and in good form in every respect. So I will look after him as if he were my own son. I shall not neglect to make him get down to his work and as a result … [41]

As was mentioned in the first chapter, letters of love are scarcely represented in the surviving correspondence and the same applies to letters written to friends and relations upon the death of someone close. The 'letter of consolation' was one of the standard forms identified by the epistolary theorists, but such letters are few and far between, and in those we do have the feelings are not very extensive and even rather coolly fatalistic. Clichés occur but that is perhaps no surprise; such letters have always been difficult to write and the cliché does not necessarily imply lack of feeling. The letter which Eirene wrote in the second century AD to the wife and husband, Taonnophris and Philo, who had suffered a recent bereavement begins not with the usual 'greetings' but with 'be of good cheer'. This is uncommon in standard letters but was a regular word used on memorials. Perhaps it was a usual convention in consolatory letters.

> Eirene to Taonnophris and Philo, be of good cheer.
>
> I was as much grieved and wept as much over Eumoiros as over Didymas and I did all that was fitting, and so did all my folk, Epaphroditos, Thermouthion, Philion, Apollonios and Plautas. All the same one can do nothing in such circumstances. So encourage each other.
>
> May all go well with you.
> 1st of Athyr.
> [Address on the back]
> To Taonnophris and Philo[42]

The family and its human relationships seem to have some recognizable constants in the letters and, without falling into stereotypes, it is perhaps not too fanciful to observe some specially Greek characteristics too. There is a particular warm but very practical concern for the children of the family and their well-being, the concern sometimes being expressed in a slightly hectoring tone – some of the young correspondents seem to have been under strict instructions to write home as soon as possible. Parents also seem to be quite as anxious about the safe arrival of children after a journey as they are in the modern world. Then, in economic matters there is a close attention to detail on the part of the person who reckons to be in charge (man or woman), not without the occasional hint that other parties need to be watched and that accounts need to be scrutinized with care. There is certainly a strong awareness of hierarchy (father/children; bosses/underlings) but there can also be pretty fierce outbreaks of independence when, for instance, a son reckons that a father or mother may be defaulting on their responsibilities. Generosity and hospitality in celebrations seem to have been, then as now, a delightful feature of Greek family life; the roses and narcissi at Sarapion's wedding must have made quite a fine show, and Demophon's party with the colourful visiting entertainers was probably quite an occasion too. It is easy and right to stress the huge differences between the life of Greeks in Hellenistic and Roman Egypt and life in Greece or Cyprus today, but it is also a mistake to miss a part of what has contributed over the centuries to that peculiarly stubborn, persistent and great phenomenon – Greekness.

3

BUSINESS LETTERS

Business letters are often humdrum items and, having served their purpose, are usually thrown away by the hundredweight. Most deserve oblivion but, for the historian and even for the general reader, much curious and fascinating detail about life and people can emerge from rummaging in ancient Greek administrative waste-baskets and the remains of business correspondence. A part of the picture that emerges emphasizes how different the ancient Greek world was from our own, but what often brings administrative letters of that time to life is the realization that some problems and situations are universal. Managers have to get it right when handling subordinates; they have to know how to work the system and how to deal with the unexpectedly awkward situation or the downright crisis. Subordinates too have to learn tactful ways of handling the boss, even to making sure that his lady-friend is looked after discreetly. Local authority officials become adept at coping with applications and complaints, and law officers are well versed in those bitter neighbourly disputes, often involving land, which still form a sizeable part of a modern lawyer's in-tray. Bureaucracy has always had its own momentum too, and some ancient Greek bureaucrats were just as obsessed as their modern counterparts with orderly record-keeping, with establishing zones of responsibility and full supporting paperwork, and with trackable accountability.

It is of course the case that nearly all the 'waste paper' from the ancient Greek world has now disappeared, and that the quite large quantity of business correspondence which survives has nearly all come from the Greek or Greek/Egyptian community in Egypt, thanks to the favourable circumstances of survival for papyrus in some areas of the country. A very great deal has come either from the original rubbish heaps on which it was originally piled when it became outdated and surplus to requirements in the office, or from random finds, or (in recycled form) from the *papier-mâché*-like cartonnage of mummy cases, the original sheets of papyrus having been separated out in modern times. There are thousands of individual documents including letters, and among them have been found those sequences of dated papers already mentioned in Chapter 1 which leave no doubt that what we have recovered are virtually the contents of an administrator's 'filing cabinet' between certain dates. Some of them give a remarkably vivid and detailed picture of what it was like to be an ancient Greek administrator and businessman at a certain point in history. Papyrologists refer to such sequences as 'archives', and they are usually called after the administrator from whose office they came, e.g. the Nicanor archive, the Diophanes archive, the Abinnaeus archive, etc. The most extensive is the Zenon archive, which was discovered by some Egyptian farmers in 1915. It consists of some of the working papers of Zenon, a Greek from Caunos in Asia Minor, who became estates manager and general administrator to Apollonios, the *dioicetes* or Minister of Finance under King Ptolemy II, who ruled Egypt between 285 and 246 BC. Apollonios was an important man at the top of the tree and Zenon must have been a loyal and trusted administrator, for the documents cover a twenty-year period from 260 to 240 BC, embracing all aspects of running Apollonios' large estate at Philadelphia (modern Darb-el-Gerza) and a great deal else besides. The archive contains mainly business letters to and from Zenon and quite a number are quoted in this chapter.

Before entering the world of Greek business and administration, two words of caution are in order. First, the fact that pretty well all the surviving business letters come from or were written to members of the Greek community in Egypt is of some significance, since it has often been argued that Egypt, especially in terms of government and administration, was always untypical of the rest of the Greek world or, for that matter, of the Roman world too. When Alexander the Great's general Ptolemy, son of Lagos, took over Egypt in 323 BC after Alexander's death and finally proclaimed himself king as Ptolemy I in 305 BC, he established Macedonians and Greeks as a ruling colonial elite and actively encouraged Greeks to come to share in the prosperity of one of the richest countries in the ancient world.[1] He and his companions, in coming to terms with thousands of years of Egyptian tradition and a much shorter period of Persian administration, inherited a well-developed bureaucracy, and it can quite fairly be argued that, though the language and modes of that bureaucracy were speedily translated into and maintained in Greek, the resultant administrative culture was not the same as that to be found in mainland Greece or the other Hellenistic kingdoms. Likewise, when Cleopatra VII, the last of the Ptolemies, committed suicide in Alexandria following the battle of Actium and Augustus established Egypt as a Roman province under tight personal control, Egypt was a province like no other. Its recent history, its wealth and, above all, its importance as one of the main grain-suppliers to the ever-growing city of Rome made it a highly sensitive area – at the start no Roman senator or member of the equestrian order was allowed to visit without the emperor's permission. It is therefore easy to make a case for saying that Egypt was always special and that what is found there is not typical nor does it offer a true sample of the kind of life lived elsewhere in the Greek world. Yet a glance at the surviving documentation gives pause for thought. While it is true that much of the economic and historical background is quite unlike situations elsewhere (and a huge amount of fruitful scholarly research has been devoted to economic affairs in Egypt), the human situations and transactions revealed in the letters are often only partly related to Egypt's peculiarity and must often reflect life as it was experienced by ordinary people elsewhere in the Greek East. For many ordinary Greeks the local administrator with considerable power over their lives has always been an overwhelmingly important horizon, and the person with legal authority (or the muscle or the contacts) to sort out disputes and right wrongs has never lacked petitioners. In those respects the world revealed in the business letters of Greeks and Greek-speakers in Egypt can reasonably be thought to be not too unlike what was happening elsewhere in Greek communities and kingdoms at that time. The second and more controversial word of caution concerns not geography but time. Many of the letters in this chapter – though not all – belong to the Hellenistic world of the third century BC, and they cannot therefore be taken as representative of a culture which flourished and fluctuated in the eastern Mediterranean with a degree of continuity right through the Roman and early Byzantine periods. The main reason for this narrow focus is simply the fact that the material in the 'archives' gives a unique opportunity, hard to resist, for a closeness to the detail of ordinary Greek administrative activity which is not available at any other period. And, even though this sounds like an excuse, it is perhaps arguable that it was the Hellenistic world which materially helped to define the 'Greekness' of later Hellenic consciousness. So, a narrow focus in the following selection may not be quite so limiting as first appears.

The ancient Greek business letter was an essential part of the administrative machine and in form it was very similar to the private letter. 'A to B, greetings' at the start and, at the end, 'Farewell' or 'Best wishes' in a single word. It differed in that it was almost always precisely dated and it also very commonly acquired a filing note or a record of action taken or to be taken, this being added by the clerk or official who dealt with the document. We possess only the tiniest fraction of what was written, but it is patently obvious that, then as now, administrators generated much paper – or properly, papyrus. If the Hellenistic monarch has sometimes been pictured as living an easy life enjoying the fruits of luxury or decadence, the picture is often misleading: he was more likely to be groaning under the weight of paperwork. In a little essay entitled 'Whether government should be entrusted to the elderly' Plutarch reports the following rueful verdict, probably from Seleucos I Nicator, founder of the Hellenistic royal line in Syria: 'people said Seleucos repeatedly declared that, if most people knew just the tediousness of writing and reading so many letters, they would not wish to pick up a diadem, even if it had been thrown away'.[2] We are told in an account of 258–257 BC that two branches of a large-ish office – belonging to the Apollonios mentioned above – used 434 rolls of papyrus over a thirty-three day period.[3] There is no standard length for a papyrus roll, but such evidence as there is suggests that it was usually between 2.20 m and 4.80 m. So Apollonios' staff in these two offices got through some one and a half kilometres of papyrus in just over a month. Not all of it would have been letters, but even half the quantity generates a fair amount of correspondence. Most senior administrators like Zenon, Apollonios's subordinate, would not normally write business letters themselves. They might dictate them or draft them on scrap papyrus, but the final version would be written by a professional secretary. The safe delivery of letters was a problem in the ancient Greek world, but less so for an administrator in Egypt. For many purposes it was a matter of finding someone or sending someone to take the letter and deliver it personally, and this is doubtless why the 'address', usually on the reverse side of the papyrus, consists often of a simple 'To A', except in the rare instances of letters conveyed over long distances by official networks like the Roman army postal service. For official purposes Egypt was in that respect unusually well organized, for the Ptolemies had a fast delivery service within Egypt for government documents.

Doing business in the Greek world has always been closely linked to personal contacts, and in the ancient world it mattered even more whom you knew and what your connections were. Whether it was St Paul in prison in Rome or a Greek giving a helping hand to a fellow-Greek newly arrived in the locality, the letter of recommendation was a vital tool. One of the earliest recorded letters of this kind is one written in 340/339 BC by the speech-writer, teacher and statesman-on-paper Isocrates to Antipater who was ruling Macedonia in the absence of King Philip. Isocrates was an old man of eighty at the time and it was a tribute to his reputation that he was able to make such a request to the ruler of a land with which Athens was currently at war. The letter is written on behalf of one of Isocrates' past pupils, Diodotos, and on behalf of Diodotos' son too who seems to have had some kind of physical disability. Like many another great teacher Isocrates was proud of his successful pupils and was pleased to offer them and their offspring a little help. The letter does not ask Antipater to give Diodotos a specific post but looks for general patronage and support for him and his son. It contains all the usual ingredients of letters of recommendation but is quite untypical in that it is a long, consciously rhetorical set-piece, and was clearly designed not only to commend an ex-pupil but also to give Antipater a literary present – an example of that stylistic fluency and persuasive advocacy for which Isocrates was famous. One strongly suspects that publication and a wider public were never far from Isocrates' mind. The opening of the letter gives the flavour:

> To Antipater.
>
> Although in our situation it is dangerous to send a letter, not only now when we are at war but in time of peace too, all the same I have decided to write to you about Diodotos, thinking it right to

take some trouble over those who have associated with me and have developed into people worthy of me, and not least this man, both because of his goodwill towards me and because of his other deserving qualities. I would have wished that he could actually have been introduced to you by us, but, since he has met you through others, it remains for me to give testimony on his behalf and to confirm your acquaintance with him. Many men from many places have studied with me, some with great reputations, and of all these, some have become experts with words, others with ideas and actions, and others have been sensible and cultivated in their lifestyle but with no gifts at all for other useful activity. This man, however, has such harmonious gifts that he is most accomplished in all the matters I have mentioned. And I would not be so bold as to say these things if I had not myself had the most particular experience of his company and anticipate that you would too, partly from your own acquaintance and partly by hearing of him from others who have encountered him. Of these there is no-one who would not agree, unless he is very jealous, that both in speaking and giving counsel Diodotos is no-one's inferior, and that he is both very just and very sensible, and is most competent in monetary affairs. Further, he is the pleasantest and nicest person with whom to spend the day – or one's life – and in addition he is very frank, not in an inappropriate way but in the proper way, which is an unmistakeable sign of goodwill towards friends.[4]

The more usual, everyday form of such letters is much more simple and straightforward, with no great display of subservience or excessive compliment. A knows B, and B is asked to trust A's judgement about the excellent C and give C a chance to show what he can do. Here is a letter which Zenon received from one Asclepiades in about 250 BC on behalf of Philon, who delivered the letter himself:

Asclepiades to Zenon, greetings.

Philon who has delivered this letter to you has been known to me for some time. He has sailed up river in order to get himself into some sections of Philiscos' offices, being recommended by Phileas and other accountants. So you would oblige me by getting to know him, introducing him to some other well-placed people, and making an effort to help him, both for my sake and for the sake of the young man himself. He is worth your trouble, as will be clear to you if you take him in hand.

Farewell

[Address on the back]

To Zenon[5]

This is a straight request for helping Philon to find a job and to make useful contacts, and Philon must have been quite persistent in drumming up supporters and suggesting the wording of their letters, since a certain Ptolemaios wrote an almost identical letter to Zenon on Philon's behalf. We do not know what Zenon thought of getting two almost identical letters recommending the same person to him – perhaps it often happened. Round about the same time Asclepiades also wrote on behalf of a relative's nephew with another request. The nephew had probably signed on as a soldier and, since he was then classified as a military settler, he would have been eligible to receive an allotment of land for cultivation, known as a *cleros*. The allotments obviously varied in quality and Asclepiades here tactfully asks Zenon to do his best for Asclepiades' relation. He does not push his case, merely asking for 'a suitable plot', but both sides must have known what was being suggested:

> Asclepiades to Zenon, greetings.
>
> Erasis who is delivering this letter happens to be a relative of mine and a friend. He is bringing up to you Erilochos, his nephew, in order to measure up the land. So you would oblige me by looking after these people so that they can get a suitable plot, preferably in Philadelphia so that it can be near you, but, if not, wherever is convenient, and so that, in the surveying of the land, they are not cheated. If they need anything else from you, undertake that diligently for them, both for my sake and for the men themselves; for they are worth the trouble.
>
> Farewell.[6]
>
> [Address on the back]
>
> To Zenon.

Needless to say, recommendations were sometimes accompanied by sweeteners and Zenon was quite accustomed to receiving sometimes quite substantial gifts.[7] In the following letter Platon, who writes very much as the equal of Zenon, makes a request on behalf of Demetrios' son but thinks it advisable to add a token gift of chick-peas along with the promise of further shopping (price of the chick-peas specified, however, so that Zenon knows the quality of what he is getting):

> Platon to Zenon, greetings.
>
> The father of Demetrios who is delivering this letter to you happens, it appears, to have taken up residence in the Arsinoe district. The young man himself therefore wants to get some work there. Hearing that you are well disposed, some friends asked me to write to you about him to ask you if you would employ him in some capacity in your office. I should be much obliged if you could do me this favour

and give some thought to his having some work – whatever you think is suitable – and look after him generally if he is of service to you. As a mark of gratitude I have sent you from Sosos two *artabs* of chick-peas (price – five drachmas apiece) and I will try in Naucratis, if there are any, to buy also about twenty *artabs* … and bring them myself to you.

Farewell. Year 31. The 12th of Dios.[8]

[Address on the back]

To Zenon.

Requests for plain introductions and therefore opportunities for advancement were common too. The unemployed son of a successful father is a not unknown phenomenon. In the 250s BC Cleon was a quite highly placed engineer, or perhaps superintendent of public works, in the Fayyum district to the west of the Nile. He seems to have been much concerned with building and maintenance works connected with the irrigation system, which was of particular importance and complexity in that district. He had a large staff and managed a labour force of thousands, and was far enough up the hierarchy to have some access to the King himself. He was a family man with two sons, one of whom, Polycrates, was out of work and looking for a job. Polycrates therefore writes to his father (not for the first time) to ask him to put a word in the royal ear. He knows he cannot press too hard, and the letter has personal expressions of concern for the recipient's well-being which are appropriate for a dutiful son:

Polycrates to his father, greetings.

I shall be pleased if you are keeping well and everything else is as you wish it. I too am well. I have written to you many times to ask you to come here and give me a recommendation so that I can escape from my present state of unemployment. Now, if it is possible and none of your commitments gets in the way, try to come to the festival of Arsinoe. If you come here yourself, I am confident that it will be easy for me to be recommended to the King. Know that I have received seventy drachmas from Philonidas, half of which I have kept back for necessities, and the rest I have deposited to make interest. This comes about because I have not received it as a lump sum but in instalments. Write to me so that I may know how you are and not be anxious. Take care of yourself so that you keep in good health and come to me in good form.

Good wishes.[9]

Into this framework of standard recommendations other letters from Greek-speakers loosely fit. One such is the letter which St Paul and Timothy wrote to their friends, Philemon, Apphia and Archippos. It is a letter of recommendation on behalf of the slave Onesimos ('Useful'), and, although its formulas are adapted and extended to include Christian messages and although its expression is somewhat fulsome, there is plainly behind it the standard pattern for the Greek letter of recommendation (or in this case perhaps rehabilitation):

> Paul, a prisoner of Christ Jesus, and Timothy our brother, to Philemon, our dear friend and co-worker, to Apphia our sister, to Archippus our fellow-soldier, and to the church in your house: Grace to you and peace from God our Father, and the Lord Jesus Christ.
>
> When I remember you in my prayers, I always thank my God because I hear of your love for all the saints and your faith towards the Lord Jesus. I pray that the sharing of your faith may become effective when you perceive all the good that we may do for Christ. I have indeed received much joy and encouragement from your love, because the hearts of the saints have been refreshed through you, my brother. For this reason, though I am bold enough in Christ to command you to do your duty, yet I would rather appeal to you on the basis of love – and I, Paul, do this as an old man, and now also a prisoner of Christ Jesus. I am appealing to you for my child, Onesimus, whose father I have become during my imprisonment. Formerly he was useless to you, but now he is indeed useful both to you and to me. I am sending him, that is, my own heart, back to you. I wanted to keep him with me, so that he might be of service to me in your place during my imprisonment for the gospel; but I preferred to do nothing without your consent, in order that your good deed might be voluntary and not something forced. Perhaps this is the reason he was separated from you for a while, so that you might have him back for ever, no longer as a slave but as more than a slave, a beloved brother – especially to me but how much more to you, both in the flesh and in the Lord. So if you consider me your partner, welcome him as you would welcome me. If he has wronged you in any way, or owes you anything, charge that to my account. I, Paul, am writing this with my own hand: I will repay it. I say nothing about your owing me even your own self. Yes, brother, let me have this benefit from you in the Lord! Refresh my heart in Christ. Confident of your obedience, I am writing to you, knowing that you will do even more than I say. One thing more – prepare a guest-room for me, for I am hoping through your prayers to be restored to you. Epaphras, my fellow-prisoner in Christ Jesus, sends greetings to you, and so do Mark, Aristarchus, Demas and Luke, my fellow-workers.
>
> The grace of the Lord Jesus Christ be with your spirit.[10]

The opening formula has been amplified to include encouraging, friendly epithets, and in place of the customary 'Greetings' we now have 'Grace to you and peace from God our Father and the Lord Jesus Christ'. The start of the letter expresses pleasure, not for the physical well-being of the recipients as many ordinary letters do, but for their spiritual health and its anticipated results. The essence of the letter is a request from Paul to Philemon and his household to take back the slave, Onesimos, who has been of service to Paul, Timothy and others in prison. We do not know what Onesimos had done to put himself in Philemon's bad books – he had probably absconded and a sum of money seems to be involved – but Paul is plainly treading on thinnish ice. The semi-apologetic tone (I didn't want to do anything without finding out what you thought), the assurance that no-one is going to lose financially, the emphasis on the closeness of Paul and Onesimos, the reminder that Paul is only calling in a much bigger debt, and the fact that he is taking the trouble to send at least part of the letter in his own hand are all in marked contrast to the usual straightforward terms of such requests, not to mention the personality of Paul himself. It would be interesting to know if Onesimos made it back and if Philemon gave him the welcome for which Paul and Timothy were asking.

The personal touch doubtless helped in many situations but it did not solve all problems, particularly where labour relations were concerned. We have already met Zenon, the estate manager and administrator for Apollonios, Ptolemy II's finance minister. When Zenon's office files were cleared out, some correspondence involving his predecessor, a man called Panacestor, was thrown away and it sheds a little light on how work got done and on the relations between foremen, their gangs and the bosses like Panacestor who were in the end responsible. By coincidence the situation also involves the same Cleon, the public works superintendent whose son wanted him to put in a word with the King about a job. On 11 October 257 BC Panacestor delivered a sharp rap over the knuckles to Cleon, backing it up with a threat of telling the minister if nothing was done:

> Panacestor to Cleon, greetings.
>
> I sent a message on the 22nd as well that we should send a slave to dig out the bends of the small canal, but you seem to have gone past us to the small lake. You shouldn't have passed us by, but landed here with us for a few minutes and, when you saw that the land had not been irrigated, you should have asked the reason for our not irrigating it. For you have not only been charged with engineering the small lake but with dealing with this complaint. Meet us tomorrow after giving instructions to us and the engineers about how the water must be diverted (?) for we are inexperienced. We will provide slaves and the rest of the workforce – as much as you require. If you do not come here, we shall be compelled to write to Apollonios that it is your fault alone that his land at the lake is dry, although we are willing to provide all the resources.
>
> Farewell. Year 29. The 21st of Mesore.[11]

Cleon probably obliged, but two other surviving letters show that he had his own problems with parts of his workforce in the quarries:

> Philoxenos and the other young men [to Cleon], greetings.
>
> The 140 quarrymen are absolutely on strike because they do not have what they need. For the advance payment made by us has been eaten up and they are idle, with no-one giving them suitable tasks. You should send them wheat from the stores – but not beyond their due – for the Minister is in a hurry. So the quarrymen must be at work in all respects.
>
> Farewell.[12]

The hungry striking quarrymen were evidently being paid, at any rate partly, in kind. An *artab* is between 30–40 kilos, so Philoxenos and his men were understandably trying to secure the medium-term future for themselves. There seems, though, to have been a history of bad industrial relations in the quarries, for another letter to Cleon was in the files from the foremen warning that, if the 'other side' did not honour its agreement, the workmen would not only down tools but actually put them in pawn:

> To Cleon greetings from the foremen of the free quarry-workers.
>
> We are being wronged. Nothing of what was agreed by Apollonios, the Minister, has come to us. So make every effort to see that we are recompensed on the terms we got from Dionysios and Diotimos, and that the work does not get behind schedule as happened before. For if the workers discover that we have received nothing, they will pawn their tools.
>
> Year 30. The 19th of Pachon.[13]
>
> [Address on the back]
>
> To Cleon.

Demarcation disputes were not unknown too, and even quite lowly persons pushed to claim their rights. The two slaves who were the official feeders of the sacred cats in the temple at Boubastis cannot have ranked very high on the social scale but they knew what their job description was and it did not include making bricks:

> To Zenon, greetings from the temple slaves at Boubastis who feed the cats.
>
> The King acted properly in giving our profession exemption from compulsory work throughout the land, and so did Apollonios too; we are from Sophthis. Leontiscos, forcing us to go, sent us to the harvest, and, so that we should not bother you, we finished the work given to us. But now for the second time Leontiscos has sent us out

to make bricks – there are two of us. He is just looking after the brick-makers in Sophthis, Amerois and Beras, who should be doing this work – for his own advantage. Would you oblige us by proceeding to follow the instructions of the King and Apollonios, his Minister. Apart from you we have no-one to complain to.

Farewell.[14]

Administrators, however, did occasionally have pleasanter tasks. Their masters sometimes had interests in places far away and needed someone to check that all was well with their investments. Such visits when there are no problems and everyone is trying to leave a good impression can be quite comfortable experiences for the inspector, and on the visit referred to in the following letter the local manager, Melas, seems to have provided appropriate hospitality, giving the inspector, Glaucias, a wine-tasting with satisfactorily inconclusive results. The quite extensive vineyard at Bethanath which Glaucias was visiting belonged to Apollonios and was located in Galilee, probably in a fertile valley which leads from the district around Acre towards the Sea of Galilee. Glaucias reports to Apollonios:

Glaucias to Apollonios, greetings.

About the matters you told me to report to Nicanor and Antiochos, I have reported them; know that they are going along with them. For the rest, I will report to you when I am back with you. When I got to Bethanath, having Melas with me, I went to inspect the vines and everything else. They seem to me to be properly cultivated and he said there were 80,000 vines. He has built both a well and satisfactory accommodation. He gave me a tasting of the wine and I could not tell whether it was Chian or local. Please prosper in everything.

Farewell. Year 29. The 7th of Xandicos.[15]

[Address on the back]

To Apollonios.

Glaucias sent this letter on 9 May 257 BC and it was received in Apollonios' office later that month (rather uncharacteristically the clerk did not record the exact day, leaving a space. On the back of the letter near the address he left his file note summarizing the contents for easy reference:

From Glaucias about what he was ordered to tell Antiochos and Nicanor and about the wine at Bethanath.

Year 29 … Xandicos – at Alexandria.

The wine trade, however, was not only a matter of large estates; local smallholders who grew vines in addition to their main jobs used their produce both as payment in kind and as a means of making money. In the next letter a Syrian camel-driver is asked to act as both transporter and salesman (though exactly why Plolos needed to write a letter to someone who was probably illiterate is not clear):

> Plolos to Horos, the Syrian camel-driver, greetings.
>
> Since I have filtered for you ten measures of old wine as transport costs, and – for myself – twelve measures, take them to the Oxyrhynchos district so that you can sell the twelve measures at the going rate in the Oxyrhynchos district and bring me the money. So don't neglect this but bring me the proceeds since I need the cash.
>
> I pray that you fare well.[16]
>
> [The address was written twice because the papyrus was awkwardly folded]
>
> To Horos, the Syrian camel-driver from Plolos the potter.

It was on another visit to Palestine that Zenon bought some slaves in Marisa, a town in Idumaea. He got them from a dealer called Zaidelos. Unfortunately on the journey back to Egypt three of them escaped and were not recaptured. A typical Middle Eastern situation now developed for, when Zenon got back, he heard from his agent in Palestine that the three slaves had turned up in the possession of someone called Collochoutos, who just happened to be the brother of the original slave-dealer, Zaidelos. Collochoutos was prepared to return the slaves but was asking for one hundred drachmas as a 'handling charge'. Zenon immediately fired off five letters and sent his man, Straton, to deliver them, the first and second letters being to fellow-Greeks who were asked to negotiate the safe return of the slaves on his behalf:

> To Pasicles.
>
> If you are well, that is good. I too am in good health. Crotos reported to me that you had written to him to say that there is information that the slaves who have run away are with Collochoutos, the brother of Zaidelos, and they are asking one hundred drachmas for returning them. You would be doing us a service if you would make every effort to recover them … handing them over to Straton who is bringing you this letter. If you do this we should be much obliged … and if you have expenses, we will pay. There is an alabaster chest which was bought … If you don't want it, the man who bought it will return it. If you need anything locally, write to us for we are grateful to you.
>
> Farewell.

> To Epicrates.
>
> When we were staying in Marisa, we bought some slaves [lit. bodies] from Zaidelos' stock, of whom, while we were on the journey to

> Egypt, two brothers escaped whose names and descriptions I have attached to this letter. It has been reported to us that they are with Collochoutos … you would oblige us if you would make every effort to recover them and hand them over to Straton. What you spend on getting them back …

The third letter is to another Greek contact in Palestine, Peisistratos, asking him to keep an eye on Pasicles and make sure that he does what Zenon has asked and keeps the slaves safe when he has them. Pasicles is clearly not entirely trusted:

> To Pesistratos [sic].
>
> If you are well that is good. I too am in good health. Crotos has sent information that Pasicles has written to tell us about the runaway slaves which we bought in Marisa from Zaidelos. We therefore wrote asking him to make every effort to bring about their recovery and to hand them over to Straton who is bringing you this letter. We should be much obliged therefore if you reminded him and took the trouble to see that they do not escape. And you will be in our debt if you write … if you need anything from the country here. For we shall act as friends do.
>
> Farewell.

The fourth and fifth letters are to the local taxation department in Palestine to make sure that Straton, Zenon's agent who is delivering the letters and will presumably see to the transport of the slaves, does not become entangled in any local tax demands following the negotiations for their return:

> To Epainetos.
>
> Some of our slaves happen to have escaped and they have been said to be in Idumaea. We have sent Straton for that task. You would oblige us by giving instructions to your son not to hinder him in matters concerning taxes so that he can recover the slaves.

> To Ammon.
>
> Ditto. You would oblige us if you could write to Dorotheos and Demainetos so that he should not be hindered in matters concerning taxes.[17]

The intriguing thing about these five letters is that we naturally no longer have the actual letters which were sent, since these were taken to Palestine by Straton. The texts we can read have been roughed out on the back of an old oil account, and what we have are therefore the drafts on scrap papyrus that Zenon made, probably in his own hand, for his secretaries to work on.

Escaped slaves were rather like stolen cars today and, on another occasion, Zenon received a memo from Sosicrates on the staff of someone called Paideas who had evidently bought some slaves from Zenon's former boss, Apollonios, and then lost them:

> Memo to Zenon from Sosicrates about the slaves, formerly belonging to Apollonios, the ex-Minister, but now the property of Paideas. If anyone finds them, arrest them and write to me.
>
> Pindaros – a Lycian servant, about 29, medium height, honey-coloured, with eyebrows that meet, hook-nosed, and a scar below the left knee.
>
> Also Philonides who is also known as Beltenouris – about 24, medium height, honey-coloured, a scar on the left eyebrow and below the lip on the right.
>
> Also from the slaves of Alexandros, the ex-hostage – Philinos, a Babylonian, shampooer, about 44, short, black-skinned, hook-nosed, eyebrows that meet, and having a mole by the left temple.
>
> Also Amyntas – a Mede, coachman, about 34, medium height, black-skinned and with a scar on forehead and nose.[18]

The scars as a regular feature of identification tell their own story. The second slave, Philonides, is unusual in having two names, the second – Beltenouris – being probably the Greek transcription of his Babylonian name, Belti-nuri or Belit-nuri, though why his Greek owner ever used this we do not know.

The official in charge of one of the regions of a Hellenistic country, both in Egypt and in some other kingdoms, often had the title of *strategos* – literally, 'general' – though his jurisdiction was not primarily military. He and his officials acted for the king, and they were the focus for innumerable requests for arbitration, for swift action on local issues, for help, for putting injustices right, for tax relief and for a kaleidoscopic variety of domestic disputes. One is left with the impression that over a period pretty well all human life and its problems passed through the office of a *strategos*. A few real petitions will give the flavour of the personal problems with which a local administrator was frequently besieged. Petitions were submitted in the form of standardized letters beginning 'I am wronged by *x*', and in Egypt were commonly addressed to the King himself. As was mentioned in Chapter 1, this convention may go back to the early days of Greek occupation when it may have been possible to have personal access to the sovereign. In later times everyone knew that very few applications would reach the

King, but would be dealt with in the office of the regional *strategos* who would probably instruct officials further down the line to take action. The record shows that many officials were quite careful and sensible in their handling of cases. Here is a father/son dispute which in 222 BC came before the *strategos*, Diophanes, who was in charge of the district round the town of Arsinoe:

> King Ptolemaios from Pappos, greetings.
>
> I am wronged by my son, Strouthos. For I had him taught … [and given] schooling. But when I became older and no longer able to look after myself … [I arranged] before Dioscourides, your … in Arsinoe, that my son would provide me with one *artab* of wheat and four drachmas every month – conditions he himself [accepted]. He has given me none of these things which he agreed to, but whenever he meets me, he insults me most shamefully and, forcing his way into my house, he seizes every time whichever of my possessions lies to hand, despising me because I am getting older and cannot see very well. So I beg you, your majesty, instruct Diophanes, the *strategos*, to write to the chief man of Arsinoe in the Themistes district, the one on the dyke, and get him to send my son to Diophanes and, if I am telling the truth in this petition, to restrain him from violence and make him give guarantees for what is due to me so that in future he may make payment properly. If this comes about, I shall, through you, your majesty, have obtained justice.
>
> Good wishes.[19]

The verdict or instruction for action from the administrator dealing with the case was usually written on the bottom of the document submitted, and is therefore nowadays given the technical name of a 'subscription'. In this case we have the note that Diophanes dictated, addressed to one Ptolemaios (not, of course, the King, but a local law-enforcement officer), and this is written at the foot of Pappos' complaint:

> To Ptolemaios.
>
> Preferably you yourself reconcile the father with Strouthos. But if he shows any sign of refusing, send him to me. Make sure that it happens thus.
>
> Year 26. The 23rd of Daisios – the 5th of Phaophi.

On the back of the document is a note of what actually happened when Ptolemaios got the two heads together. Case closed – but someone in the office made a mistake over the dating: this last note is clearly dated to the day *before* the instruction to Ptolemaios was sent:

Year 26. The 4th of Phaophi.

In the hearing Strouthos said he would give Pappos, his father, two copper drachmas each month for his keep. Pappos was present and said he was content with this, and, if Strouthos paid up properly for a year, he would inscribe his share for the temple.

Relationships between an occupying power and the natives often involve racial and other sorts of tension. On the whole Greeks and Egyptians co-existed with only occasional serious clashes; Egyptians took it for granted that Greeks would have the top jobs in the administration, and learning Greek became a passport to some of the lowlier posts in the administrative offices for some Egyptians. In time there was an increasing degree of integration and intermarriage.[20] Greeks, though, were often conscious of their status and particularly resentful of perceived insults to their dignity. The *strategos*, Diophanes, who dealt with Pappos and his son, had a complaint from a fellow-Greek, Heracleides, about a very determined assault on Heracleides' dignity by an Egyptian lady called Psenobastis. It may have started as an accident in the street, but both parties were plainly on a short fuse and it is frustrating not to know what action Diophanes took; we only have the filing note:

To King Ptolemaios greetings from Heracleides, one of those from Alexander's island, dweller in the city of Crocodilopolis in the Arsinoe district.

I am wronged by Psenobastis who lives in Psya in the aforementioned district. For in the 5th year of the tax-calendar on the 21st of Phamenoth I went to Psya in the same district on some private business. As I was going along … an Egyptian woman, whose name is said to be Psenobastis, leaned out and poured urine all over my clothes so that they were soaked. When I was angry and reproached her, she was abusive. When I was abusive back … Psenobastis, grabbing with her right hand at the hood of the cloak I had round me, tore it and assaulted me so that my chest was laid bare, and she spat in my face in front of some people I called to witness. I charge her with what she did: assaulting me and starting things by laying hand on me unlawfully. When she was reproached by some of those who were present for what [she had done to me], she thereupon left me and went inside the house from which she had poured the urine on to me. So I beg you, your majesty, not to ignore the fact that I have been assaulted so unreasonably by an Egyptian woman, me being a Greek and a visitor, and to tell Diophanes, the *strategos*, since … to write to Sogenes, the chief, to send Psenobastis to him so that he may give judgement to me on these matters and, if the facts of the petition are true, she may meet with whatever punishment the *strategos* decides. If this happens, I will, through you, your majesty, receive justice.

Farewell.[21]

[File note]

Year 4. The 3rd of Dios – the 27th of Phamenoth.

Heracleides against Psenobastis concerning assault.

Justice, however, was not in theory one-sided and it was possible for Egyptians to complain about Greeks too. In 221 BC Diophanes received the following note from an Egyptian farmer about the behaviour of a Greek, Geroros, who seems to have been given an allotment of land under some settlement scheme in Pasis' village, Polydeucia, and to have taken a high-handed fancy to Pasis's house instead of the one he had been given. It is unlikely that Pasis spoke or wrote Greek himself so he must have been to the trouble of getting a professional letter-writer:

To King Ptolemaios greetings from Pasis, farmer of Polydeucia.

I am wronged by Geroros, who has seventy *arourai*. I had a house in the village and I was thrown out of it by him and my cattle are wandering about in the open air. He was violent, even though in the village he had … given to him as lodgings. So, I beg you, your majesty, if it pleases you, to order Diophanes, the *strategos*, to write to Sosibios, the supervising officer, and have the man sent to him, and, if what I say is true, not to allow him to throw me out of my house so that I may be able to get down to my farming and through you, your majesty, the common saviour of all, I may get justice.

[Year] 1. The 28th of Gorpiaios – the 12th of Tubi.[22]

It was a simple case and the following note from Diophanes to the police-chief obviously invokes standard procedure. It is worth noting that the tribunal mentioned was mixed, i.e. it probably had both Greek and Egyptian members:

To Sosibios.

Preferably reconcile them. But if not, send them over to be judged by the mixed tribunal.

Such disputes over land allotments sometimes took a nasty turn. One local Greek official, Antiochos, received a sharp letter on the subject from the King himself – the local *strategos* had to walk a tricky tight-rope:

King Ptolemaios to Antiochos, greetings.

About billeting the soldiers, we hear that too much violence is being used when the troops do not get lodgings from the administrators, but charge into the houses themselves, throw people out and take over the houses by force. Issue orders therefore that in future this is not to happen. Preferably let the soldiers fix accommodation themselves but, if they have to be given billets by the administrators, let the administrators give them what is necessary. When the soldiers leave the billets, let them surrender them having made them good, and not simply abandon them until they return, as we hear happens now. For whenever they go away they let the billets and run off after sealing up the dwellings. Take particular care over Arsinoe near Apollonopolis to see that, if soldiers arrive, none of them is billeted there, but that they stay in Apollonopolis. But if there is some necessary reason for them staying in Arsinoe, let them make small huts for themselves as previous arrivals did.

Farewell.[23]

Greek society has always been notoriously male-dominated, but that did not prevent determined Egyptian ladies from pursuing real or imagined wrongs with the Greek administration. The redoubtable Aunchis had been running a successful beer-shop with the help of her daughter, but she was now getting on in years and the daughter had gone off to have an affair with a married man, so that Aunchis could no longer manage. She applied to Zenon for her daughter's return. Alas, we have no record of the action Zenon took – the note of receipt on the document merely has the year, the month and Aunchis' name; perhaps she was an all-too-regular correspondent and the name was enough. The time is the spring of 253 BC:

Aunchis to Zenon, greetings.

Getting beer from the large beer-shop I have a daily through-put of four drachmas' worth and pay regularly. But Demetrios, the vineyard worker, having deceived my daughter, has taken her off and hidden her away, saying that he is going to set up house with her but without me. She herself helped me mind the shop and was looking after me since I am elderly. So now, with her having left, I am making a loss and I don't have the necessities of life myself. He has both another wife and children here so he can't set up house with the woman he has deceived. So I ask you to help me because of my old age and give her back to me.

Farewell.[24]

[File note]

Year 32. Mecheir. Aunchis.

Children not supporting parents proved sometimes to be a problem with the Greek community too. Ctesicles, now an old man, had already been taking his daughter to court in Alexandria and had obtained a settlement for a regular monthly pension. She, however, had not kept her side of the bargain and her partner, Dionysios, was blamed for it. Ctesicles may well have written his letter himself, for he takes a swipe at Dionysios – unusual in this kind of letter and perhaps not very good tactics:

> To King Ptolemaios, greetings from Ctesicles.
>
> I am wronged by Dionysios and my daughter, Nice. For though I had brought up my daughter, educated her, and brought her to adulthood, when I became disabled in body and my eyes became defective, she would not supply me with any of the necessities of life. When I wanted to obtain justice from her in Alexandria, she asked my pardon and in Year 18 she gave a written Royal Oath in the temple of Arsinoe-on-the-Shore that she would pay me twenty drachmas every month, working with her own body. If she didn't do this or transgressed any of the terms of the contract, she was to pay me five hundred drachmas or become liable under her oath. But now, seduced by Dionysios, who is a bugger, she doesn't do any of the things required by the contract, despising me because of my old age and my present disability. So I beg you, your majesty, not to ignore the fact that I am wronged by my daughter and that bugger, Dionysios, who has seduced her, but tell Diophanes, the *strategos*, to call them before him and listen to us … and that Diophanes deals with the man who seduced her as he thinks fit and compels my daughter, Nice, to act justly by me … If this happens, I shall be wronged no longer but, having gone to you, your majesty, for help, I shall obtain justice.[25]
>
> [File note]
>
> It has been referred to Euphor …
>
> [On the back]
>
> Year 1. The 30th of Gorpiaios – the 13th of Tubi. Ctesicles against Dionysios and Nice, his daughter, concerning a contract.

The legal system was certainly not perfect and, once caught up in it and put in prison, it was easy to be forgotten, particularly if you were an Egyptian. Zenon received this rather pitiful plea for help from someone who had been imprisoned without trial for five months. The change from 'I' to 'we' in two sentences may mean that Pais is thinking of his family too. It is a personal application to Zenon, and Pais obviously could not afford a very good scribe for the hand-writing is crude:

> To Zenon, greetings from Pais, brother of Patis.
>
> Since coming to these parts I have neither robbed nor stolen nor has any serious complainant come to you about me. It is now five months since I was arrested and all my resources are gone so that I

lack even the necessities. So now we have come to you as suppliants. We have no other help but you. I swear by your good luck and the King's guardian-genius that I was wrongly arrested. You yourself know that I am one of the reliable ones. Go bail for me and, when I get out, I will provide guarantees for you.

Good wishes.[26]

Religion is often a source of friction between communities with different traditions, but in many ways the Greeks seem to have respected the age-old religious practices of Egypt, and the Egyptians in their turn were happy to accommodate a degree of assimilation and switches of identity between their deities and those of the Greeks. In the following letter the priests of Hathor (tactfully describing themselves as the priests of Aphrodite) remind Apollonios that royal approval has been given for a large quantity of myrrh for the ceremonial burial of the Hesis, the sacred cow who was worshipped as an incarnation of Hathor. They will pray for Apollonios to receive a blessing in the shape of the king's favour:

The priests of Aphrodite to Apollonios, the Minister, greetings.

Following the King's written instructions to you to give one hundred talents of myrrh for the burial of the Hesis, you would oblige us by requiring this amount to be given. For you are not unaware that the Hesis is not brought up to the district unless we have ready all that is necessary and needed for the burial because [embalming is done?] on the same day. Know that the Hesis is Isis. May she give you the favour of Aphrodite before the King.

Farewell. Year 28. The 15th of Hathyr.[27]

Managers and executives have always been on the look-out for perks, and the likes of Zenon and his predecessor in office, Panacestor, were no exceptions. In 257 BC Panacestor had obviously asked his boss, Apollonios, the minister, for a personal boat on the Nile and a crew to go with it. For Apollonios this was evidently a perk too far, but he didn't want to disappoint or disincentivize a useful subordinate, so suggested a compromise straight out of the handbook of management studies: Panacestor could hire a boat when he needed it, but the provision was to be outsourced by a hiring arrangement with an agency:

Apollonios to Panacestor, greetings.

We would have despatched a boat to you before but we foresee great expense with regard to the sailors. If, however, you are able to make a payment to some of the people in Cerce who work and manage the sailors and will hire them out when you need a boat, write to me about it. For I will send you [the money]. If not, I do not see how I can possibly pay the sailors for spending most of their time sitting about.

Farewell. Year 29. The 2nd of Phaophi.[28]

But if bosses had to handle staff judiciously, staff had to tread carefully with their superiors. Philoxenos let Zenon borrow a millstone and needed it back. He therefore sent a note to remind Zenon and to arrange transport:

Philoxenos to Zenon, greetings.

Give the millstone to Python so that he may bring it to us. You would oblige me if you could supply a baggage-animal if one is free so that he may bring it back. Consider how we can transport the oar too.

Farewell.[29]

In spite of this and some follow-ups and in spite of personal reminders, the millstone still wasn't returned. How to write a really firm request whilst keeping it respectful?

Philoxenos to Zenon, greetings.

I have asked you previously to send me back my millstone, and have written several times. You would oblige me by returning it if possible, for I need it. But if it is not possible to get it here, write to me; for I am embarrassed to be pestering you on a number of occasions about something trivial.

Farewell.[30]

[Address on the back]

To Zenon.

Sometimes it wasn't just a millstone but arrears of pay. One of the vineyard workers had to write on this subject:

Menon, the vineyard worker, to Zenon.

For the month of Hathyr three drachmas are owed to me for my pay. I would be obliged if you would arrange for it to be given to me. For you see that I, like the rest, have neither vegetables nor anything else, but I am relying on my pay.

Good wishes.[31]

And Menon took care to remain in Zenon's good books. The slightly toadying tone of his next letter grates a little but Zenon probably took it for what it was worth and sent him the wine:

Menon to Zenon, greetings.

> You yourself know how I carry out my work for you profitably and blamelessly, and I shall try to manage things even better. Therefore, if you are so minded, give instructions for me to be given a measure of sweet wine so that I can make a libation for you and Apollonios to the spirit of this place; this is the universal custom.
>
> Good wishes.[32]

Bosses have human failings – including lady-friends – and subordinates need to handle these with discretion. Here is one of Zenon's staff, Antimenes, ensuring a comfortable journey for Doris on board the ship of another Zenon:

> Antimenes to Zenon, greetings.
>
> If you are well, that is good. I too am in good health. At the outset because of Zenon, son of Heracleides, being on a journey and because Doris was not fit and could not sail, we refrained from writing to you, but now, know that we have despatched her with Ariston in Zenon's ship and we have told Zenon to take every care of her and we ourselves have equipped her with everything she asked for the voyage.
>
> Good wishes.[33]

And the perpetual bureaucrat lurks among the files, even in the ancient world. Here, at a rather later time in the Roman period, an official who is deputizing for another official writes to himself in his original capacity to inform himself of a transaction approved by his *alter ego* acting as deputy:

> Hephaistion *aka* Ammoninos, royal clerk at Nesut, taking over the duties of *strategos*, to Hephaistion *aka* Ammoninos, royal clerk of the same district, his very good friend, greetings.
>
> A document has been submitted to me by Eudaimon, son of Psois and Tiathres, from … under the signature of the chief finance officer, the noble Claudius Apollonius … about a change of name … this reply is sent to you, my very good friend, so that you may be informed and take appropriate action.
>
> Farewell.[34]
>
> Year 3 of the Emperor Caesar Lucius Septimius Severus Pertinax Augustus
>
> Hathyr

This letter is accompanied by a copy of the original petition submitted by Eudaimon in 194 AD and it is an interesting example of someone of obviously Egyptian parentage attempting to move racially up-market by changing not his own name, which is already Greek, but the two names of his parents so that he will appear to come of good Greek stock. Henceforth he will be Eudaimon, son of Heron and Didyme, rather than Eudaimon, son of Psois and Tiathres.

Great occasions often provoke anxiety in the officials responsible for them and in 254 BC Ptolemy II received a visit from a delegation sent by Pairisades II, king of the Cimmerian Bosporus, a place far away in the region of the modern Crimea. We do not know why they came (connections between two of the major grain-producing areas – the Black Sea and Egypt – have been tentatively and rather improbably suggested), but Egypt with its spectacular sights and luxuries must have been a favourite place for 'fact-finding' missions. Ptolemy may have been economizing on this occasion for, along with the delegation from Pairisades, there was another party from Argos in mainland Greece which had religious connections. Whatever the visitors' motives, state visits have to run smoothly and this not infrequently involves last-minute arrangements on the part of the administrator in charge. In this case the two parties of distinguished visitors had probably made their way from Alexandria via Memphis and on 21 September were due to arrive at Ptolemais, the regular starting point for tourist visits to the region round Arsinoe. The minister, Apollonios, may well have been with them, at least as far as Memphis. At all events on the day before their anticipated arrival he sent this rather panicky note to Zenon to rush the carriages and mules needed for transport to Ptolemais as soon as he had read the letter:

> Apollonios to Zenon, greetings.
>
> As soon as you have read this letter, send to Ptolemais the chariots, the other conveyances for the journey, and the luggage-mules for the ambassadors from Pairisades and the delegates from Argos whom the King has sent to see the sights in the Arsinoe district. Take care they are not late for when they are needed, for when I wrote this letter to you, they had already sailed up-river.
>
> Farewell. Year 32. The 26th of Panemos – the 1st of Mesore.[35]
>
> [Address]
>
> To Zenon.

Zenon plainly realized the urgency of the situation and was perhaps anxious to cover his back too, for the file note on Apollonios' letter most unusually notes the actual hour at which the letter reached him as well as the date:

> Year 32. The 2nd of Mesore. Apollonios. The 10th hour.
>
> About the transport for the ambassadors from Pairisades and from Argos.

Foreign delegations were one thing, visits from the king himself quite another. One of Zenon's fairly wealthy friends, who doesn't however seem to be an official, was either giving a banquet for the king or was much concerned with the arrangements for it. He wrote to Zenon asking probably for a few outstanding items needed for the banquet (the quantities are much too small for this to be a main provision order); Zenon had clearly agreed to help:

> Philinos to Zenon, greetings.
>
> You would oblige me by giving to Poseidonios the jar of sweet wine as you agreed, and likewise send me the boiled grape-juice and the honey. Send the pig too quickly so that we are not too late for the arrival of the King.
>
> Farewell.[36]
>
> [Address]
>
> To Zenon.

The full food order for a distinguished visitor's formal dinner was pretty impressive. When the head of the royal bodyguard came (someone carrying the same rank as Apollonios, the Minister, himself), the hospitality was quite elaborate (not to mention the roadworks):

> Ammeneus to Asclepiades, greetings.
>
> Just as you wrote, I have prepared for the visit of Chrysippos, Head of the Bodyguard and Minister, ten whiteheads, five domestic geese and fifty fowls; for the wild birds, fifty geese, two hundred fowls and a hundred pigeons. I have borrowed five riding-mules and of them the … and I have arranged also for forty luggage-mules. I am dealing with making the road.
>
> Farewell. Year 22. The 4th of Choiak.[37]
>
> [Address]
>
> To Asclepiades.
>
> [File note]
>
> Year 22. The 7th of Choiak. Ammeneus about the hospitality arrangements.

When both the power and importance of Rome were increasing in the eastern Mediterranean in the second and first centuries BC, Greeks in Egypt, seeing the way the wind was blowing, prudently began to treat visiting Romans as rather special guests. During 112 BC the Roman senator Lucius Memmius was on a sight-seeing trip to parts of Egypt, the Memmii being one of Rome's elite and noble families (a raffish, ambitious and unprincipled member of the family was the patron of the great Roman poet Lucretius, and an acquaintance of Catullus). The event-organizer in Egypt, Hermias, writes to two subordinates about the arrangements, even reminding them of the titbits necessary for persuading the sacred crocodiles to do their stuff and put in an appearance for the visitors (Petesouchos was a local god incarnated in a crocodile):

> Hermias to Horos, greetings.
>
> A copy of the letter to Asclepiades is appended. So take care that everything happens accordingly.
>
> Farewell. Year 5. The 17th of Xandicos – the 17th of Mecheir.
>
> To Asclepiades.
>
> Lucius Memmius, a Roman senator who is regarded with much respect and honour, is journeying up-river from the city [Alexandria] to the Arsinoe district to do some sightseeing. Let him be received with due magnificence, and take care that in the appropriate places the guest-rooms will be ready and the landing-places there..... will be finished, and that at the landing-place the under-mentioned gifts will be presented to him. Take care that the preparation of the guest-room, the tit-bits for Petesouchos and the crocodiles, and the arrangements for going to see the Labyrinth ... prescribed sacrifices and ... of the sacrifice ... will be attended to. Generally in every respect take the utmost care to see that the gentleman gets a good impression and make every effort ... [38]

Some comfortably-off administrators feel an obligation to support the young, and Zenon was at one stage giving a helping hand to the education of a young man in Alexandria and offering a little amateur sports sponsorship too (provided the sporting side of things did not get out of hand). He had a friend in Alexandria called Hierocles who – rather oddly – wrote three very similar letters to Zenon about Zenon's young protégé, Pyrrhos. Pyrrhos was a promising pupil but also a promising athlete (he was, of course, going to win), and he had been lucky enough to find a trainer – another Ptolemaios – who had an obligation to Zenon:

> Hierocles to Zenon, greetings.
>
> If you are in good health and in all else getting along as you would wish, that is good. You wrote to me about Pyrrhos that, if we know for certain he will win, he must be trained but, if we do not, it must not happen that he is distracted from his schooling and needless expense falls on you. Well, he has not been at all distracted from his schooling, but he is making progress – and in other studies too. As for knowing for certain, the Gods would possibly know, but Ptolemaios says that he will easily beat his present competitors, although at the moment he is trailing because they started a long time ago and we have only recently begun training. And know that Ptolemaios is not charging fees like the other coaches, but simply

hopes you will get the crown – in return for the favours you willingly did him previously, although you were not acquainted with him … what you are doing about the *palaistra*. Take care to see to the mattress about which I wrote to you previously and bring it down; and send two jars of honey so that we can have some, for it is handy.[39]

[Address]

To Zenon.

It is really a personal letter and, comparing the distinctive script with other letters from Hierocles, we can be reasonably sure that the papyrus is in Hierocles' own hand-writing. Personal letter or no, Zenon had to remember to take some things with him when he went to Alexandria to see Hierocles and Pyrrhos, and so the letter went into the filing-system and on the back there was the usual filing note:

Hierocles about the young man.

Year 29. The 2nd of Xandicos. In Memphis.

Youth however is not always grateful, especially when the artistic temperament is involved and when there are perceived injustices. Zenon and another man called Nestos had been appointed as guardians to a young man, Heracleotes, who was a budding lyre-virtuoso. He had been living with his teacher, Demeas, who clearly had a fine instrument, and when he died, Demeas had bequeathed it to his pupil. Demeas had not only been teaching Heracleotes but also periodically issuing his living allowance, doubtless as part of some kind of contract, but, after Demeas' death, everything had gone wrong. Demeas' beautiful lyre was discovered to be in the hands of a pawnbroker (musicians often seem to have money troubles), and the living allowance to Heracleotes had been drastically reduced. Heracleotes therefore demands that his guardians first find him an instrument and then practically double his living allowance:

Memo from Heracleotes to Zenon and Nestos, my appointed guardians.

I have given you previously a memo about the instrument which was left to me in his will by Demeas, my teacher, and, when it vanished from his quarters, asking that you should either find it and give it to me, or give me another not inferior one on which I can practise and compete, so that I am not left behind by many of my fellows through being out of practice.

I sent you another memo about the instrument asking that, since Hieron agreed he was keeping the lost instrument at his place as security for a one hundred and five drachma loan, you should get it back and give it to me or else buy me another one not inferior so that I can practise and compete and not be left behind by many of my fellows because I am out of practice. You have not bothered about any of these matters.

And I sent you a third memo asking that since Demeas, my teacher, left in his will that I should be supported with all that a free man should and must have who is being trained in lyre-playing up to the stage of entering a competition; and since you are providing me every month with three drachmas four and a half obols for meat, three drachmas and three *choes* for oil, two drachmas and a half-obol for fish and seven and a half measures of wine; and since I said these were not enough for my training, I asked you for Demeas' sake and for the sake of not making a fuss to give me a monthly allowance of: for meat, seven drachmas three obols; for oil, six drachmas, six *choes*; for fish, seven drachmas three obols; and fifteen *choes* of wine. You have done none of what I asked in my memos.

So I ask you once again that either my instrument should be given back to me, the one that Hieron says he has and that was left to me in the will, or that another, not inferior, should be bought and given to me so that I may practise and enter the competition and should not be left behind by many of my fellows for the reason that I do not have an instrument. And I ask that you provide me with the necessaries specified in my letter to you according to the requirements of the will that I should be provided with all that a free man should and must have who is to be trained in lyre-playing up to the stage of entering a competition.

If it is not your choice to make this provision, I ask you to give me the monthly monetary equivalent for two years so that, looking after myself and finding a manager, I may enter the competition proclaimed by the King and not rot here – but be able to help myself.

Farewell. Year 6. In the month ... [40]

This is not strictly a letter, and Heracleotes took care to describe it as a memo. However, it has the customary 'Farewell' at the end, even if it rings a little hollow. Two previous memos are quoted almost verbatim and one wonders whether Heracleotes anticipated that these documents might be needed in court or before the *strategos* – hence the repetitive formality.

Behind a lot of the commercial and administrative activity there of course lay large numbers of financial transactions, and, while much of the business of poorer people must have been carried on by barter and exchange, the banker's table (*trapeza* – still the Greek word for a bank) became a vital and in some cases quite sophisticated part of commercial life. The evidence is not entirely clear, but in Egypt there seem to have been two types of bank: the 'royal' banks, which were much more numerous, and the private concessionary banks. Royal banks could be found in the chief town of each administrative district and sub-branches were also to be found in some of the villages. They seem to have provided simple banking functions, though not a unified system of the modern type, and they served as points for the deposit of official tax collections. The private banks seem never to have been involved with state revenues.[41] Here is a cheque written by Ammonios to his banker, Nicanor, in 241 BC:

> Ammonios to Nicanor, greetings.
>
> Transfer from my account to Apollonios, on the staff of Antiochos, the cost of two white calves – five hundred and forty copper drachmas.
>
> Farewell. Year 6. The 20th of Choiak.[42]
>
> [Another hand – in Nicanor's office]
>
> Pay 540 copper drachmas.

The zealous administrator has always had an eye for mistakes in the bank statement, particularly if the account is his own, and the following letter is evidence of the indefatigable Zenon pursuing one such discrepancy in one of his private accounts at a bank in Memphis. It is interesting to see the banker perhaps using a familiar device to underline his own importance – keeping the client waiting:

> Poseidonios to Zenon, greetings.
>
> I have given Pyron the up-to-date statement of your account and showed him the mistakes in the discrepancy. He was delayed for a few days here because I was occupied.
>
> Farewell.[43]

Cheques or money-orders that have gone astray have always been a nuisance and sometimes an embarrassment, but papyrus documents in Egypt were liable to an unusual hazard. Zenon's brother, Epharmostos, had to write to him about providing a duplicate money-order on one occasion:

> Epharmostos to his brother, greetings.
>
> The letter which you wrote to Menon about Callicon's money has been eaten by mice. You would oblige me by writing quickly so that Callicon may not be delayed.
>
> Farewell.[44]
>
> [Address on the back]
>
> To Zenon.

And some five hundred years later the same problem was still being reported: 'as far as the letter which you sent … I received it today nibbled by mice'.[45]

Most of the letters quoted in this chapter date from the Hellenistic period in Egypt when Greeks were the dominant race and the Ptolemies were beginning to exercise their oddly dual role as kings and heads of the Greek administrative machine and also as inheritors of the divine and priestly traditions of the Pharaohs. When Egypt became a Roman province, the Greeks in turn became subordinate to a layer of Roman administration and there are a great many documents which show Roman officialdom in action, and, in time, Roman, Greek and Egyptian elements in the population growing closer together. But the impression remains of an essentially Greek culture, certainly continuously modified but going on in recognisable form right into the Byzantine period. The growth of Christianity introduced a new dimension, and the language of many official and state transactions slid eventually into what sometimes became an elaborate code of flattery and self-abasement.[46] Yet somehow the Greek spirit survived. The meteoric rise of Islam and the Arab invasions of the seventh century AD changed much of the eastern Mediterranean for ever, and few things are more poignant than the last traces of the Greek administrative letter from those large parts of the Greek or Byzantine East which fell under Arab rule. In the following letter, written in AD 710, Kurrah ibn Sharik, the Arab governor of Egypt, wrote to his Greek subject Basileios, the administrator of the village of Aphrodito, about casualty figures in an Arab raid on Sicily. The heading of the letter is in Arabic but the text is in Greek; the multi-lingual scribes are now working between Greek and Arabic, and the letter has been delivered by one Said. The dating is still according to the Egyptian calendar, but the Arabic names do not transliterate very easily and it is clear that, by a curious twist of history, it is the Greeks who are – for the second time – being addressed as the subjects of a colonial elite:

> [In Arabic] To the Lord of Ashkuh as to that which has happened regarding the sailors of Africa.
>
> [In Greek] In the name of God, Kurrah, son of Sharik, the governor, to Basileios, *dioicetes* of the village of Aphrodito.
>
> We give thanks to God. Following this we have not learned the number of sailors who came back in your district – those who went out on the expedition to Africa with Ata, son of Rafi, those whom Musa, son of Nusair, sent back – and of those who stayed in Africa. So, when you receive the present letter, write to us giving the number of those aforesaid sailors who have arrived in your district, getting information from them and asking them about those who stayed in this same Africa and for what reason they stayed there – likewise the number of those who died in the aforesaid place and on the journey back after they were demobilized – and, to put it simply, give a complete and clear picture of their situation without wasting time and send it to us with all urgency after your reading of the present letter.
>
> This was written on the 4th of the month Mecheir. The 8th indiction.
>
> [File note on the back]
>
> The 15th of the month Mecheir. The 8th indiction. It was brought by Said.
>
> About listing for him the sailors sent with Ata, son of Rafi ... [47]

4

LETTERS OF STATE

Examples of official letters about politics, governance or security or the military operations of Greek states and city states, or letters which convey the thoughts and instructions of prominent public figures, are rarely available for the Classical era. It would be wonderful to have the letters of Pericles or Cleon as we have those of Cicero or Pliny, but any genuine collections have long since vanished. Tantalizingly both Herodotus and Thucydides make use of official letters in their two different modes of history-writing, but even in Thucydides we can never be sure that we have the precise words of a quoted letter. It was also the case that most Greek city-states (particularly those with democratic constitutions) conducted their affairs by recording resolutions and decrees rather than by writing letters. Generals in the field wrote reports and dispatches which might be classified either as letters or as speeches delivered by proxy, and the delegation bringing the dispatch would often be coached as to subject-matter and the answering of questions. This type of document is occasionally recorded but, though the sense may be preserved, the original words are probably beyond our grasp. In the Hellenistic world from the time of Alexander the Great onwards, the situation changes remarkably. Monarchy was in the end a personal exercise of power and the king wrote to his subjects person to person in letter-form, the writer of the letters uttering the royal voice: the head of the royal chancery in Syria was known as the *epistolographos*, the Letter-Writer. After Alexander's death and the formation of the Hellenistic kingdoms, royal correspondence is frequent and – fortunately – frequently permanently recorded, for it was often in the interests of both ruler and ruled to have the king's decisions and instructions unarguably available in public; they were normally cut as inscriptions and fixed in one or more prominent and central places.[1] Civil servants often evolve their own codes and formulas of expression, and the chanceries of the Hellenistic kings soon devised formal patterns for the conduct of typical royal correspondence. These are easily recognizable and doubtless provided a framework of mutual understanding for both officials and subjects. The royal letters very occasionally hint at the thoughts and words of the king himself, but they are mostly of interest because of the direct insight they offer into the workings of Hellenistic government and diplomacy. They show these in remarkable detail, whether it is a matter of larger cities adjusting their allegiances and jockeying for position or of a world increasingly nervous about the expansion of Roman influence and the unmistakeable signs of a *Drang nach Osten* from that direction.

The earliest genuine piece of state correspondence we have from the Greek world is not strictly a Greek letter, for originally it was probably written in Aramaic or Old Persian. However, it is a letter partly about Greeks and for Greeks, and the text which has survived is in Greek and came from a Greek city, Magnesia-on-the-Maeander. The opening shows that the letter originates from a very grand person indeed, Darius, the lord of the Persian empire, and it was sent to his provincial governor or satrap who was probably in charge of the western part of Asia Minor in which a number of flourishing Ionian Greek cities were located. The address bears eloquent witness to the gap between the absolute monarch and even a quite important subordinate: ' … Darius … to Gadatas, his slave … ' The Persian kings took an interest in the cultivation of trees and crops[2] and Gadatas too was evidently something of a horticulturalist, for he had been responsible for transplanting a particular variety of fruit trees into southern Asia Minor. The fruit trees were native to the Syrian region – from the Persian point of view the land 'across the Euphrates' – and Gadatas is rewarded with a conventional formula of Persian royal praise ' … great gratitude … in the house of the King'. However, the surprising part of the letter concerns some rather lowly Greeks, 'the sacred gardeners of Apollo'. The situation would seem to be that some Greek gardeners attached to the temple of Apollo at Magnesia felt aggrieved on two counts: first, they were becoming liable to fresh taxes – in their view unjustifiably – and second, they were being compelled to cultivate land outside the sacred precincts and therefore beyond their job description (perhaps transplanting the fruit trees?). Somehow they seem to have managed to get their complaint to the ears of the King of Kings himself, and surprisingly he ruled in their favour and sent the following abrupt letter to his satrap. The gardeners must have been glad to see their success recorded in Greek on Apollo's temple wall and it must have been a useful assurance of their rights for the future. What Gadatas thought of this can only be guessed but perhaps the royal approval for the fruit trees mollified his feelings:

> The King of Kings, Darius, son of Hystaspes, to Gadatas, his slave, speaks as follows:
>
> I discover that you are not obeying my instructions in all respects. Because you are taking much trouble over my land, transplanting fruit trees from across the Euphrates to the lower parts of Asia [Minor], I praise your enterprise and because of this, great gratitude

> will be laid down for you in the house of the King. But because you are effacing my arrangements on behalf of the gods, I will give you, if you do not change your mind, experience of my anger when I am wronged. For you have collected taxes from the sacred gardeners of Apollo and you have ordered them to cultivate unsanctified land, ignoring the intention of my ancestors towards the god who has spoken whole truth to the Persians and to the … [3]

One obvious place to look for state correspondence is in the work of historians. The two greatest Greek historians, Herodotus and Thucydides, regarded letters as part of the fabric of history and both wrote the texts of letters into their narratives. So, in Herodotus Harpagos writes to Cyrus, the Persian king, the Egyptian Pharaoh Amasis writes to Polycrates, the Greek tyrant of Samos, Oroites, a Persian, also writes to Polycrates, Darius writes to Megabazos, Histiaios writes a top-secret letter to Aristagoras, Demaratos, the Spartan king now living at the Persian court, writes clandestinely to let Sparta know about the imminent invasion of Greece by Xerxes, and a Greek traitor, Timoxenos, secretly corresponds with the Persian Artabazos by means of letters delivered by arrows.[4] There seems little doubt that, where the texts of letters are quoted, Herodotus composed the letters himself and was more concerned with giving an appearance of reality to his story than with the authenticity or otherwise of the documents.[5] The form of these letters is, however, of interest because they presumably reflect the kind of letter which Herodotus took for granted and thought appropriate to the events he described. So, when the Egyptian Pharaoh, Amasis, wrote to his friend, Polycrates, who had been enjoying an unusual run of success raiding and plundering in the Greek islands, he did so in Greek, with some conventional Greek moralizing on the theme of *hybris*, and in a form which is presumably that of the contemporary Greek letter:

> Amasis to Polycrates says thus:
>
> It is pleasant to discover that someone who is a friend and with whom one has a connection is enjoying success. But for me your great good fortune is not a source of delight since I know that the gods feel envy. As for myself and for those I care for, I want to succeed in some things and to fail in others, and to spend my life alternating between the two rather than enjoying total success. For I have never heard tell of anyone who finally, after enjoying total success, did not experience total ruin. So now, follow my advice, and in the face of success, act as follows: think carefully about what you value most and about what your heart would most grieve to lose and throw this away beyond human ken. If, then, in future success does not alternate with suffering, use the method I have put before you as your remedy.[6]

There is, however, one instance of a public 'letter', advertisement or proclamation which was carved on stone and which Herodotus appears to quote verbatim. It is a notice, carved into the rocks of the coastline, in which Themistocles, following the victory at Thermopylae, urges the Ionian Greeks who were fighting with the Persian army to rebel against Xerxes and join their fellow-Greeks. Whether Herodotus saw the inscription and copied it is open to very considerable doubt; it was probably the fact of its use as a 'secret weapon' in war that took Herodotus' fancy. It has – curiously – been regarded as a 'letter', though the form of it is more akin to a patriotic notice; it neither reads nor feels like a letter, even an open letter, and the text is probably an exercise in historical imagination.[7]

With Thucydides the search for authentic letters becomes more serious, for with him the rules of evidence change. It is very unlikely that he saw the originals or copies of all the letters that he purports to quote, and it has been suspected on reasonable grounds that he must have adopted the same practice with letters as with the speeches he reports:

> And, as for the words each person spoke, either on the eve of war or in the course of it, it was hard for me to recall the exact words of what I myself heard as it was for those who reported speeches to me from here and there. I have used the words which it seemed to me that each person would have spoken in accordance with the occasion, holding as far as possible to the overall sense of what was actually said.[8]

There may be, though, a difference between speeches and letters, for the carefully wrought speech was becoming a fashionable commodity at the time Thucydides wrote, and the notoriously crafted style of his speeches is not reflected in the quoted letters. Letters are integral parts of sections of Thucydides' history and there is a vein of conscious realism in their quotation. For instance, in Herodotus the Egyptian Pharaoh writes to his friend, the Greek tyrant, in dialect Greek; in Thucydides, however, when the Athenians intercept a letter from the Persian Artaxerxes to the Spartans, it cannot be read until the Assyrian characters have been deciphered.[9] Thucydides normally has a careful and consistent way of introducing quoted documents, whether speeches or letters: the expression 'as follows' (*tade* or *tauta* in Greek) indicates a near-representation of the original; the expression 'in something like the following way' (*toiade* or *toiauta*) introduces Thucydides' version of what the situation seemed to require. In Book i.126–38 a longish section describes the uneasy period of the late 430s BC which immediately preceded the outbreak of the Peloponnesian War between Athens and Sparta. Thucydides reports various diplomatic skirmishes, one of which involves the Athenians reminding the Spartans of the treacherous behaviour of their king, Pausanias, at the time of the Persian Wars. Pausanias had been the victor of the crucial battle of Plataea and, being also the uncle of the legendary Leonidas, was an unquestioned war hero. However, he had had dangerous ambitions and had secretly opened negotiations with Xerxes. His first move was made by sending back some prisoners of war, including people close to Xerxes himself. A man from Eretria, Gongylos, managed the transaction and also took the following letter to the Persian king:

> Pausanias, the Spartan leader, wanting to do you a favour dispatches to you these men who were captured in battle, and I make the suggestion, if you too think it is a good thing, of marrying your daughter and of bringing Sparta and the rest of Greece under your control. I believe I can do this if we plan jointly. So, if you are at all attracted by this, send across the sea a man you can trust through whom we can communicate in future.[10]

It seems too good to be true with its clumsy bluntness (fitting the Spartan stereotype), and the letter has been much suspected. However, Thucydides introduces it with 'as follows' – normally signifying a near-quotation – and reinforces that with the expression 'as was afterwards discovered'. Moreover, at the end of the letter Thucydides continues, 'This was what the written message revealed … ' It seems clear that, whatever some modern scholars might feel, Thucydides himself believed that he was giving a pretty true quotation. The same can probably be said of Xerxes' reported reply. Xerxes took Pausanias' bait and sent his envoy, Artabazos, to replace the local satrap and to deliver a letter to Pausanias in Byzantium, guaranteeing its authenticity with the Persian royal seal:

> Thus says King Xerxes to Pausanias:
>
> As for the men who you saved for me, sending them across the sea from Byzantium, gratitude will lie for you in our house forever recorded, and I am pleased by what you say. Let neither night nor day hold you back so that you slacken in the performance of any of the things you promised me, and do not be hindered by the need to spend gold and silver or the need for military support if you require it at any point, but, along with the good Artabazos whom I have sent to you, confidently pursue my interests and yours so that there may be the best and most excellent outcome for us both.[11]

This invites even more questions: how could Thucydides or his source have come upon such texts? Yet Thucydides introduces the letter with 'as follows', and there are touches which suggest authenticity: 'gratitude will lie for you in our house' recalls Darius' expression of thanks to his satrap who had successfully transplanted the fruit trees. It is of course possible that Thucydides composed the letter himself and added a touch or two of oriental spice to make it look right, but there are no other instances of Thucydides using decorative detail of this kind to add spurious reality to an invention of his own. It looks as though Thucydides believed that he was giving a genuine text.

A little later, as part of a counter-accusation by the Spartans to the Athenians, the career of the great Themistocles is described after he had been ostracized and had left Athens. His first approach to Artaxerxes, who had succeeded his father Xerxes, was by means of a letter and Thucydides quotes this, introducing it not by 'as follows' but 'the written message revealed that':

> I, Themistocles, have come to you, I who of the Greeks did the most harm to your house during the time when I necessarily defended myself against your father who was coming upon us, but did even greater good when in turn the retreat meant that I was safe but he was endangered. Gratitude is owed to me (he wrote here about the warning he gave to retreat from Salamis and the fact that the bridges over the Hellespont were not destroyed, which he falsely claimed was due to him) and now I am here, able to do great things for you and pursued by the Greeks because of my friendship for you. But I wish to hold off for a year before revealing the reasons for my coming.[12]

This is of a piece with the letters of Pausanias and Xerxes, and its documentary credentials are at first sight strengthened by Thucydides' abbreviation of part of the letter (if you are inventing it anyway, why bother?). According to Thucydides' practice elsewhere in his history, all three letters are offered as the real thing, but it must be admitted that few modern historical commentators are without serious doubts. There are two possibilities: that Thucydides composed them himself adding supposedly authentic touches, or that he took them from another source sincerely believing that they were genuine. The first sits unhappily with Thucydides' normally rigorous standards, and the explanation that they are youthful indiscretions looks thin. All that can probably be said is that, if the letters are made up, the results were good enough to deceive one of the most careful ancient historians.[13]

Probably the most celebrated 'letter' to be found in Thucydides is the one written by the Athenian general, Nicias, to the Athenian Assembly in 414 BC about the dire plight of the Athenian forces on the Sicilian expedition. Thucydides emphasizes that Nicias wrote a letter for a particular reason: he was afraid that envoys might not convey the starkness of the picture, either because they did not express themselves well enough or because they had lapses of memory or because they would try to tell a large crowd in the Assembly what it wanted to hear.[14] He had been accustomed to send reports back to Athens, but this time the situation in Sicily was so serious that he wanted to be sure that the facts were truly understood at home. A delegation was therefore thoroughly briefed verbally and equipped to answer questions, but most importantly of all it also brought a written statement intended to be read publicly verbatim. The crucial importance and historical significance of this document for Thucydides is shown by the trouble he took to compose a quite lengthy reconstruction of it (introduced by 'in something like the following way' – *toiade*). There can be little doubt that a similar communication was sent by Nicias and was read to the Assembly, nor is there much doubt about its status: it was an urgent military dispatch which not unnaturally assumed the form of a public speech:

> As for what has been done previously, Athenians, you have learnt about that in many other letters. But now is no less the right moment for you to understand the situation we are in and to take decisions. For when in the majority of battles we had beaten the Syracusans against whom we were sent here and had built the fortifications in which we now have our positions, the Spartan Gylippos arrived with an army from the Peloponnese and from some of the Sicilian cities. In the first battle he was defeated by us, but in the following one, forced back by many horsemen and javelin-throwers, we retreated within the fortifications.[15]

The worsening situation is described at length and in urgent detail and serves both as an explanation of the Athenians' plight and as an evocation of a dramatic moment in the Athenian Assembly. Perhaps Thucydides allows himself a moment of personal pique when Nicias is made to reflect on the Athenian corporate character – Thucydides himself as an army commander had suffered at the hands of the Assembly for his failure against the brilliant Spartan general, Brasidas, in 424 BC:

> And at the same time knowing your character – that you want to hear what is most pleasant, but afterwards turn to accusation if some event does not turn out like that – I thought it safer to reveal the truth.[16]

These are the only quoted letters in Thucydides' history; five others are mentioned but no text is given.[17]

One other military dispatch survives from the time of the Peloponnesian War. It is reported by Xenophon in his *Greek History* and is very likely to be genuine, for it is laconic both in its telegrammatic form and its Dorian dialect. Xenophon says it was sent back to Sparta in 410 BC after the Athenians had won a great and unexpected victory over the Spartans at Cyzicus in Asia Minor. The three Athenian commanders, Alcibiades, Theramenes and Thrasyboulos, had taken the Spartan admiral, Mindaros, by surprise and, fighting both on shore and at sea, not only relieved Cyzicus from the Spartan siege but inflicted such a resounding defeat that the Spartans actually sued for peace. In fact, the dispatch never reached its destination but was intercepted by the Athenians and, being short, memorable and perhaps a kind of war-trophy, entered the historical record. The tone is desperate:

> The good times are finished. Mindaros is dead. The men are starving. We have no idea what we should do.[18]

In the fourth century BC it was the growing power of Macedon and the extraordinary conquests of Alexander the Great which dominated the Greek historical scene. Alexander's tough and remarkable father, Philip II, laid the foundations, and his ambition and plans for expansion were fiercely resisted by people like the Athenian orator and politician, Demosthenes. Philip's methods were the familiar ones of power politics: military strength and its use excused by linking it to supposedly justifiable causes. In the text of Demosthenes' famous speech *On the Crown*, a letter of Philip II is quoted, addressed to his allies, especially those in the Peloponnese. What Philip actually wanted at this time was to get a large force under Macedonian command into central Greece with a view to securing the town of Amphissa and the district of Locris (just to the east of Delphi). In the letter, what he says he wants is 'to come to the help of the God [Apollo] and to defend him' – a noble cause to which all can assent. The final sentence proclaiming that all who are not with us are against us is a familiar enough device of *Machtpolitik*:

> Philip, King of the Macedonians, to the magistrates and councillors of the Peloponnesians who are in alliance with us, and to all our other allies, greetings.
>
> Since the Locrians, those called Ozolians, who live in Amphissa, are causing offence in regard to the temple of Apollo at Delphi and, entering sanctified territory, are plundering it by force of arms, I want, along with you, to come to the help of the God and defend him against those who are to an extent transgressing the bounds of what is held sacred among men. Therefore, assemble with us under arms in Phocis, having provisions for forty days, within the present month of Loios as we term it, and, as the Athenians call it, Boedromion, and, as the Corinthians, Panemos. And those who do not assemble with us with all their forces we shall treat as liable to punishment.
>
> Good wishes.[19]

That an actual letter from Philip was read at this point in Demosthenes' speech is not in doubt and it is possible that, when Demosthenes prepared his speech for publication, he included the original text of the letter. It is certain, however, that the letter we now read is not the one that Philip wrote. It is not known when the letters which occur in the text of *On the Crown* were composed or by whom, but the writer of this letter had quite a keen appreciation of the language of aggression (in spite of his rather academic excursus on dating) and it is a reasonable guess that Philip's own letter adopted a not dissimilar tone.[20]

The letter now became a regular means of conveying the royal will, and we have an undoubtedly genuine letter from Philip's son, Alexander the Great, to the people of Chios, probably sent in 332 BC when Alexander was occupied with the conquest of Asia Minor; the letter survives on an inscription. Chios, a large prosperous island lying just off the modern Turkish coast, was culturally Greek but always liable to the ebbs and flows of Persian influence, and in the mid-fourth century BC had been under the control of Mausolos, the ruler of Caria; it was then therefore within the orbit of Persian power. In 336 BC the oligarchy sympathetic to Mausolos was overthrown and a precarious independence achieved, but three years later a small group betrayed Chios back to the Persians and the island remained under Persian control until it was 'freed' by the Macedonians. What freedom meant is shown by the tone of the letter: Alexander issues instructions to his new free subjects as confidently as any Persian autocrat. And, in spite of handing over the pro-Persian traitors to what looks like an independent inquiry – the 'Council of the Greeks' refers to the Greek allies of the League of Corinth founded by Philip II – Alexander in fact dealt with them himself. The Macedonian garrison was withdrawn after a year.

> In the term of office of Deisitheos, from King Alexander to the people of Chios, greetings.
>
> All the exiles from Chios should return and the constitutional body on Chios should be the people. Law draughtsmen should be chosen who will write and revise the laws so that there may be no impediment to democracy or to the return of the exiles. What has been revised or written should be referred to Alexander. The people of Chios should provide twenty manned triremes at their own expense, and these should sail for as long as the rest of the Greek fleet sails with us. As for those who betrayed the city to the barbarians, those who have departed should be exiled from all the cities which are parties to the peace and should be liable to arrest according to the Greek decree. Those who have been left behind in the city should be brought to court and judged in the Council of the Greeks. If there is any disagreement between those who have returned and those who have remained in the city, judgement between them in this matter will be made before us. Until the people of Chios are settled, a garrison sufficient for the task will be with them from King Alexander; the people of Chios shall maintain it.[21]

Kings, kingdoms and cities

Alexander's imperious correspondence ushers in an era of government in which many important matters are dealt with by the official letter sent from the royal chancery. After Alexander's death in 323 BC the short-lived cohesion of a huge Macedonian empire fragmented and was replaced by a mosaic of smaller kingdoms. The Hellenistic monarchs rarely enjoyed stability and the spheres of influence of kingdoms, city-states and cities waxed and waned according to the balance of military power, economic changes and the political acumen of kings and their advisers. Hence it was not surprising that cities often made arrangements for mutual support, and for particular reasons they might join together in confederations or leagues with treaty obligations which could involve agreeing to fight together – the *symmachia.* One of the first and most powerful of these leagues had been occasioned by the Persian threat to Greece in the fifth century BC – the League of Delos, a defensive alliance which Athens – the lead partner – transformed into a short-lived empire. In the Hellenistic period and on a more local scale, individual cities often sought advantages in partnership, and occasionally two cities would even agree to an outright merger in which the entire population of one city would transfer to another, thereby creating (it was hoped) a larger, more secure, more viable unit. Such a process of setting up house together (the literal meaning of the technical term – *synoikismos*) usually required a new or adapted set of laws and must also have sparked all kinds of local disputes and the need for fair, and sometimes external, arbitration in compensation and settlement claims. If it succeeded, however, the resulting city was a bigger and stronger centre for the local area, and it was a process encouraged and sometimes imposed by the Hellenistic kings, who preferred larger and more stable units under their control. In the following letter King Antigonos of Macedon is trying to advise on or arrange just such a merger between two cities on the western coast of modern Turkey. The immediate cause of it is not clear but it may have something to do with the major earthquake which hit the region in 304–3 BC. Lebedos was a small place on the coast about thirty-six kilometres north-west of Ephesus, and it was one of the poorest of the Ionian Greek cities. Teos, its partner city and the proposed centre of the new merged community to whose town Council and people Antigonos' letter is addressed, was also on the coast and little to the north west of Lebedos. It was a much more substantial place and was comparable to cities like Miletus and Ephesus.[22] Before this letter was written considerable negotiation had gone on, traces of which can be followed in a surviving edict of Antigonos. The project does not seem to have been popular with either city for there was considerable dragging of the feet, but things had progressed far enough for the king's wishes and advice to be published in two letters inscribed and displayed on Teos. Here the question of how to fund immediate compensation for the people of Lebedos is addressed. The solution of setting up a loan-fund from contributions by the 600 richest citizens of Teos can hardly have appealed to many of the city fathers there. The letter goes on to deal with the tricky matters of valuing the houses of the dispossessed and drafting the laws of the new merged city, and it seems that, for the valuations, independent assessors are to be brought in from the island of Cos. Cos is some way to the south and at this period owed its allegiance to Ptolemy in Egypt, not to Antigonos, so it looks as though considerable efforts were being made to obtain impartial arbitrators and law-givers. Indeed, the laws, by mutual agreement, were to be copied from those of Cos which famously derived from the legendary law-giver Charondas. The king and his staff were obviously well aware of the likelihood of delaying tactics and therefore set a tight timetable. The final part of the letter refers to arrangements for the temporary billeting of the people of Lebedos on their first move to their new city – this is entrusted to local arrangements, again within a time-limit.

> King Antigonos to the Council and people of the Teans, greetings.
>
> When we looked before at how the merger would be most quickly completed, we did not see from where the necessary money could be provided for you to reimburse the people of Lebedos for the value of their houses, since the money from revenues accrues over too long a period. When we received your people and those from Lebedos and asked them if they had any source of funds to suggest, they said they had not, except the money from taxes. On examination of what has been settled we find that it is only your richest citizens who regularly pay the property tax. It seems to us, therefore, a fair decision that six hundred should be chosen as the richest men, and that they should contribute according to their assets so that a quarter of the valuation money should be very quickly available to the people of Lebedos, and that repayment should be made to these contributors first from the revenues of the city after a year's interval, all the revenues being allotted for that purpose. And it seems right to us that the men who are to convey the valuers of the houses and those who are going to copy the Cos laws should be chosen as soon as the winding-up vote is taken, and should be dispatched within five days from the date of their being chosen. Those dispatched to get the laws, having conveyed them from Cos, should deliver them within the period we indicated to you in our [previous] answer to you, and those dispatched to get the valuers should bring the valuers as soon as possible. We think it necessary that the houses in your city which must be given to the people of Lebedos as temporary accommodation should be counted up within fifteen days of the reading of this answer and that those who are going to count the houses and allot them to the temporary occupants should be chosen by each tribe at the first available Assembly.[23]

In spite of the fact that so much trouble had been taken and a royal letter published, the merger between the cities never actually took place for, a little later, the inhabitants of Lebedos were moved into Ephesus. Antigonos himself was killed at the battle of Ipsos in 301 BC. The Tean draggers of feet achieved their end.

Under the Hellenistic rulers, Greek kingdoms were constantly jockeying for position, either by mounting military expeditions or more commonly by diplomatic alliances and agreements. In this process the allegiance of some of the great Greek cities of Ionia was a matter of considerable concern. They were too large and too prestigious simply to be coerced, and their room for independent manoeuvre meant that, when crises threatened, attempts were frequently made to secure their support. In the year 288–7 BC there was the need for just such an initiative. Demetrios, king of Macedon, was known to be preparing a major military expedition to enlarge his territories and influence, and this had provoked an impressive defensive alliance consisting of Pyrrhos, king of Epirus, Lysimachos, king of Thrace, Seleucos, king of Syria, and Ptolemy, king of Egypt. Pyrrhos and Lysimachos had already seen action against Demetrios with some success, but this did not prevent Demetrios from taking an expedition across the Aegean in the autumn of 288 BC. To the dismay of his opponents, many of the great Ionian cities welcomed his approach and he seems to have had friendly connections there; among these cities was Miletus which was nominally under the control of one of the alliance kings, Lysimachos. At this stage a military solution was evidently not thought appropriate, so Miletus became the recipient of a politico-religious initiative. Seleucos and Antiochos who in name ruled jointly in Syria therefore sent their agent, Polyanthes, to Miletus with a massively generous offering to the oracle of Apollo at Didyma, along with an official covering letter from Seleucos which made it clear that they were instructing the authorities in Miletus actually to present the offering on their behalf. This was plainly to be interpreted not only as a request for the god's favour but also as a signal honour for Miletus and of course the dutiful act of god-fearing kings. The oracle at Didyma was about twelve kilometres south of Miletus and was of some antiquity and reputation, the shrine having been destroyed by Darius in 494 BC and re-founded in some grandeur in the time of Alexander the Great. Consultation ceremonies at the oracle were quite elaborate and a dedication of this size may well have involved some extended pomp.[24] The gesture from the kings was evidently accepted, for a copy of the letter was inscribed and publicly displayed, and it was prefaced by an explanatory note giving the names of the Milesian officials on whose authority it was put up. The tone of the letter is curious: while an honorific gesture is being made to Miletus, Seleucos makes it clear that he is instructing rather than asking Miletus to act for him, and he thereby conveys an unmistakeable message about where he expects the city's loyalties to lie. The letter did not, however, achieve its purpose, for Miletus did not return to her original allegiance until matters came to a military head seven years later when Demetrios was defeated by Seleucos at the battle of Corupedion.

King Seleucos to the Council and people of the Milesians, greetings.

We have dispatched to the temple of Apollo at Didyma Polyanthes, bringing you the great lamp stand and the gold and silver cups (bearing inscriptions) as an offering to the Saviour Gods. You, therefore, as soon as he is with you, having received the gifts with goodwill, present them to the temple so that you can pour libation and make use of them for our health and prosperity and for the continuing safety of the city – which is my wish and your prayer. Carry out the instructions given to Polyanthes and the dedication of the objects dispatched, and perform the sacrifice which we have detailed to him. Join him therefore in taking care that things are done properly. I have appended a list for you of the gold and silver dispatched to the temple so that you may know both the nature and the weight of each item

Farewell.

A list of the golden objects dispatched

One *phiale* – date pattern – 'Of Good Fortune' – weight 247 drachmas
Another – date pattern – 'Of Osiris' – weight 190 drachmas
Another – date pattern – 'Of Leto' – weight 198 drachmas, 3 obols
Another – date pattern – 'Of Hecate' – weight 113 drachmas
One pair of *rhytons* with double deer-heads – 'Of Apollo' – weight 318 drachmas, 3 obols
Another *rhyton* with double deer-head – 'Of Artemis' – weight 161 drachmas
A horn inscribed 'To Zeus the Saviour' – weight 173 drachmas, 8 obols
A wine-pourer – 'Of the Saviour Gods' – weight 386 drachmas
A wine-cooler – foreign, set with gems inscribed 'Of the Saviour Goddess' – seven dates fallen off – weight 372 drachmas
A gold bread-plate – weight 1,088 drachmas

Total weight of gold objects – 3,248 drachmas, 3 obols

A silver *skyphos* with relief figures – [cord pattern?] – weight 380 drachmas
A large wine-cooler of silver – two-handled – weight 9,000 drachmas
10 talents of frankincense, 1 talent of myrrh, 2 *minai* of casia, 2 *minai* of cinnamon, 2 *minai* of spice
A large bronze lamp stand.
[Polyanthes] also brought a sacrifice for the god – 1,000 sheep and 12 oxen.[25]

But if rulers in the Hellenistic world sometimes needed to flatter and entice other important cities, it was much commoner for the cities to ask favours of their king. In the following letter King Antiochos II is replying favourably to a request from the city of Erythrai for independent status and for what seem to be substantial tax exemptions. Erythrai was a large Greek coastal city in Asia Minor lying opposite the island of Chios. It had been a member of the Delian League in the fifth century BC and its high tribute-assessment of seven talents testifies to its size and importance.[26] Its prosperity continued under Alexander the Great and his successors, including Antigonos I under whom it received tax-exempt status; under what circumstances taxes were reimposed we do not know. From the letter it is possible to reconstruct the typical process of petitioning the king. First, doubtless, came lengthy deliberations in the city Council of which we have now no trace. Once the terms of the request were decided, a package of compliments was devised. In this instance this consisted of a decree passed by the city Council setting out praise of the king and granting him city honours, and probably titles like 'benefactor'. In addition he was voted a *stephanos*, a crown; the gesture was so frequent that the word sometimes simply signified 'honours', but here it is mentioned separately by the king and was quite probably one of those elaborate leaf-gold wreaths which were the common coin of diplomatic exchange in the Hellenistic world. The king was not only flattered with words and titles, however; gifts of carefully calculated value (in this case gold) were also sent. The petition and the decree were delivered personally by a delegation of three senior figures from Erythrai and were evidently presented with a carefully crafted speech which not only flattered the king and 'made the ask' but also reminded him of historical precedent for the request. The members of the city delegation were in this case successful; the king's secretaries summarized the process of negotiation (including mention of historical precedent), thanked Erythrai for its friendly sentiments, its honours and its presents, and elaborated the royal grant with reciprocal compliments. The whole thing well demonstrates the careful and subtle modes of Hellenistic diplomatic courtesy, not forgetting the word of thanks at the end to the members of the delegation. At the foot of the king's letter the decree of the Council of Erythrai formally thanking the king was inscribed; only end-fragments of the first five lines survive. The original *stele* on which the whole thing was inscribed unfortunately no longer exists today, and its fate is a curious example of the accidents of survival of sources from the ancient world. The original *stele* was found at the site of ancient Erythrai by a Mr Christoiannaki, who presented it to the museum of the Evangelical School in Smyrna in 1874–5; it was transcribed and given scholarly publication by E. Curtius in Berlin that same year. Later, when a Greek school for girls was built in Smyrna, called the Homereion, it was felt that the inscription was a suitable ornament and the stone was accordingly built into the wall of the school playground. However, the builders found its irregular shape inconvenient and chopped off the last twelve lines of text to square the block. A pressed copy – a 'squeeze' – was taken and is in the collection of the Austrian Archaeological Institute. The school itself was burnt down in the great fire which destroyed large parts of Smyrna in 1922 and the stone was never found, in spite of the effort of two diligent scholars who searched the ruins.

> King Antiochos to the Council and people of Erythrai, greetings.
>
> Tharsynon, Pythes and Bottas, your representatives, presented us with the decree according to which you voted us honours and brought us the crown with which you crowned us, and likewise the gold too meant as a friendly gift, and having themselves spoken about the goodwill you have for our house in all circumstances, and in general about the gratitude felt by the people towards all their benefactors, and further about the prominence enjoyed by the city under previous kings, they asked with all enthusiasm and zeal that we should maintain a state of friendship with you and at the same time, in all that relates to honour and glory, we should join in promoting the city's affairs. We have been pleased to accept the honours and the crown and likewise the gifts, and we praise you for showing your gratitude in all things; for you appear generally to adopt this posture. Because of this we shall continue the goodwill we had for you from the beginning, observing that you conduct yourselves with sincerity and honesty in all matters; and now we are drawn to you much more, appreciating your nobility from much else and not least from the decree which was presented to us and from the words of your delegation.
>
> Since Tharsynon, Pythes and Bottas demonstrated that in the time of Alexander and Antigonos your city was independent and tax-immune, and our forebears were always zealous for it, we, observing that they showed good judgement and ourselves not wishing to be left behind in benefaction, will along with you guard your autonomy and we agree that you should be tax-immune in all respects including from tax collected for the Galatian business. You will also have … [and if] there is any other benefit that we may think of or you [may ask]. We ask you also remembering … goodwill as is right and … and what you have done previously … you will properly remember [those by whom] you have been benefited. [More about these things and] the others of which we have spoken will be reported to you by your representatives whom [we praise] both for the other things [they did] and because of the zeal they displayed for [the interests of the people].
>
> Farewell.[27]

The actual machinery of government in some of the large Greek cities offers another facet of the tricky balance between the desire of kings to exercise control, the requirements of local self-esteem, and the appearance of partial independence. Pergamum is a case in point. The city had its citizen body (the *demos*) and its local Council (the *boule*), but a board of five annually appointed 'generals' (*strategoi*) presided over meetings of the city Council and had the exclusive right to introduce measures to the Council and the assembly. These five were appointed by the king and, while they acted as his political and financial watchdogs, they could also be seen as an arm of the local administration and as collaborators in the local enterprise. The following letter from King Eumenes I of Pergamum shows this process in action. He writes – unusually – directly to the people of the city (not to the Council and the people) commending to them the five *strategoi* of the previous year who had plainly been cleaning out the city's administrative stables for the benefit of all, and conveys the broadest hint that the people should follow him in giving public acknowledgement of their services. Needless to say, the people obliged, and inscribed with the letter is the decree in which the people resolved to award to the *strategoi* gold crowns at the next Panathenaia festival and, at the king's own festival, the Eumenaia, to give them every year a sheep for sacrifice. The system of five supervisory officers was plainly successful for *mutatis mutandis* it lasted well into Roman times. The decree makes financial provision for having both the letter and the decree recorded on stone and placed in the *agora*, and the inscription we have is the result. It was discovered in Pergamum in 1883, built into a Turkish gateway tower. Some of the text of the letter is missing but it can very plausibly be restored from the complete text of the decree which follows it. The date may be any time between 260 and 240 BC.

> Eumenes, son of Philetairos, to the people of Pergamum, greetings.
>
> Palamandros, Skymnos, Metrodoros, Philotimos and Philiscos, the *strategoi* who were appointed … appear to have performed the duties of their office well on all occasions. All other matters of administration relating to these have been carried out fairly, and they have not only managed properly the city and temple income which falls under their remit on behalf of the city and the gods, but have also tracked down what has been overlooked by previous office-holders and, sparing no-one who has withheld anything, have returned it to the city. They have given their attention to repairing offerings in the temple and, since they have reinstated the aforementioned matters, the *strategoi* who come after them, following their guidance, will be able to run the affairs of state smoothly. Therefore, thinking it right not to belittle those who have discharged their duties in this way so that subsequent appointees may try to preside duly over the people, we have ourselves resolved to award them crowns at the next Panathenaia, and we thought we should write to you about them so that, in the meantime, after discussing

the matter, you should honour them in the manner you think they deserve.

Farewell.[28]

Things are not always quite what they seem in royal diplomatic transactions. In about 240 BC King Ziaelas of Bithynia, a monarch who had seized the throne in a mercenary coup, received a delegation of three representatives from the island of Cos. Bithynia had a long coastline on the Black Sea and, by a combination of diplomacy and force, had managed to remain independent of the larger kingdoms. The delegation's ostensible purpose was to secure a continuing guarantee of inviolable status for the famous shrine of Asclepius on Cos, with its medical associations. Cos lay far to the south and Bithynia was therefore unlikely ever to have to honour its guarantee. This is the window-dressing; the delegation's real purpose is revealed in the second half of the king's reply. Cos was a thriving trading centre and it looks as though its merchants were regularly operating in the Black Sea and becoming somewhat nervous of their reception among the native Bithynians; the Bithynians were not Greeks and had a certain reputation for stern, unfriendly masculinity.[29] Ziaelas is anxious to dispel suggestions of xenophobia, to show that Greeks are welcome, and to stress points of common ground such as the friendly relations with Egypt. The letter was found inscribed on a prism of marble along with two other royal letters in the shrine of Asclepius on Cos; it is written in a Greek which contains a few loose colloquialisms and gives a hint perhaps that Ziaelas' Greek secretaries were not quite of the calibre usual in more central parts of the Greek world.

The King of the Bithynians, Ziaelas, to the Council and people of Cos, greetings.

Diogeitos, Aristolochos and Theudotos, your representatives who came before us, asked us to recognize the temple of Asclepius situated in your midst as inviolable and asked us in all other respects to maintain a good relationship with your city in the same way that Nicomedes, our father, was well disposed to your people. We do actually take trouble over all the Greeks who come to us, being persuaded that this kind of thing makes no small contribution to our reputation. Most of all we continue to honour our father's friends and you because of our father's acquaintance with your people and because King Ptolemaios, our friend and ally, is well disposed to your affairs; still more because your delegates recounted particularly favourably the goodwill you have for us. In the future, as you may ask, we will try to show favour both to individuals privately and to all in public as far as we are able; and for those who sail the sea, we will look out for all your people who chance to enter the places which we control so that their safety may be guaranteed;

and for those who happen to be cast up on our territory because of some accident on the voyage, we will make every effort to see that they are not injured by anyone. We recognize then your temple as inviolable just as you think it should be, and about these things and our other wishes I have instructed Diogeitos, Aristolochos and Theudotos to report to you.

Farewell.[30]

Local city pride was naturally highly developed and the quest for self-esteem and commercial advantage often looked to a city's public events. A four-yearly Games festival, for instance, could bring both, especially if it was recognized by other cities as a prestigious event in the calendar. Magnesia-on-the Maeander was a city just inland from Ephesus with some memorable history.[31] Its patron goddess, Artemis of the White Brow, had appeared to her priestess, Aristo, in the city during the late 220s BC, and there was also an apparition of Apollo at the same period. On each occasion a deputation was sent to Delphi to ask for oracular advice – the reply given by the oracle to the second deputation is recorded – and the citizens decided that the replies warranted and required putting the four-yearly festival, which had been held for centuries in honour of their patron goddess, on to a more impressive footing. The city therefore determined to try to get a higher status for the Games associated with the festival, and to get them recognized in the inter-city league as 'crowned' – that is, Games prestigious enough for the prizes to be wreaths, not crude cash. The first attempt failed, but fourteen years later three delegates were sent to King Antiochos armed with a decree setting in train the next festival, and asking that the four-yearly Games for Artemis should be elevated to the 'crowned' league and should receive the formal status of equality with the renowned Pythian Games at Delphi (the Pythian Games being one of the Big Four on what was known to athletes as 'the circuit' – the *periodos*). The three delegates tactfully made their submission to the king in Antioch in Persis, a faraway Greek city on the eastern shore of the Persian Gulf which Magnesia had recently re-colonized.[32] Their journey of some 2,000 km was rewarded, and, as the king's letter shows, the festival was duly upgraded; prestige followed and a number of later inscriptions found in the temple of Artemis testify to the new-found respect for Magnesia felt by other cities. Antioch on the Persian Gulf naturally made a special point of recognizing the success of its sister-city and passed a fulsome decree, mentioning the three delegates by name and celebrating the newly promoted festival.[33]

King Antiochos to the Council and people of Magnesia, greetings.

Demophon, Philiscos and Pheres who were dispatched by you to us with the task of announcing the Games and the other things which the people voted as a tribute to the mistress of the city,

Artemis of the White Brow, having met with us at Persis, handed to us the decree and themselves gave an enthusiastic address, following what had been resolved in the decree, asking us to recognize the Games which you are establishing for the goddess every four years as 'crowned' and of Pythian status. Therefore, having had from the beginning the most friendly disposition towards your people because of the goodwill you have shown on all occasions towards us and our affairs, and wanting to make our decision public, we approve the honours voted by you to the goddess and we have resolved to further these in whatever ways you advise or that we ourselves conceive. We have written also to those in charge of affairs so that the cities may give consequential approval.

Farewell.[34]

The royal courts were not concerned solely with higher-level inter-state and inter-city politics; in the name of the king all kinds of matters were dealt with relating to local administration and the provision of local services. It was not uncommon for the Hellenistic states to use mercenary soldiers in their frequent clashes with neighbouring kingdoms.[35] Mercenaries, however, had to be rewarded, and the reward sometimes took the form of a land-grant. The following letter illustrates both the problems this could cause for an employer and the chancy business of retirement from the mercenary calling. In 181 BC King Eumenes II of Pergamum received a petition from what was probably a group of mercenaries recently settled in a village near Telmessos in Lycia in the far south-west of Asia Minor. The petition was accompanied by comments from the local governor, Artemidoros, and the situation of the settlers is pretty clear. Their land was not productive and their orchards were not producing fruit, so there was little income and the tax bill became impossible. Moreover, they had bought some extra land and were in no position to pay for it. Some people had therefore moved away, if only temporarily, and additions to the community were welcome. Finally, the village settlement needed a secure stronghold and the existing fort needed repair. The king's reply to his governor follows his governor's recommendations: no payment required for the newly purchased land, tapering tax remissions for the existing villagers with specially attractive tax-breaks for returners or new settlers, and a builder supplied at royal expense to help repair the fort. We do not know whether this solved the ex-mercenaries' problems.

King Eumenes to Artemidoros

The comments you appended to the submission which the inhabitants of the village of Cardacos made have been read by me. So, since after examination you find that they have come off poorly in their private affairs because the fruit from their trees is so scanty and the land poor, give instructions that they should allowed to keep the land which they bought from Ptolemy and the money for it that they did not pay because most of them were ruined, and do not exact the cash. And since it is necessary for each person of eligible age to make up the arrears of the poll-tax, four Rhodian drachmas and one obol, and since they are burdened by weakness in their private affairs, give instructions to exempt them from the arrears for the sixteenth year and from one Rhodian drachma and one obol for the seventeenth year. And for all those they bring in from beyond the boundaries, there should be tax remission for all for three years, and, for those who left the place and now want to return, exemption for two years. Give instructions to repair the fort they previously had, so that they can have a stronghold, with them providing the other resources while I myself pay for a skilled craftsman

[Year] 17. 4th day from the end of Dios.[36]

Monarchs and rich men in the large Greek cities often made endowments and benefactions of different kinds and these often involved new appointments At some time in the third century BC a new priesthood – possibly dedicated to Zeus – was founded at Pergamum, probably sponsored and supported by King Attalos I. The following portion of a letter was almost certainly written by court officials in legalistic style, and it throws some interesting light on the perks and privileges which had to be attached to a new office so that the honour should be attractive enough. Unfortunately the first part of the letter is lost so the doubtless fulsome explanation of the king's purposes and generosity is missing; what we have are the 'terms and conditions'. The newly endowed priest is to be chosen by lot and his vestments are prescribed, the purple in the olive wreath discreetly demonstrating the royal connection. Priesthood, it was often recognized, could mean loss of income, and compensation for the new incumbent is here offered in the shape of meat from the animals sacrificed and the use of their skins. In addition and more substantially, the incumbent is to lease some workshops which the king has established and linked to the foundation and enjoy the income from them. The priest is, however, to maintain the workshops properly and bear the costs of that. While he holds the priesthood, he is not to be liable for liturgies – financial and administrative obligations as a form of tax. He is finally to take good care of the silver and the dedications which will be made. The document is direct and to the point, and can be identified as a royal letter by the formal signing-off.

Let the man chosen on each occasion wear a white mantle (*chlamys*) and a wreath of olive with a purple ribbon, and let him receive as perquisites the skin and hind-parts of the animals sacrificed and the income from the workshops I have dedicated. Let the man chosen on each occasion lease them, and let him, on leaving office, hand them over well-maintained or pay back the cost of maintenance. Let him be exempted from all liturgy-taxes for as long as he wears the wreath. Let him look after and hand over to the incoming priest the silverware belonging to the God and the other dedications.

Farewell.[37]

A further example of the kings of Pergamum becoming involved in religious affairs can be found in the following letter, which dates to the last years of independence in the kingdom before Rome took over. The last reigning king, Attalos III, here makes an arrangement for a temple-sharing agreement between Athena, Bringer of Victory, and Zeus Sabazios. A cult of Zeus Sabazios had already been established by Attalos' royal predecessors some seven years earlier, in 142 BC, and the priest mentioned in this letter, Athenaios, had been put in charge of it. King Attalos III was unmarried and without children, and his mother, Stratonice, obviously had considerable influence over him and had taken the cult and its priest under her wing. It is perhaps not too imaginative to hear in the letter a rather poignant note of the bachelor son still much under his mother's thumb and befriending a local priest, 'my Athenaios'. On the *stele* which contains this letter two other letters were recorded showing the royal family's close connection with both the priest and his father. Stratonice persuaded her son not only to make arrangements for transferring the cult of Zeus Sabazios to Athena's temple, but to do so by permanent legal provision rather than simply by royal edict (an edict would no longer be automatically valid after the king's death). Two years after this, King Attalos III died and in his will bequeathed his kingdom to Rome; perhaps he hoped that the legal provisions he had made would give his mother's wishes some permanence. The city of Pergamum certainly published his letter and two others concerning the priest, Athenaios; it did enter the instructions in the city laws, and it ordered the copy we have to be displayed in the temple of Athena – it was found, still there, by German archaeologists in the 1880s.

King Attalos to the Council and people of Pergamum, greetings.

Since Queen Stratonice, my mother, the most pious of all women and exceptionally devoted to my father and to me, was reverently attached to all the gods and especially to Zeus Sabazios, whom she introduced to our country as an ancestral god and who stood by us and helped us in many matters and in many moments of danger, we have decided, because of his manifestations, to grant him a jointly consecrated dwelling with Athena, Bringer of Victory. We thought this would be a place worthy of him and fitting, and we have given instructions in consequence about celebrating the sacrifices, processions and mysteries for him before the city at the proper times and places. We have also created for him there an hereditary priest, my Athenaios, who is exceptional in piety, a gentleman and truly loyal to us. We have decided on account of these things that the honours for the God and the benefits for Athenaios should remain fixed and unchangeable for all time, and that the instructions we have written should be entered in your sacred laws.

Year 4. 4th of Dios. Lytos [delivered this] from Pergamum.[38]

A doctor's service to his community often inspires gratitude and affection, and even if the ancient physician was notably less successful than his modern counterpart, he still not infrequently received sincere tributes. In the last quarter of the third century BC the city of Gortyn on Crete evidently felt the need for a first-class doctor to work in the city and sent to the best medical school of the day on the island of Cos. Although so much hiring and firing in the Greek world was on a strictly personal level, the medical school on Cos had a kind of agency arrangement with its local authority, and requests for doctors were sent formally to the Council and people of Cos, who presumably saw to the selection of a suitable candidate. In response to its request, the city of Gortyn received Hermias, son of Emmenidas, on a five-year agreement; he was evidently a kindly physician for, in addition to his contractual obligations to Gortyn, he unhesitatingly offered his services to others in emergencies. An uprising in Gortyn had resulted in a bloody battle in which forces from Cnossos (who were responding to an alliance agreement) became involved. There were casualties to men of both cities and Hermias attended to both the Cnossians and the Gortynians with no distinction; he did the same in a later battle near Phaistos. The local authority of Cnossos therefore passed a formal decree of gratitude to Hermias and sent a letter to the Council and people of Cos about him. Their account of Hermias' services survives, but the end of the letter is missing so we do not know what honours Cnossos voted to him. However, Hermias' employer, the city of Gortyn, wrote to Cos in grateful terms at the end of Hermias' five-year contract, mentioning his generosity to allied troops and recording the city's thanks to the people of Cos for sending them 'a good doctor and a remarkable man'. They sent two city representatives to accompany him on his return to Cos (and doubtless to read out the letter), and they voted in addition the unusual honour of citizenship both to him and to his descendants. Hermias was obviously not averse to 'foreign' tours of duty for we know that he also did a stint at Halicarnassus. The copies of the letters sent by Cnossos and Gortyn were found not in Crete but on an inscription from the shrine of Asclepius on Cos. Medical schools have always been proud of their successful students and conscious of their reputation; the letters were evidently a useful public testimony to the quality of Cos graduates.

The magistrates and city of Gortyn to the Council and people of Cos, greetings.

Since Hermias, son of Emmenidas, who was chosen by your vote and dispatched to us as a doctor, has completed his period of service among us in a way which is worthy of you who sent him and of the man himself, and further of us who charged you with the choice of a doctor; and since he has completed his five-year period of service with no accusations against him in all his dealings, caring both for citizens and the other residents of Gortyn, and has, by his professional skill and other sorts of care, keenly and eagerly saved many from great dangers, never sparing his zeal; and since, at a time when many allies were with us and we were at war, he exercised the same care for them too and saved them from great dangers, wanting to show his goodwill to our city; and since he has come to the Assembly and asked us to let him go back to his own city, we have met his wishes and sent with him our citizens, Soarchos and Cydas, wishing to thank him, and we resolved to praise Hermias for his excellence and his kindness to the city and to praise also the people of Cos because they sent us both a good doctor and a remarkable man. And so that everyone may appreciate that we know how to render gratitude, we resolved also to grant citizenship to him and to his descendants.[39]

Kings – some more personal letters

Royal marriages have often been beset by problems, especially when power and political expediency become involved. One such situation arose in 253 BC when King Antiochos II, lord of the huge Seleucid kingdom, received a tempting offer from Ptolemy II, king of Egypt. Antiochos had been laying claim to territory in the neighbourhood of Damascus which was part of the Ptolemaic sphere of influence (the area was known as 'Hollow Syria'); conversely, he was anxious to recover some of his lands in Asia Minor which Ptolemy had conquered. The 'road-map' to a peaceful settlement proposed by Ptolemy was a simple one: Antiochos should marry Berenice, Ptolemy's daughter, and Berenice would bring with her as her dowry the land in Asia Minor which Antiochos wanted, while he would abandon his territorial ambitions around Damascus. There was only one problem: Antiochos had for years been married to his cousin, Laodice, and they had four children. Moreover, she seems to have enjoyed many queenly perquisites, even having a city named in her honour – Laodicea, which St Paul later visited and which became one of the 'Seven Churches of Asia'. Political advantage won the day, however; Laodice was divorced, and Berenice made a ceremonial progress from Egypt, accompanied as far as the Egyptian frontier by someone already very familiar, Apollonios, Zenon's boss and Ptolemy's Minister of Finance.

Laodice was, however, given a generous divorce settlement in the shape of an extensive estate and its revenues, together with tax-immune status. Nominally she purchased the estate from the king, but the price was so low as to make it clear that this was a formality. She also received a transferable right to attach her property to the territories of any city she chose.[40] In the following letter, King Antiochos writes to the governor of his Hellespontine satrapy, Metrophanes, instructing him to make the necessary arrangements via Laodice's property agent, Arrhidaios, and to take immediate action to mark the boundaries. One curious thing about the letter is the bald mention of Laodice without any of her royal titles; it may follow the letter of the law after the divorce but it looks oddly discourteous. On the other hand, unusual care is taken to see the arrangements are properly documented and widely disseminated – the ex-queen's future is being made as secure as possible. The settlement is not only to be recorded in the archives at Sardis but to be published on stone in sanctuaries at Ilion, Samothrace, Ephesus, Didyma and Sardis itself. It is the inscription put up at Didyma which we have, and most of it came to light in the excavations of 1896 (an additional fragment was discovered ten years later). One noticeable feature of the letter is the comparative looseness of the drafting – strange little asides like the mention of the peasants who have moved away punctuate the normal careful logic of such contractual arrangements, almost as though they are thoughts occurring on the spur of the moment. The intriguing possibility has been raised that, unlike the processing of most official correspondence, the king himself may have been involved in the final draft, the scribes dutifully recording the rather unsystematic royal thoughts from dictation.

> King Antiochos to Metrophanes, greetings. The month of Daesios.
>
> We have sold to Laodice Pannoucome and the great house and the land which belongs to the village, the boundary being the Zelean land and the old road which lay above Pannoucome but which has been ploughed up by the farmers nearby so that the land could be cut off (the present Pannoucome happens to have been established later) – and any places falling within this territory, and the existing inhabitants with all their households, and with the revenues of the 59th year, at the price of thirty talents of silver – and likewise any people from this village who have moved to other places. The terms are that she pays nothing in tax to the throne and will have the right to attach the property to any city she wishes. People who can buy it or receive it from her will have the same right and can attach it to any city they wish, unless Laodice has previously attached it to a city, when they will obtain it as attached according to Laodice's indication.
>
> We have given instructions to make payment to the military treasury in the district of Strateia in three instalments: the first in the

month Audnaios in the 60th year, another in the month of Xandicos, and the third in the following three-month period.

Give instructions to hand over to Arrhidaios, the manager of Laodice's affairs, the village, the great house, the land which belongs to it, and the inhabitants with all their households and all their existing possessions, and to record the sale in the royal archives in Sardis and on five *stelai*. Of these, one is to be set up in Ilion in the temple of Athene, another in the temple in Samothrace, another in Ephesus in the temple of Artemis, the fourth in Didyma in the temple of Apollo, and the fifth in Sardis in the temple of Artemis. Give instructions at once to set the boundaries and to put markers in the area and to record the boundaries set on the aforementioned markers.

Farewell.[41]

The inscription also includes two other documents. A letter from the governor, Metrophanes, to one of his subordinates, Nicarchos, gives orders for cutting the inscriptions, setting them up in Ephesus and Didyma and telling him that another letter has gone to the archivist in Sardis with instructions to file the sale and survey documents. The second document from a lowlier official instructed by Nicarchos is a report to say that all the arrangements have been made.

Unfortunately, like so many other Middle Eastern peace plans, this one soon foundered. Laodice and the new queen, Berenice, had an obvious conflict of interest, especially over Laodice's four children and their rights, and, when King Antiochos died shortly after summoning his ex-wife to meet him at Ephesus, this conflict erupted into armed hostilities between the Seleucid and Ptolemaic kingdoms. Laodice therefore had the dubious privilege of giving her name not only to a city but also to a war – the Laodicean or Third Syrian War.[42]

King Antiochos' letter may or may not reveal traces of royal dictation; state correspondence was normally dealt with by professionals and was conducted in a fairly uniform register of official language. It is quite rare to find unmistakeably personal notes in such state correspondence, but they can be found in a set of seven letters which survived until the late nineteenth century, written between two Hellenistic monarchs and a priest-king on the borders of Galatia (only one is complete).[43] The letters date from a period between 160 and 156 BC. King Eumenes II of Pergamum and his brother Attalos, who succeeded him, were evidently on friendly personal terms with the chief priest of the great shrine of the goddess Cybele at Pessinos on the borders of Galatia, some 250 miles to the east of Pergamum. Galatia was a strange and uncomfortable element in the mosaic of kingdoms in Asia Minor. Quite extensive, it occupied a central area of modern Turkey, with modern Ankara as roughly its centre. In the first quarter of the third century BC it was occupied by an aggressive migration of Celtic tribes who overran the country, implanting an alien language and giving constant trouble to their neighbours; the kings of Pergamum and later the Romans both had to meet them in battle.[44] The chief priest of Cybele at Pessinos was rather more than his title might suggest. Each chief priest took the name Attis, after the young man associated with the Cybele myth, and was in fact the local ruler, a priest-king, able if necessary to take military initiatives in the locality. How Eumenes and Attalos had become friends with this particular Attis is not known, but a letter whose end is missing shows the personal touch and uses the familiar elements of the Greek personal letter; it must have been written or dictated by the king himself.

> King Eumenes to Attis, greetings.
>
> If you are well, I am glad. I too am in good health and I got your letter in which you made clear what had been written about your brother, Aioiorix. So you were right in your violent opposition. Would that the goddess, caring for her priests when they have been and are being insulted, would take away from the man who did this the things he most desires. If she does not, may he, becoming sound of mind and god-fearing, send back the offerings and … [45]

Just what brother Aioiorix had done we do not know – some serious thefts from the shrine seem to be involved, as well as insults to the Attis – but his name points to an oddity: it is a Celtic name and presumably the Attis himself was a Celt too. He was not, however, a supporter of his fellow-Galatians, as the next letter clearly shows. This was written by Eumenes' brother, Attalos, who succeeded to the throne in 159 BC after his brother's death. It has the marks of a personal communication too and also shows how the shadow of Roman power was falling over the Middle East in the second century BC. Attalos had been seriously considering an attack on neighbouring Galatia and felt no need to inform anyone else; he thought it prudent, though, to bring the plan before the 'kitchen cabinet' of special advisers which seems to have acted as his sounding-board. One member, Chloros, was much concerned by the likely reactions of Rome to the success or failure of such a project. There was good reason for this since Rome maintained good relations with Galatia and regarded it as a useful buffer against formidable powers like Armenia further to the east. Success for a Pergamum expedition would mean a highly suspicious and probably hostile Rome; failure would be total, for Rome would be delighted. Discussions went on over several days and general opinion shifted from support for the king to agreement with Chloros; in the end the king changed his mind and decided to keep Rome constantly in the picture by sending personal representatives whenever required. One gets the impression that he was rather glad to share his dilemmas with his friend.

King Attalos to Attis the priest, greetings.

If you are well, that is how I would want it; I myself am in good health. When we came to Pergamum and I brought together not only Athenaios, Sosander and Menogenes but many others too of my closest people and put before them the debates we had in Apamea and spoke about what I had decided, there were exceedingly long discussions and at first everyone was inclined to the same opinion as us, but Chloros was really up-tight, putting the fact of Rome before us and advising us that on no account should we do anything without them. At first few took his part, but afterwards, as we constantly discussed this day after day, he convinced more of us, and making an attack without them seemed to involve great risk. For, if we were successful, there would be envy and withdrawal and vicious suspicion (which they had towards my brother), and, if we failed, self-evident ruin; for they would not care about us but be glad to see it, if we made such a move without them. But now, if – may it not happen! – we were defeated in any situation, provided we had done everything with their approval, we would get help from them and live to fight again with the gods' goodwill. I have therefore decided to send to Rome people who would give regular reports in matters of dispute and have decided that we ourselves should prepare carefully so that, if we need to help ourselves … [46]

From the last years of the third century BC the western areas of the Greek world became increasingly aware of actual and likely expansionist pressure from Rome. Philip V, king of Macedonia, ruled for forty-two years from 221 to 179 BC and during his long reign deployed his very considerable talents to trying to block the spread of Roman influence. His efforts were brought to an abrupt end when his army was defeated at the battle of Cynoscephale in 197 BC and the Second Macedonian War came to a decisive conclusion.[47] In the early part of his reign he seems to have lost no opportunity to try to strengthen key positions in northern Greece against the threat of Rome, and in the autumn of 217 BC he was in correspondence with the important city of Larisa in Thessaly. The city and some other parts of Thessaly were in name independent, but the iron hand shows through the velvet glove; Philip's concern is to see that a strategically placed city maintained its citizen-body at full strength and his letter has a note of firmness and urgency: he will send a list in due course but meanwhile local residents who are not citizens (including those from other parts of Greece) are to be offered citizen status.

King Philip to the magistrates and city of Larisa, greetings.

Petraios, Anancippos and Aristonous, when they arrived after their mission, made it clear to me that because of the wars your city is in need of more inhabitants. Therefore, until we should propose others who deserve citizenship with you, I judge that for the present you should vote that citizenship should be granted to those of the Thessalians and other Greeks who are resident among you. For when this has been accomplished and all are settled down together through the favours received, I am convinced that many other advantages will follow, both for me and for the city, and that the land will be better worked.

Year 4. The 21st of Hyperberetaios.[48]

The city duly passed a decree quoting the king's letter and following his instructions. However, something went wrong, for less than two years later the new citizens whose names had been published had lost their new-found rights and had seen their names removed from the public lists. The king was not pleased and sent another letter to Larisa to make his displeasure clear. He treads carefully, however; some of the new, hastily created citizens had plainly been making trouble and giving reasonable cause for disqualification, while others had been running into local resentment at the sudden extension of privilege. The king, all the same, wants no kangaroo courts and wants to take a personal hand in future decisions. His rebuke is therefore tactful, the blame being shifted to unspecified 'advisers' and his wishes being recommended by argument rather than threats. Philip points to Rome's successful policy of using the extension of the citizenship to promote expansion, and though he pushes his argument somewhat – freed slaves were not at this time eligible for holding political office at Rome and the word 'nearly' covers an appreciable exaggeration in the number of *coloniae* – the people and magistrates of Larisa were probably not disposed to question the niceties of history.

King Philip to the magistrates and people of Larisa, greetings.

I learn that those enrolled as citizens in accordance with my letter and your decree and who were identified in writing on the *stelai* have had their names erased. Therefore, if this has happened, your advisers have mistaken both what is advantageous for our country and my judgement. For I think none of you would deny that the best state of affairs is for the city to be strong – as many as possible having a stake in the constitution – and for the land not to be shamefully barren as it is now. It is legitimate to contemplate too others who employ similar schemes of citizen-enrolment, among whom are the Romans, who admit even slaves to the political process when they have been freed and give them a share in political offices, and, by such means, have not only enlarged their own country but have sent out *coloniae* to nearly seventy places. Further, even now I ask you to approach this matter without jealousy for privileges and to restore citizenship to those who have been chosen by the citizens, and, if any have done something intolerable or are, for some other reason, undeserving of being entered on the *stele*, postpone these matters until I have returned from the campaign and can give them a thorough hearing. However, caution those who intend to accuse these people that they should not appear to be doing this out of jealousy for privileges.

Year 7. The 13th of Gorpiaios.[49]

The city magistrates in fact responded at once and a decree was passed in the city Council restoring the effaced names of the new citizens and proposing a further list.

For the Greek kings of Asia Minor the growth of Roman power and influence soon began to pose awkward dilemmas. On the one hand they were keenly aware of Roman ambition and military might, and doubtless often felt that prudence should recommend a friendly and reasonably co-operative stance towards Rome. On the other, they could equally not afford to be seen to be lukewarm in their support for Greek coalition and resistance. The ruler of Pergamum from 197 to 160 BC, King Eumenes II, had on the whole adopted a pro-Roman stance for much of his reign, but his kingdom had influence in Asia Minor and the Romans had become suspicious of a kingdom which might become an obstacle or even a counter-force. Relations on their side cooled noticeably, and an attempted visit to Rome by Eumenes had been pointedly snubbed in the Roman Senate by the sudden enactment of an edict banning all royal visits.[50] This was only one in a chain of such incidents and they had an effect which was probably something of a surprise to Eumenes: his popularity soared in the rest of the Greek world, which was not enamoured of 'liberation' at the hands of the Romans and was eager for the prospect of strong leadership. In 167 BC, soon after Eumenes' visit to Italy had been refused, the League of Ionian Cities – a loose grouping of the Greek cities in western Asia Minor – therefore passed a fulsome decree of gratitude to the king, together with an expensive promise of his gold statue to be located anywhere in Ionia and a golden crown. Representatives of the League met Eumenes on the island of Delos to present the honours. The king's reply is a model of diplomacy; in accordance with the usual pattern of such exchanges it gratefully repeats the terms of the League's decree and promises that future policy will reflect the same spirit as before. As to the gold statue, the king neatly sidesteps any feeling of obligation by paying for the statue himself and locating it in Miletus, a city in which he is already honoured with a shrine and which is one of the most prominent Ionian cities. And the end of his letter makes clear that the royal speech-writers had been more than equal to giving a suitable reply at the presentation ceremony on Delos.

King Eumenes to the Ionian League, greetings.

Of your representatives, Menecles did not join us, but Eirenias and Archelaos, having met me on Delos, delivered to me a fine, friendly decree, in which you began with the fact that I chose the most honourable deeds from the beginning and proved myself the common benefactor of the Greeks and engaged in many great encounters with the barbarians, making every effort and taking every care to see that the inhabitants of the Greek cities should be in every respect at peace and in the best situation; and making compensation for the attendant risk and choosing rather to be zealous and ambitious in matters concerning the League following my father's chosen path, I have given manifest proof of these things in many deeds, both publicly and privately, being well-disposed to each of the cities and arranging for each of them many matters proper to their public reputation and glory which, because of my deeds, [demonstrate] my ambition and the gratitude of the League.

Because of this you resolved – so that you might always be seen to be awarding due honours to your benefactors – to crown us with a golden crown as a sign of excellence and to set up a golden statue in whatever place in Ionia I should wish, and to proclaim these honours at the Games you celebrate and, in the cities, at the Games established in each, and to send me greetings from the League and congratulations on my health and that of my closest family and on our affairs being in due order, and to request me to take note of the people's gratitude and to take proper precautions to see that the Ionian League is increased and in every respect enjoys the best possible circumstances; for in this way too in the future I will acquire all that is proper to honour and glory. Pursuant to all that was agreed, your representatives spoke too with particular enthusiasm in explaining the people's most eager and unalloyed goodwill towards us.

I gladly accept the honours, and, having neglected nothing that is in my power with regard to the continual preservation of all that is proper to honour and glory, both for everyone collectively and for the individuals in each city, I shall try now too not to depart from such a policy. May events follow the path of my wishes. For thus you will appreciate the sincerity of my announced policy more through actual deeds. And so that in future at the Panionian Festival, when you keep a day in my name, you may celebrate the whole event with more splendour, I shall deposit with you a sufficient contribution from which you will be able to make a fitting remembrance of me. As for the gold statue, I shall make it myself, choosing that your favour should involve no public expense at all. I wish it to be set up in the shrine voted to us by the people of Miletus. For since, in celebrating the Festival, you voted the honour to us in this city, and since up to the present it alone of the Ionian cities has opened a shrine for us and regards itself as kin because of

> the people of Cyzicus, and since it has performed many splendid and memorable deeds on behalf of the Ionians, I reckoned that it was most suitable that the statue should be erected there. As for the detailed provisions of my goodwill, both collectively to you all and in respect of each city, your representatives have heard them and will report them to you
>
> Farewell.[51]

Interfaces between Rome and parts of the Greek world continued to produce dangerous crises. The annexation of Greece itself in 146 BC and its establishment as a province had profound consequences for Roman cultural development but was naturally a cause of deep-seated resentment in Greece. In 133 BC King Attalos of Pergamum left his kingdom to Rome in his will and this formed the core of the new Roman province of Asia. In spite of concessions to some of the larger Greek cities and their designation as 'free', the burdens of Roman taxation and its often brutally unscrupulous tax-collectors soon became a source of dissatisfaction. Other nominally independent kingdoms like Cappadocia and Bithynia became 'friends and allies of the Roman people' – a status which spoke more of control than friendship. Thus, by the 90s BC there was among mainland Greeks and the inhabitants of the Greek cities of Asia Minor a strong undercurrent of fear and anti-Roman resentment, and this became an important ingredient in a very serious crisis which burst upon the Roman Republic. King Mithridates VI – the 'Good Father' as he was known – was the able, ruthless and ambitious ruler of Pontus. This was in north-eastern Asia Minor, with a long coastline on the south-east of the Black Sea where one or two Greek cities were located, functioning largely as trading stations. The royal house had been established at the end of the fourth century BC and the kingdom, with its rich agriculture and metal mining resources, had flourished and expanded. Mithridates VI had carried the expansion much further – to the Greek cities of the Crimea and north-eastwards into Colchis. As a result he now disposed of a large army and navy. Pontus was culturally a mixture; it belonged naturally to the East and the kings probably traced their ancestry to Persian nobility. However, Greek influence had also made its mark and Greek was spoken and written at court; moreover, Mithridates had already posed as the defender of the Greeks in the Crimea when they were threatened by northern tribesmen, and this was a role he now adopted towards Rome. A preliminary encounter, provoked by Mithridates' advance into Bithynia and Cappadocia, resulted in a spectacular defeat for the Romans and their allies and the execution of the Roman head of mission, Manius Aquilius. *Pour encourager les autres* and to exact retribution for Roman greed, Aquilius, after being publicly paraded, was killed by having molten gold poured down his throat. Mithridates now swept through Asia with little resistance and, whether by choice or necessity, most of the Greek cities welcomed him and his promise of freedom. A further brutal act set him on a certain collision course with Rome: an order was given that on a certain day all Romans and Italians still to be found in Asia should be massacred, together with their families, and some 80,000 are said to have been killed. An invitation from Athens to Mithridates to liberate Greece ratcheted up the danger and brought it appreciably closer to Rome.[52] In this highly charged atmosphere, friends and enemies became sharply divided, and from early in the conflict Mithridates was plainly determined to stamp hard on any prominent Greeks who were showing pro-Roman sympathies and who were therefore 'traitors' to the cause. In the following letter, written in 88–87 BC before the slaughter of the Romans, he puts a price – a not inconsiderable one – on the heads of the Greek Chairemon and his two sons, Pythodoros and Pythion; live capture would be better but the dead heads would do. Chairemon was from a very wealthy Greek family and had been a material supporter of Roman power, having made a huge gift of provisions for Roman troops stationed in Asia for which he received an official letter of thanks from C. Cassius, the proconsul; one of his grandsons would marry one of Mark Antony's daughters.

> King Mithridates to the satrap, Leonippos, greetings.
> Since Chairemon, son of Pythodoros, who has the most hostile and warlike intentions towards our affairs, has from the start joined up with our most hated enemies and now, learning of my presence, has taken away his sons, Pythodoros and Pythion, and has himself fled, issue a proclamation that, if anyone brings in Chairemon or Pythodoros or Pythion alive, he will receive forty talents, and, if anyone brings in the head of any of them, he will receive twenty talents.[53]

A little later Mithridates wrote again to his subordinate, Leonippos, because Chairemon had sought sanctuary in the famous temple of Artemis at Ephesus after helping a number of Romans and his two sons to escape to Rhodes. Chairemon's whereabouts had therefore been pinpointed and his fate was sealed. We do not know what happened to him but he probably died in the large-scale massacre of the Romans, when even rights of sanctuary were ignored.

> King Mithridates to Leonippos, greetings.
> Chairemon, son of Pythodoros, has previously removed those of the Romans who fled, along with his children, to the city of Rhodes, and now, learning of my presence, has fled to the temple of Artemis at Ephesus and from there is corresponding with our common enemy, the Romans. The shamelessness of this man for the wrongs that have been done is the starting point for those who are acting against us. Think how you may best bring him to us, whether under guard or in prison, until I am back from dealing with the enemy.[54]

After Mithridates had been decisively defeated by Sulla in 85 BC, people like Chairemon were no longer traitors but honoured friends of Rome (albeit posthumous ones), and Chairemon was commemorated in his home town, Nysa, with a monument on which the proconsul Cassius' thank-you letter for the army provisions was recorded, together with the two letters of Mithridates – anyone who had been so high on Mithridates' wanted list was plainly sound. This is the monument which has survived; it first came to light in the ruins of Nysa about 1860 and is now in the Istanbul Museum.

It would perhaps be appropriate to leave this awkward and uneasy relationship between Rome and Greece with a letter written in Greek from Rome. There were, of course, in later times many official missives from Rome to parts of the Greek world (the well-known letter of the Emperor Claudius to the people of Alexandria, for instance), but the following letter is from a time when political realities and diplomacy still required a certain delicacy in dealing with the Greek world. It was written by the young Octavian, the future Augustus, to the city of Ephesus in 39–38 BC, when Octavian was still only twenty-five but had already shown himself more than equal to the ruthlessness of power politics. Fresh from a consulship obtained by threats of violence, he was now a triumvir and, along with Antony and Lepidus, commanded the Roman world. Antony controlled the East, and both Ephesus and Aphrodisias, two of the cities mentioned in the letter, were clearly within his sphere of influence and therefore off-limits to Octavian. Nevertheless, Octavian has been approached by a Greek representative from Aphrodisias and Plarasa, pleading for help since those cities have been plundered in the recent war with Parthia (Labienus, a disaffected Roman general, led the invasion). Octavian therefore promises to get Antony to do his best to restore things, and also uses the occasion to get Ephesus to send back to Aphrodisias a statue of Eros which Julius Caesar, Octavian's adoptive father, had presented to the city. The request to Ephesus is couched in the politest terms and hints that Ephesus too may well figure on Octavian's goodwill list.

The letter is interesting on two counts: first, it shows the future Augustus fishing in a pool in which he strictly had no business and displaying that attention to detail and eye for every main chance which many another dictator has employed on the path to power. The rich cities of Asia Minor were influential centres and their welfare is here carefully regarded; the matter of the statue is linked to Octavian's proper duty as a respectful (adopted) son of a father who traced his ancestry back to the goddess Venus. Eros and Aphrodisias were therefore fitting objects for Octavian's special care. The second point of interest is the form and tone of what is written. It begins with a formal address but continues with the conventional formula of a personal letter – 'if you are well, that is good. I myself too am in good health ... ' And it remains personal, with no mention of the Senate and People of Rome. It is doubtful if Antony ever saw the letter, but if he had, he would not have been too pleased to read that Octavian intended to give him 'instructions'.

Aphrodisias probably did get its statue of Eros back, for two hundred years later the inscription was still felt to be worth recording and a newly cut copy was fixed to one of the walls of the theatre at Aphrodisias. That copy too had a history, for in the sixth or seventh century AD the city's name was thought to be too provocative for a Christian country and was changed to Stauropolis (City of the Cross); with due diligence the words 'Aphrodisias' and 'people of Aphrodisias' were scraped off.

> The *imperator* Caesar, son of the god Julius, to the magistrates, Council and people of Ephesus, greetings.
>
> If you are well, that is good. I myself too am in good health along with the army. Solon, son of Demetrios, representative from Plarasa and Aphrodisias, explained to me how much their city had suffered in the war with Labienus, and how much public and private property had been plundered. I have given instructions in all these matters to my colleague-in-office, Antony, so that, as far as he can, whatever he can find should be restored to them. I have decided to write to you since you have a city which can conveniently help them if they make a claim for a slave or some other private possession. I received a report that, as a result of the looting, a golden Eros which had been dedicated to Aphrodite by my father had been transferred to you and had been dedicated to Artemis. You will therefore be acting rightly and worthily of yourselves if you return the offering given to Aphrodite by my father; for Eros is an unsuitable dedication for Artemis. It is necessary for me to show to the people of Aphrodisias for whom I have done so many good things that goodwill which I believe has come to your notice too.[55]

5

THE LETTER AS TRACT

In this chapter there is an attempt to follow the development of the letter used as a tract for the purposes of persuasion and instruction, or as a public statement which is written with the intent of reaching a listening public beyond the overt addressees. The letter-form is used in a way which is not on the face of it 'natural' to the genre; it is a form which gives letter-signals to the reader's expectations (though usually not for long), but then replaces them with serious intents which go beyond the boundaries of ordinary private or administrative correspondence, in terms of both length and tone. The letter-form here can be regarded as a kind of informal costume or dress which is assumed in order to put the reader at ease and offer encouragement to tackle the true character of what lies beneath; the author presents himself as wanting to win the reader to a closer, less formal relationship, and to listen to one side of a conversation, even though this takes the form of a monologue or even a contrived speech. A magisterial – sometimes pompous or even hectoring – tone is a frequent characteristic of such letters, the writer speaking as the head of a school, a leader of opinion, a senior adviser or chief instructor. It is a genre with a long subsequent history.

The addressees of these letters may be problematic too. The name or names at the head of the letter indicate appropriate and perhaps original recipients, but they commonly do not denote the whole anticipated readership. Thus, when Isocrates writes to Philip, or Plato to the sons of Dion, or Epicurus to Pythocles, they are conscious of a potentially much wider audience and sometimes admit as much. This leads to another phenomenon: when letters like this enter or are entered into the public domain, they, like all works of literature, acquire a life of their own, and it can be argued that some of the early Christian letters, for instance, have been 'promoted' by the Church to an instructional and definitively doctrinal status which was not their original intention.

This kind of letter had already been identified in antiquity. Demetrius in his essay *On Style* wrote:

> Letters which are too long and in addition too weighty in their style would not truly be called letters but written works which have the

> addition of the word 'Greetings', like the many letters of Plato and the letter of Thucydides.[1]

The 'letter of Thucydides' is the long military dispatch from the Athenian general Nicias to the Athenian Assembly mentioned in Chapter 4, and in fact neither Nicias' nor Plato's letters have the conventional 'Greetings' at the start. However, it is with Plato's alleged correspondence that we first encounter the letter-form with a new purpose. Thirteen letters attributed to Plato survive, and there has been much debate about their authenticity.[2] The letter which has always aroused the greatest interest is *Letter vii*, and, if it is not by Plato himself, it was certainly written by someone close to him who knew the circumstances of his visits to Sicily and the disappointments they brought.[3] If it is by Plato, it is of particular interest since none of his other works takes the form of a first-person statement about both his life and his philosophy. But, authentic or not, it is unquestionably the letter in a new guise. It is ostensibly a reply to Dion's friends and companions who had asked for Plato's advice. Plato had met Dion on his first visit to Sicily in about 388 BC when Dion was a young man of about twenty and they had become close friends. Dion's sister was married to the ruthless and powerful tyrant of Syracuse, Dionysios I, and it is not at all clear why Plato should have visited a ruler in a distant country whose style and reputation was so alien. Twenty years later, when Dionysios I had died, Plato's friend thought that there might be some chance of turning Dionysios' son, who had succeeded to the tyranny, into the semblance of a 'philosopher-king' and invited Plato again to Syracuse. This visit was unsuccessful and, indeed, some four months after Plato's arrival Dion was exiled. Six years later Dionysios II invited Plato to Sicily once more, but this visit too was abortive and a mightily disillusioned Plato eventually returned to Athens in 360 BC. Three years later the exiled Dion attempted a *coup d'état* and invaded Sicily, but was eventually murdered in 354 BC. It was in the period following his murder that Dion's relations and companions wrote to Plato asking for advice. *Letter vii* is nominally Plato's reply to them, and indeed a section of the letter is devoted to discursive and repetitive general advice, but it is quite clear that the main purpose of the letter is Plato's personal *apologia pro vita sua* intended for a wider audience. It opens with the hope that Dion's relations and companions really do share Plato's own convictions, the reasons for which are said to be 'worth the attention of young and old' – a sign of the letter's public intentions. Plato first describes his own pilgrimage of experience which led him to the central conviction of his political philosophy – the overriding need for a 'philosopher-king':

> Plato to the relations and companions of Dion, greetings.
>
> You wrote to me to say that I must consider your views to be the same as those which Dion held and furthermore you asked me to

make common cause with you both in deed and word as far as I could. If you have the same opinions and aspirations as his, I agree to make common cause with you, but, if not, I shall have to think again very carefully. What his opinions and aspirations were, I would like to explain to you clearly, not by guesswork but from knowledge. For when I first arrived in Syracuse – I was about forty – Dion was the same age as Hipparinos is now, and Dion held fast to the same opinions which he had then, that the Syracusans should be free men living under the best laws. So it would be in no way surprising if some divine being made Hipparinos of the same mind as Dion about politics. How these opinions had their origin is worth the attention of young and old, and I will try to explain from the beginning; for the present business offers the opportunity.

When I was young I had the same experience as many others: I thought that, if I was going to be quickly master of my own affairs, I should go into public life. And the situation of the city's affairs which I encountered was something like this: since the then constitution was reviled by many, there was a revolution and fifty-one men emerged as leaders of the revolution – eleven in the city, and ten in the Piraeus (each group had to manage the *agora* and the administration in the cities), and thirty were set up as rulers with full powers over all. Some of them happened to be my relations and acquaintances, and indeed they invited me straightaway to take part in matters that seemed to suit me. And because of my youth, what happened to me was not surprising; for I thought they would govern the city, taking it from being an unjust society to one characterized by justice, and I devoted particular attention to them to see what they might do. But when indeed I saw that they had in a short period made the previous government look like a Golden Age – among other things there was that dear, older friend Socrates, whom I would not be embarrassed to call the most upright man then living, whom they dispatched with others to arrest one of the citizens by force with a view to execution so that Socrates would bear responsibility for these matters along with them, whether he wanted to or not. But Socrates was prepared to risk everything rather than join them in their wicked deeds – so, observing all this and much like it of no mean importance, I was disillusioned and withdrew myself from the wrongs that were then being done. Not long after, the Thirty and that whole government fell, and the urge to take part in public and political life began gradually to attract me again. Inasmuch, though, as there had been disturbance, much was happening with which one was deeply dissatisfied and it was not surprising that in a time of revolution some took more violent revenge on their enemies. All the same the people who then returned to

> power acted with much moderation. However, by a turn of fate some of those who were in authority took my companion Socrates to court, bringing a charge which was outrageous and least of all appropriate to him; for some of them prosecuted him for impiety, and the court condemned and executed the man who had not been willing to be party to the wrongful arrest of someone who was a friend to those who were then in exile and suffering ill-fortune.
>
> And, observing these events and the men who were involved in politics and the legal and moral climate, the more I looked at the situation and the further I advanced in age, the more difficult it seemed to me to manage political affairs in a proper way. It was impossible to take action without friends and reliable colleagues and it was not easy to find them as things were, for our city was not being run by the standards practised by our fathers and it was not possible to acquire new friends easily. Both written law and social customs were being corrupted and this was progressing at an astonishing rate so that, whereas I was at first full of great enthusiasm for getting involved in public affairs, when I looked at the situation and saw everything in total confusion, I ended up by getting dizzy; I did not stop trying to see if there could be some improvement in what I have described and the whole condition of the state, always looking out for the right moment for action, but I ended up thinking that all existing cities are badly administered – for their constitutional state is pretty well irremediable, short of a miracle, and a lucky one at that. I was driven to say, in approval of true philosophy, that the following is the key to seeing what is right in both political and private affairs: human beings will have no escape from trouble until either people come to power who practise genuine and true philosophy, or until – by some divine providence – those who rule become true philosophers.[4]

The next section of the letter moves from Plato's early general disillusionment with politics to his experiences in Sicily. The description of his first impressions of western Greek society has a curiously contemporary ring and is probably coloured by his later disappointments.

> Having this conviction I paid my first visit to Italy and Sicily. But when I arrived, the so-called sweet life there pleased me not at all with its constant concern for Italian and Syracusan cooking, life consisting in gorging oneself twice a day and never going to bed alone at night, and all the accoutrements of that life-style.[5]

However, Plato soon met up with Dion, a young man who became completely converted to Plato's way of thinking and who moved in social circles which gave hopes of influence at the court of the reigning tyrant. Nevertheless,

Plato then returned to Athens, and it was not until twenty years later that Dion saw what he believed was a chance of realizing the ideal of the philosopher-king. Dionysios I had been succeeded by his son, and Dion thought that the disposition of Dionysios II was favourable enough to Plato's ideas to make a visit worthwhile. Plato was taken with the possibility of putting his ideas into practice and travelled to Syracuse, but things soon went awry. About four months after Plato's arrival, Dion was accused of plotting against the government and was sent into exile. Plato was naturally nervous about his own position, but Dionysios was sensible enough to realize that he had a celebrity on his hands and kept Plato for a while, not allowing him to leave Sicily. His security was assured and Dionysios made himself personally agreeable, but he made no political concessions and studiously avoided discussions of philosophical or constitutional theory. Eventually Plato left for Athens having achieved nothing of importance.

The next section of the letter returns to the present and contains the advice which Dion's friends and companions had originally asked Plato to give. It is quite a substantial part of the letter but, if Dion's adherents hoped for a penetrating analysis and a clear indication of a way forward, they must have been very disappointed. After a warning that advice is only worth giving if the recipients are disposed to hear it, Plato offers a mixture of historical details about Dion's experiences and murder (which Dion's friends presumably already knew), some familiar philosophy of a personal and general nature (the desirable way of life gives mastery over oneself and makes a necessary circle of loyal friends; absolute power is bad for the person who wields it as well as for his subjects; the accountability of the soul after death), and finally some rather lame and unoriginal suggestions for looking for allies abroad and for choosing fifty of the best men in Greece in order to frame a new law-code once Dion's friends had won power.

Plato then returns to his own later experiences and again makes it clear that this is the main subject of the letter and that he is returning to the expectation of a wider readership:

> So much then for my advice and the letter, and for my first visit to Dionysius. Whoever is interested may see from what follows how naturally and also fittingly my second journey and voyage came about.[6]

This second visit came about as the result of what appeared now to be remarkable enthusiasm on the part of Dionysios. A trireme was specially sent from Syracuse to invite Plato to return, and with it a small delegation led by Archedemos, one of the pupils of Archytas, a western Greek philosopher whom Plato admired. The delegation assured Plato that Dionysios was now taking philosophy seriously, but also brought a letter from him which rather bluntly and unpromisingly suggested that Dion's future welfare depended on Plato's acceptance of the present invitation. However, corroborative letters of encouragement came from Archytas himself and Plato accordingly set out once more. On arrival in Sicily he became at once wary of Dionysios' new-found ardour and proposed to give him the infallible philosopher-test:

> There is a certain way of giving a test on such matters which is not demeaning but really suitable for tyrants, especially those that are full of second-hand notions – a malady from which I discovered on arrival that Dionysios suffered rather badly. One must show such people what the subject is in its entirety, its nature and how much is involved, and the hard work that will have to be put in. If the person who hears it is a real philosopher, suited to philosophy and worthy of it, with a touch of divine inspiration, and believes he has discovered a path which is wonderful, he has to order his existence to be like that and life is not worth living in any other way. And after this, putting himself and his guide along the way to full stretch, he does not relax until he either reaches his final goal or finds the capacity on his own account and without his tutor to make his own way … But those who are not true philosophers, with opinions which are skin-deep (like those who get a tan for their bodies in the sun), seeing how much learning is involved and what kind of hard work, and the daily discipline required which befits the subject, they, thinking it hard and impossible for themselves, cannot practise it, and some persuade themselves that they have a sufficient general understanding and have no need of such subjects.[7]

Plato never got through the whole of his test, for Dionysios wrong-footed him by claiming that he already knew from others what was necessary (and, as a final indignity, Plato heard later that Dionysios had published a pirated version of some of Plato's ideas). The letter continues with some curious reflections on the huge difficulty of pinning down complicated philosophical conclusions in adequate words and an odd remark that 'on these matters there is no written statement by me nor would there ever be'.[8] Nevertheless, there follows a difficult philosophical exposition of the theory of Forms (though Plato never here uses the words *idea* and *eidos* which usually denote the Forms in his other works). Dion's associates must have skipped this section if it is indeed authentic, and it is actually described as a digression (*planos*). However, the previous mention of Dionysios' pirated publication provokes Plato – like any aggrieved author – into a stinging denunciation of the tyrant's intellectual capacities.

The last section of the letter deals with the succession of quarrels and patched-up understandings which characterized Plato's last months in Sicily. One phrase sums it up:

> Up to this point that was how I came to the assistance of philosophy and my friends; but after this Dionysios and I lived with me looking to the outside world like a bird longing to fly away, and with him plotting some way of scaring me.[9]

Eventually, with the aid of representations from his fellow-philosopher, Archytas, Plato got away and travelled back to Athens via Olympia, where he met Dion. He offered his services as mediator between Dionysios and Dion, who were then at loggerheads, but Dion would have none of it and set off on the course which led to his eventual murder. Plato ends the letter with a renewed reference to his purposes in telling his story:

> The advice I offer subsequent to the events I have described has for the most part been given, and let that be the end. But it seemed to me essential that the reasons for my second journey to Sicily should be described because of the strangeness and illogicality of what happened. If anyone feels that what I have said makes things more intelligible and gives proper explanations for events, then what I have set down here has been reasonably adequate.[10]

Whatever this is, it is clearly not the usual kind of letter. It was occasioned by a request for advice and some advice is given, but it is mainly a public statement about Plato's visits to Sicily for anyone who wants to know, and about his intentions there; and, though a central feature of his philosophy is expounded in one section, the author is mainly concerned to show how his sincere efforts and those of Dion were thwarted by the capriciousness of a tyrant who had been canny enough to lead Plato and Dion to believe that he might be 'converted' to their way of thinking. Plato had a very considerable reputation by this time and must have staked a lot of intellectual capital and personal commitment in an enterprise which, in his view, might have started to change the world. Alas, in this letter and even more in *Letter viii* (if that is genuine), there is the unmistakable sense of a well-intentioned intellectual out of his depth in the messy, violent and ruthless world of Sicilian *Machtpolitik*.

The other twelve letters in the Platonic collection have been discussed frequently.[11] In all these necessary investigations there has been a tendency to concentrate on the genuineness or otherwise of the letters, but at least as interesting is the question of why it was felt that letters written in the name of a great teacher were a suitable and legitimate medium for extending the range of his teaching. Perhaps the supposed coming to light of letters, with their natural function of bringing messages from places far away, was an acceptable fiction, and the writers may have believed that the views they expressed were so akin to Plato's own that they were merely amplifying his established teaching. In this way the canon of works available to students in the Academy could be enlarged and points of doctrine or history given further explanation. This is a phenomenon which continues. We do not have the collection of Aristotle's letters made by Artemon but it would not be at all surprising if the collection grew over the years to include letters written by close associates or teachers at the Lyceum. At a later period, Cynic philosophy was surrounded by letters allegedly written by the founder, Diogenes, and prominent followers like Crates, though they were in fact written by much later disciples. And in the New Testament it appears certain that some of the letters attributed to Paul were written by others who made quite considerable efforts to make their letters seem genuine; the canon became quite tolerant.

The next examples of the letter as tract are the work of Isocrates, and here the focus shifts markedly from defensive biography and philosophical exposition to the obsessive advocacy of nationalist conviction allied to not a little personal vanity.[12] Isocrates was born in 436 BC and was probably a slightly younger contemporary of the celebrated legal speech-writer, Lysias. Lysias had made a commercial success of writing speeches for clients in the law-courts, but his skill and way with words had also established his speeches as saleable and entertaining reading for a select public.[13] Isocrates too began his career as a legal speech-writer – a *logographos* – having accepted that neither his vocal powers nor his self-confidence were up to life on the public stage. Six of his law-court speeches survive, but at first he does not seem to have enjoyed the same literary success as Lysias, and later he himself regarded his early calling with some disdain. The key stage of his career began about 388 BC with the opening of a select school or college in Athens and, working intensively with a very small group of high-fee students, he soon established a kind of *grande école* for politicians, tyrants and statesmen which quickly won a very high reputation (though not all the students turned out well). Looking back, Cicero wryly observed that the college was rather like the Trojan Horse: it disgorged pure leaders (*meri principes*).[14] This new career ushered in a new kind of writing for Isocrates; he now began to compose discourses which took the form of real speeches or addresses but which were primarily intended to be read, not spoken, and were certainly not intended for only one particular occasion. Such works might indeed be 'performed' but the focus was on the skill of the writer and his message, and only secondarily on the art of the performer. The first and best-known example of this was the *Panegyricos* – the *Festival Speech* – a discourse published in 380 BC over which Isocrates had laboured for over ten years. The underlying theme was Isocrates' cherished vision of Athens and Sparta uniting in a crusade against Persia, with of course Athens in the lead. In some other discourses Isocrates exercised the rhetorician's skill of *ethopoieia* and wrote as another character, e.g. Archidamos III, King of Sparta, or an anonymous citizen of Plataea, but the register of a speech as literature remained the same. Three works which hover between addresses and letters are discourses simply addressed to individuals: *To Demonicos*, *To Nicocles* and *To King Philip*. Here Isocrates presents himself as a speaker making a formal address but he admits that these discourses are not for real delivery but for private reading. They are curiously diffuse pieces – unorganized collections of unexceptionable, trite, gnomic sayings with rather ordinary amplification by the author. They do not have the identity or purposefulness of letters and are described as discourses (*logoi*) or even in one place as a book or pamphlet (*biblion*).[15]

When we come to the letters proper, six of the nine extant letters belong to the last thirty years of Isocrates' long life, the last being written when he was ninety-eight.[16] It is not clear whether Isocrates only took to the letter-form late in his working life or whether the letters we possess are a random survival, but it is reasonable to assume that, if there had been a substantial corpus of public letters from earlier dates, some would have survived or at any rate have been mentioned. The first letter, dated about 368 BC, is addressed to Dionysios I, the tyrant who has already been mentioned in connection with Plato. Although it is for his eyes and accompanied by almost courtier-like flattery, it is also part of the relentless public pressure Isocrates kept up for his project of a war with Persia led by a Greek consortium. The letter begins with a respectful greeting and an apology for not coming in person, incorporating a discreet reference to Socrates' views on the limitations of writing (this may well have been lost on Dionysios, who by all accounts was not a literary man).[17]

> Isocrates to Dionysios, greetings.
>
> If I were a younger man, I would not be sending you a letter but I would myself have sailed and talked with you there. But since the right moments in my life and your affairs have not coincided and I am past it, while your business has come to a head, I will try, as far as I can in present circumstances, to make myself clear in these matters. I certainly know that for those who are trying to give advice it is much better to have a meeting, not through letters but by being there themselves, not only because it is easier for someone to talk face-to-face about the same matters than to try to make them clear by letter, nor because everyone trusts what is said more than what is written, listening to the former as proposals for action and the latter as artificial compositions. And further, in meetings, if someone does not know what is being discussed or does not believe it, the man who is on the spot presenting the case can help on both counts, but, in the case of written communications, if something like this happens, there is no-one to put it straight. For, since the writer is not there, there is no helper either. All the same, since you are going to be the judge of these matters, I have great hopes that I shall appear to be saying something needful; for I think that you, having

> set aside all the aforesaid difficulties, will give your attention to the matters themselves.
>
> And yet some of those close to you have already attempted to frighten me off, saying that you respect those who offer flattery and despise those who give advice. If I had believed the words of those men, I should have kept very quiet. But as things are, no-one could persuade me that it is possible for someone to be so superior in thought and action unless he has become in some things a learner, in others a listener, and in others a discoverer, and unless he has brought together and collected from all sides the means of exercising his intellect.[18]

Isocrates goes on to explain why he has addressed himself to Dionysios at this moment: the Spartans are now in great difficulties and Dionysios, who is at war with Carthage, will therefore not face opposition on that front if he takes a leadership role in Greece. The bulk of the letter is missing, but there is little doubt that in it Isocrates was asking Dionysios to take the initiative on behalf of Greece in his favourite project, the drive against Persia. Needless to say, nothing came of it.

The same general theme lay behind Isocrates' second letter written to Philip II of Macedon before the outbreak of hostilities between Athens and Macedon, probably in 342 BC; Isocrates was then ninety-four. He urges Philip, who was fierce, pugnacious and not at all averse to the riskiest kinds of hand-to-hand combat, not to take so many chances with his life.[19] Isocrates wants him as the leader of a joint Macedonian–Athenian crusade against Persia, not as a dead hero. Unlike the first letter, this and the other seven in the collection do not have the conventional greetings at the start but simply begin by identifying the addressee ('To Philip'); this may well be due to an early editor of the letters. It begins rather pompously, though seeming to show due deference; soon, however, the tone changes and a surprising note of hectoring surfaces:

> To Philip.
>
> I know that everyone is usually more grateful to people who praise than to those who offer advice, especially if someone undertakes to do this unasked. And if I had not previously given you counsel with the best of intentions as a result of which you would, I thought, act in a way that was appropriate, perhaps I would not even now have undertaken to make clear my views on what has happened to you. But since I then chose to concern myself with your affairs, both for the sake of my own city and for the other Greeks, I should be ashamed if I seemed to have given you advice on less important matters, but, where more urgent business was concerned, said nothing, particularly in the knowledge that these

> former affairs had to do with your reputation while these matters concern your personal safety, about which everyone who has heard the criticisms levelled at you thinks you are too careless. For there is no-one who has not condemned you for putting yourself at risk more recklessly than a king should and for caring more about being praised for bravery than about the total outcome of an action. For both the following bring equal disgrace: not being superior to others when surrounded by enemies, and hurling yourself, when there is no need, into the kind of fighting in which, if you did well, you would have done nothing remarkable, but, if you had lost your life, you would have undone all your present success. One should not consider all deaths in time of war as good ones; some incurred for one's country, parents and children are praiseworthy, others which do harm to all these and spoil fine previous achievements should be thought shameful and should be avoided as causing a great loss of reputation.[20]

Isocrates goes on to offer examples of cities and autocrats like Xerxes and Cyrus who have properly safeguarded the common interest rather than indulging personal recklessness. He notes too that Philip is already waging war with the Thessalians and has moreover been wounded in the process; Isocrates reminds him that the real enemy lies elsewhere – Persia. This part of the letter is even more wordy than usual and – rarely for Isocrates – the writer himself seems to become aware of it:

> But in addition to this I fear I may have chosen the wrong moment. For even now, proceeding by small steps, I have not seen that I have run aground by not observing the proper proportions of a letter, extending the length of my discourse.[21]

He returns, nevertheless, to a lengthy attempt to persuade Philip to look with favour on joining forces with Athens in an anti-Persia initiative, and at the end gives Philip a not very convincing nor very flattering assurance that he and Isocrates are after all in nearly the same boat because the majority of ordinary people misunderstand and dislike them. He, however, can do something about it by following the advice he is given; Isocrates is too old and will just have to put up with it.

The sixth letter is rather different. It is addressed to the two children of the ruler of Thessaly, Jason. He had been murdered and after a bloody succession-struggle his two children, Thebe and Tisiphonos, had taken over the government. Isocrates received an invitation from the two of them to move from Athens and live in Thessaly, doubtless to act as government consultant there. At the start of the letter he declines, pleading old age and political uncertainties, and in the first section (the rest of the letter is unfortunately lost) he, like any good consultant, insists that the objects of the exercise should be defined and specific targets set; he argues from his experience as a teacher.

> For I am accustomed to say to those who are devoting time to my field of study that this is the thing that must first be examined: what is to be accomplished by the speech and the parts of the speech? And when we have discovered this and defined it, I say that one must look for the forms with the aid of which this can be worked out and the end-result we posited be brought about. I say this about making speeches but it is a fundamental principle both in all other matters and in your affairs too.[22]

There is then a short section on not being taken in by the apparent advantages of monarchy, and this doubtless set the scene for advice on a constitutional solution to the future of Pherai in the missing part of the letter.

One earlier section throws some revealing light on how Isocrates expected his 'political' letters might be read. Here he is anxious to assure the two addressees that he really is writing a genuine, personal letter to them and not a piece in which the medium is more important than the message.

> And please do not have any idea of this kind – that I have written this, not because of my friendship with you but wanting to produce an exemplary public statement. For I have not reached such a state of madness that I do not realize that I could not write anything better than what I have previously published, being now so far past my best, and that, if I did bring out something inferior, I would get a much less substantial reputation than the one I have now. Moreover, if I had been focused on an exemplary public statement and not giving my energies to you, I would not, out of all the possibilities, have chosen this subject on which it is hard to speak appropriately, but I would have discovered much better ones with more in them to grasp. But neither in the past nor at any time was I enamoured of subjects like these, but rather of the other kind which most people have not noticed. So now it was with no such intention that I undertook this business, but, because I saw you involved in many important matters, I wanted myself to reveal to you the opinion which I have about them.[23]

Isocrates' modesty is not remarkable, but he seems here to acknowledge that the type of letter he is writing may easily be mistaken for a public essay in display mode – for a piece in which the writer is above all trying to be clever and stylistic, and is simply using his subject-matter as the occasion for elegance and literary virtuosity. The Greek for 'an exemplary public statement' – *epideixis* – refers to a composition of much this sort. Isocrates is assuring the sons of Jason that he is writing in earnest, and it is quite honest of him to admit that his chosen and habitual mode of writing is close to the borderline between direct communication and a contrived, artificial display intended to excite cultured admiration.

After Isocrates the next surviving set of letters comes from a practising orator, in fact the greatest of all the Greek orators, Demosthenes. Six letters survive under his name but it is likely that only four can be considered as genuine.[24] They were all written in 324–322 BC at a particularly difficult time in Demosthenes' life. He had been condemned by the court of the Areopagus in Athens on a charge of appropriating twenty talents belonging to one Harpalos, money which had been lodged by the city on the Acropolis at Demosthenes' suggestion. Demosthenes had been found guilty, fined the huge sum of fifty talents, and was now in exile in Trozen. The four letters written from there are quite formal and are couched in conventional form with 'greetings' at the start and a farewell at the end. They are, however, addressed to the Council and the people of Athens and Demosthenes is obviously conscious that they will be read aloud to a large audience. The mode is accordingly the text of a speech rather than one side of a conversation, and the style is such that anyone reading the letters in public could hardly do other than assume the role of an orator.

The letters have two characteristics: first, they show a man who has enjoyed power and influence trying desperately to hang on to a part in the conduct of affairs from a considerable distance, and second, they show a resentful exile losing no opportunity for pressing the case for his return. The third letter, which carries a title *Concerning the sons of Lycurgus*, is a good example of this combination. It begins with a plea on behalf of the sons of Lycurgus, a prominent figure in public finance and the promotion of city building and restoration programmes. In spite of Lycurgus' remarkably successful career which had brought great benefits to Athens, his successor in office, Menaichmos, alleged that he had left a deficit and prosecuted his sons after their father's death. The sons had not been able to pay the required sum and were therefore imprisoned. Demosthenes cannot appear in court himself but he does the next best thing – sending a letter which is in effect a speech for the defence. It begins in the conventional way:

> Demosthenes to the Council and people, greetings.
>
> I sent an earlier letter to you about my own situation and what I thought it was right for you to do, and you will come to an agreement on this at your discretion. On the subject about which I am now writing, I would like you neither to overlook it nor to hear it with a view to point-scoring but to look to what is right. For, although I am living abroad, I happen to hear many people criticizing you for what has happened to the sons of Lycurgus.[25]

He begins with a measured, favourable summary of Lycurgus' public career in order to set the scene but quite soon takes the matter above the level of a quarrel among politicians; it is actually the international reputation of Athens which is at stake, and who better than an exile to know what is being said abroad? And the reason for the risk to Athens' reputation is the unquestionable integrity of Lycurgus – the encomium is beautifully engineered.

> All the same, as I said at the beginning, I would have written this letter just for his benefit, but, considering it was in your interest that you should be aware of the criticisms made by people abroad, I was that much more eager to send you this letter. I ask those who have private reasons for quarrelling with Lycurgus to wait upon the truth and to listen to justice on his behalf; for be sure, gentlemen of Athens, that the city is getting a bad reputation because of what has happened to his children. For no Greek is ignorant of the fact that you gave Lycurgus exceptional honours in his lifetime, and, although many accusations were made by those who were jealous of him, you found not one of them to be true; and you so trusted him, considering him public-spirited beyond all others, that you settled many questions of justice with 'Lycurgus said so' – and no more was needed; it would not have occurred to you to do otherwise. Well, all people now, hearing that his sons have been put in prison, feel sorry for the dead man and sympathize with his sons in their undeserved suffering – and they criticize you bitterly in words I would not dare write down.[26]

The letter is for the sons of Lycurgus and Demosthenes does his best for them, but the last part of the letter is a plea for the author. Demosthenes is as hurt and obsessed by his own plight of exile as Ovid was to be with his (though not so full of self-pity), and he loses no opportunity of reminding his readers/audience of his own situation.

> I should like, in a spirit of goodwill and friendship, to make a complaint to you – for the moment in brief, but a little later in a long letter which you may expect to receive – if I am still alive – unless I get justice from you in the meantime. You, who are (what could I say, so as not to seem wrong or misleading?) so uncaring, neither feel shame before others nor before yourselves when you have exiled Demosthenes on the very same grounds that you acquitted Aristogeiton. And you allow those who have brashly cared nothing for you to have things (without your permission) which you do not grant to me – the ability to settle my affairs with you by collecting what is owed to me and borrowing from my friends – rather than be

> seen wandering about in a foreign land with old age and exile as a reward for all my hard work on your behalf, a reproach to everyone who has done me wrong.[27]

The second letter is solely concerned with Demosthenes himself and it too is a speech in the guise of a letter with once again an address to the audience – 'gentlemen of Athens' – built in. As before it asks the Council and people to exonerate the writer and allow him to return from exile on grounds of constitutional precedent, external perceptions of Athens and the honour due to a devoted and uncorrupted public servant. It is a clever piece from a master tactician. At the start Demosthenes is the respectful, loyal citizen – wronged, it is true, but regarding the mistaken process of his condemnation more in sorrow than in anger. But now mistakes have been properly rectified and Demosthenes asks that he too should benefit from their rectification.

> Demosthenes to the Council and people, greetings.
>
> As a result of my involvement in public life, I used to think that, since I had done you no wrong, I should never suffer anything like this but even meet with your pardon if I were to commit some ordinary offence. But since it has turned out in this present fashion, as long as I saw you condemning all of us on undisclosed information from the Council, there being no overt evidence or proof from that body, and, reckoning that you were giving up things no less important than those of which I was being deprived, I chose to put up with it all, since for jurymen under oath to go along with whatever the Council – with no demonstrable testimony – said was to act contrary to the constitution. But, since you have done the right thing and realized the dominance which some members of the Council had engineered for themselves, and since you are deciding cases giving regard to evidence and have found these people's secrecy reprehensible, I think it necessarily follows – provided that is your will – that I should meet with the acquittal afforded to those who incurred charges like my own, and that I should not be the only one to be deprived on a false charge of my country, my possessions and my closest family.[28]

Now a harder edge appears: if you don't do something for me, your reputation in the Greek world will suffer. This extension of the particular to the general is a commonplace of Greek forensic oratory, but here it is cleverly understated with the excuses of fear of envy (familiar to any Greek politician) and a subtle reminder of Athens' present troubles. The lack of detail enables Demosthenes to make a pretty comprehensive claim for his own virtues, and this is clinched by reference to his uncorrupted record in the face of many offers of sweeteners from Philip II at their official meetings. At the end of all this, the loyal, respectful citizen is almost in a position to give orders to his audience.

> And you would rightly be concerned about my acquittal, gentlemen of Athens, not only on the ground that I have suffered dreadful things in spite of doing you no wrong, but for the sake of your good reputation among people elsewhere. Do not think, if no-one reminds you of the times and occasions on which I was exceptionally useful to the city, that other Greeks do not realize or have forgotten what I did for you. I am embarrassed to put these down in detail at this point for two reasons: first, I am afraid of jealousy, before which there is no point in speaking the truth, and second, we are at the present time compelled to do much that does not measure up to those deeds of mine because of the cowardice of the other Greeks. To sum up, the quality of the deeds for which I rendered account to you was such that you were universally admired for them, and I had hopes of receiving the greatest rewards from you. When Fate, irresistible and mindless, gave judgement on the struggle for the freedom of the Greeks in which you were engaged, not according to right but as she pleased, not even in the times that followed did I abandon my goodwill towards you nor did I try to trade anything for it – not favour, not expectations, not wealth, not power, not security. Yet I saw all these passing into the possession of those who were politicking against your interests.
>
> Although many important matters would provoke me to speak frankly, there is one particularly important one, I consider, and I shall not be embarrassed to write to you about it. Of those who are remembered in history, Philip was the cleverest at using face-to-face contact to persuade people to his way of thinking or to corrupt notable folk in each of the Greek cities with money; I alone was never subverted in either respect – a fact which brings you honour too – and, although I met Philip often and discussed matters upon which you had sent me as your representative, I kept my hands off the large sums he kept offering me (many people who know about this are still alive). It is right for you to consider what opinion these men will have of you; for treating a man of this calibre in this way would, I am convinced, be for me a misfortune, not wrongdoing, but for you, it would be heartlessness – get rid of that with a change of heart.[29]

From this point the tone relaxes a little and Demosthenes takes his readers carefully through his political services and the more detailed circumstances of his condemnation to exile, as well as his contributions to drama and the navy. He again pleads for the same treatment as has been given to those who faced similar charges. Then Demosthenes the wronged patriot returns. Why did I go into exile? The shame of prison, and look at my age! Where did I go? – a place hallowed by Athenian history.

> Surely my departure into exile could not justly provoke anger against me? For it was not that I had severed my ties with you or that I was looking elsewhere when I left, but, first, because in my view it was very hard to bear the shame of imprisonment, and second, at my age my body could not have tolerated the suffering. Also, I did not think you were averse to me being out of range of insult which was of no help to you and was destroying me. You can see from many indications that it was to your interests I was looking and to no others. For I went to a city in which I was not going to do great things for myself but to which I knew that our ancestors had gone when the Persian crisis came upon them and where I was aware we enjoyed great goodwill. This is the city of Trozen, upon which may all the gods look kindly because of its goodwill towards you and its good deeds towards me – and may I, if I am delivered by you, be able to express my gratitude.[30]

The letter ends with an impassioned peroration, assuring the readers/listeners that Demosthenes' loyalty is firm and demonstrable. It is in his finest public style, but is perhaps let down a little by the two postscripts (25–6) which respectively try to excuse his dwelling on his personal sufferings as an exile, and offer a rather limp olive branch to his opponents.

The fourth letter is the very stuff of internecine personal politics, albeit conducted at long range, and it perhaps gives a flavour of some of those colourful exchanges in the Council and the Assembly which have otherwise left little trace. Demosthenes has heard that one Theramenes has accused him of being an agent and a victim of bad luck – not a charge heard nowadays, but luck was more commonly acknowledged then and Demosthenes was clearly stung by the suggestion. The letter, addressed like the others, gets the audience into the mood with an abusive salvo:

> Demosthenes to the Council and the people, greetings.
>
> I hear that Theramenes, among the other slanders he has uttered against me, has produced an accusation of my being prone to bad luck. I am not at all surprised that this fellow does not know that abuse which points to no wrongdoing on the part of the person addressed cuts no ice with reasonable people. Brash in his life-style, no citizen in his true nature, brought up from childhood in a brothel – it is more reasonable to think that he has no feelings at all for such matters than that he simply does not understand them. If I ever come back in safety, I shall try to have a debate with this man

> on the subject of his drunken ramblings against me and before you, and I think, although he has no scruple of shame, that I shall make him more reasonable. To you, however, I want to explain in a letter my views on these matters and this is for the common good.[31]

The fact that Athens – and by implication its most influential adviser – are in fact blessed with luck is first demonstrated by the verdicts of Zeus in his oracles at both Dodona and Dione, and those of Apollo at Delphi. Divine approval then leads on to human comparisons: Spartans, Persians, Cappadocians, Syrians, Indians and other wild men of the earth are clearly inferior to Athenians, but what about people from Thessaly, Argos and Arcadia who threw in their lot with Philip? They may seem to have better luck, but Athens actually still has the moral high ground; that is what counts. The letter ends with another vicious personal broadside:

> So, on these grounds the gods are giving you favourable oracles and turning unwarranted slander back on to the head of the man who utters it. Anyone would know this if he chose to tot up the pursuits in which Theramenes spends his life. He does from choice the things one would include in a curse on him: he is hostile to his parents but a friend to the catamite Pausanias, he has the brashness of a man but gets used like a woman, he is a bully to his father but submissive to degenerates, his mind delights in the things which make him disliked by everyone – his foul language and stories which his hearers loathe. And he constantly carries on as if he were a man of open frankness. I would not have written these things had I not wanted to stir your memory about his particular sins. For there are things one would be guardedly embarrassed to say or to write, and be disgusted if one heard them – each of you knows that much that is awful and disgraceful can be attributed to him and that consequently there is nothing shameful in my speaking of them and in this man being seen by everyone as a monument to his own wickedness.
>
> Good wishes.[32]

What the Council and the people made of this kind of thing or how Theramenes replied to it is not known; perhaps they were quite used to such exchanges.

The first of Demosthenes' letters is not like the others in that it is oddly prefaced – almost in the manner of a modern church sermon – with a prayer that the words which follow may be those which are best for the people of Athens. The reason for the solemnity is clear from what follows; a significant historical moment has arrived, for Alexander the Great is dead and, with the anticipated collapse of Macedonian power, a prospect of freedom is offered. Athens is at a crossroads and needs advice. The tone of the letter is therefore grave and paternal and, apart from its subject-matter, it could almost have come from the pen of Isocrates. A senior statesman is offering his wisdom, and even his personal difficulties (of which he usefully reminds his readers) must take second place.

> It is fitting, I think, that anyone who sets out on a serious project, whether in words or deeds, should start with the gods. I pray then to all the gods and goddesses that both now and in the time to come what I contrive to write and what the members of the Athenian Assembly choose to do should be what is best for the people of Athens and for those who are well-disposed towards them. This is my prayer and in the hope of the gods giving me good discernment I send the following letter:
>
> Demosthenes to the Council and people, greetings.
>
> Concerning my return home I think all of you will always be able to deliberate on that, so on this occasion I have written nothing about it. But seeing that the present opportunity, if you choose to do what is required, can bring at the same time glory, security and freedom not only for you but for all the rest of Greece (though if you do not recognize it or are diverted from it, taking it up again will not be easy), I thought I ought to put the view I have formed on these matters into the heart of the debate. However, it is a hard task to make a consistent case in a letter, for you are accustomed to oppose many things before taking the time to understand them. Someone who is speaking can feel what it is you want and can easily set your misconceptions straight; a written document, however, has no such recourse against those who make a noise. All the same, if you are willing to listen in silence and take time to understand everything, I think that – if I speak with the gods' favour – I shall clearly demonstrate that, though my words are few, I am acting with complete loyalty by doing what is needful for you and what is beneficial to you.[33]

After a plea for unity he addresses that eternal question for a newly liberated community: what to do about those who are now called collaborators.

> Further, I say that you should not blame or punish in any way a general or politician or any private citizen who appears in the past to have supported the then state of affairs, but allow that all those in the city have done their civic duty, since the gods, by their favourable actions, have saved the city and have given you the chance of deciding what you want in a fresh start. You should think you are in a ship, with some recommending making way with the sails, others with the oars, and all that is said by both groups aims at a safe

> outcome, though what is actually needed to deal with the situation derives from the gods. If you take this attitude to past events, you will both be trusted by all, you will be acting as gentlemen should, you will further your own interests not a little, and you will make those who have opposed you in the cities either change their minds as a group or you will isolate quite a small number of them who were at the back of all this.[34]

There then follow some rather obvious general guidelines and an optimistic exhortation to seize the proffered opportunity. The letter ends with a rousing call to action in the best leadership tradition:

> So do nothing like that but, whatever you are going to do with your whole hearts that is noble and timely, offer your support to that, and, once you have voted for it, call upon Zeus of Dodona and make him your guide along with the other gods who have vouchsafed to you many splendid and true prophecies, and, having prayed to them all with vows of victory-offerings, with good fortune on your side bring freedom to the Greeks.
>
> Good wishes.[35]

In fact, Demosthenes' pleas were heard, his exile did not last long and he returned to Athens within a year; tragically, however, he was again condemned and committed suicide.

Plato had introduced the idea of the letter as a vehicle for philosophy and had combined that with a strain of defensive biography. With Epicurus the pure philosophical letter appears for the first time. Epicurus was born in 341 BC on the island of Samos and after a period in Athens he moved back to Ionia, where he first began teaching. In 306 or 307 BC he returned to Athens and bought a house with a garden, the garden becoming both the centre of his philosophical community and a familiar icon for his way of thinking. Epicurean philosophy aimed to promote happiness in personal life and the founder was not ashamed to value true pleasure very highly. Pleasure, however, did not mean luxury and he and his followers, in trying to live out their convictions, observed a modest and plain way of life, including even slaves and women in their community. Epicureanism was in essence an all-embracing, all-explaining world-view which, with the help of Democritus' atomic theory, accounted in physical terms for the existence of the gods and everything else, and which therefore freed mankind from fears of divine intervention and judgement and – most potently of all – from the fear of death and what might follow it.[36] The message was, however, very variously understood, and this can be seen by contrasting two Roman points of view. For the Roman poet Lucretius, the discovery of the philosophy of Epicurus was a life-changing, liberating experience at the deepest level:

> When previously human life lay foul before the eyes, crushed upon earth by the weight of religion which thrust its head out from the realms of the sky to dominate mortals with its fearful appearance, it was a Greek man first who dared to raise his mortal eyes against it and first stood squarely in its way. Neither tales of the gods nor thunderbolts nor the sky with its grumbling threats intimidated him but only served the more to spur the keenness of his excellent mind with a desire to break the close-fitting locks of the gates of heaven. Because of this the lively power of his mind won through, and he advanced far beyond the flaming ramparts of the world and in his mind and intellect wandered through the immensity of space. From there he returns victorious, bringing us an account of what can come to be and what cannot, and a rationale for each thing's limited potentiality and its deeply fixed end-point. And so religion in its turn is abolished, trodden underfoot, and the victory makes us equal with the heaven.[37]

The depth of feeling and the struggle to embrace the message of Epicureanism is unmistakable. Yet only a few years later the serious and scientific side of Epicurus' philosophy could be trivialized in Roman society banter by the association of Epicurus with self-indulgent pleasure-seeking – a caricature which has persisted to this day. The poet Horace in gently self-mocking mood wanted to present the picture of his own easy-going life-style and described himself as 'a pig from Epicurus' herd' – *porcus de grege Epicuri.*[38] The implications of this throwaway phrase are light-years away from Lucretius' convictions.

Epicurus himself was a famously prolific writer and Diogenes Laertius, one of our chief sources of information, says that his works ran roughly to three hundred papyrus rolls (his great work *On Nature* alone took thirty-eight).[39] Quite apart from the community over which he presided in his Athenian house and his garden near the Academy, he kept in touch by letter with followers and like-minded communities elsewhere, and after his death his letters were carefully preserved and used as part of his philosophic legacy.[40] Some of them were personal, and Diogenes Laertius cannot resist a quote from a letter to a girl-friend: 'O Lord Apollo, dear little Leontion, with what a wild heart-beating you filled me when I read your letter'.[41] Epicurus' austere life-style is represented too by a request to a friend: 'Send me a little pot of cheese so that, whenever I want, I may dine sumptuously.'[42] Other letters, though, had a more serious purpose and were written in a totally different mode and at much greater length; they were expositions of Epicurus' doctrines and were plainly intended as a kind of supplementary support for would-be disciples or beginners. Diogenes Laertius preserves three of these addressed to Herodotus, Pythocles and Menoiceus; the subjects are the nature of the physical universe, the understanding of natural phenomena and some aspects of ethics.

The letter to Herodotus opens with a clear statement of the purpose for which it has been written; it is a summary of what is to be found in Epicurus' harder and more extended work *On Nature*. This idea of a self-help 'rough guide' to complicated philosophical exposition was not entirely new; Aristotle had distinguished between works for outside consumption (*logoi exotericoi*) and works for the really serious philosopher (*logoi cata philosophian*).[43] Unfortunately we have no examples of the first category written by Aristotle. Epicurus' first letter begins with the explanatory introduction:

> Epicurus to Herodotus, greetings.
>
> For those who are not able, Herodotus, to give detailed attention to what I have written about Nature or to examine thoroughly the larger books among my compositions, I have myself produced a summary of the complete system with a view to giving the memory an adequate grasp of the main ideas. The aim is that, whenever occasion arises, people may be able to help themselves with the most important points in proportion to their engagement with the study of Nature. And those who are sufficiently advanced in an overview of the whole subject ought still to keep in mind an elementary outline of the complete system, for we frequently need a comprehensive approach, but not a detailed one in the same way.[44]

He continues in this vein for a little and then launches into the treatise proper with a preface about the importance of clarity in the agreed meanings of words and the need to pay attention to the direct evidence of sense-impressions. Then follows a statement of one of the cardinal principles of the atomic theory which Epicurus took over from Democritus.

> The first point is that nothing is created out of what is not. For [otherwise] everything would have come into being from everything with no need for seeds. And if that which disappears were done away into what is not, everything would have been destroyed, since that into which it was dissolved does not exist. Furthermore the totality [of matter] was always the same as it is now and it always will be. For there is nothing into which it will change since there is nothing beyond the totality which could enter into it and bring about change.[45]

This is not the stuff of casual reading; it demands hard thinking and detailed study and it is written for the committed. As so often in the letter, one is brought up short by the essential directness and modernity of the argument; there is a huge time-gap between this and the emergence of modern theories about a 'steady-state universe'. One or two further examples reinforce the point; there is the dizzying prospect of infinity.

> Moreover, there is an infinite number of worlds, some like this one and some unlike. For atoms, being infinite in number as was shown just now, are carried to the furthest possible distances. For the atoms from which a world might come into being or by which it could be made are not used up in [making] one world or a finite number of worlds, whether they are like this one or different. So there is nothing which stands in the way of an infinity of worlds.[46]

The atomic theory embraces not only cosmology on the grandest scale but also deductions about the behaviour of individual atoms. Once again, how far forward does one have to go in the history of science before encountering again the notion that all bodies fall at the same speed in a vacuum?

> Further the atoms must move with equal speed whenever they are borne through the void with nothing resisting them. For neither will the heavy ones be carried more swiftly than the small, light ones (when, that is, nothing meets them), nor will the small ones be carried more swiftly than the large ones since they have a proportional passage (when nothing resists them). Neither will their upward motion nor their sideways motion caused by impacts be swifter nor their downward motion caused by their own weight. And so long as either condition obtains, their speed will be constant until there is resistance either externally or from the weight of the atoms counteracting the force of a collision.[47]

It is perhaps misleading to give examples only from cosmology and the behaviour of atoms, for the system outlined in the letter is designed to account for all the phenomena of the world – thought, sense-perception and the soul, as well as the obvious physical manifestations of matter. Everything is constituted from atoms and explained by their movements, and however hard some of the atomic constitutions may be to describe and understand, the system is ultimately a source of freedom and comfort, for there is nothing beyond the atomic world: it explains everything and there are no punishments in Hades or vicious divine retributions to fear. Epicurus ends his letter with qualified encouragement for the reader who has studied the treatise and who has at least got some notion of the theory.

> These, Herodotus, are the main points summarized concerning the nature of everything. So if this account of things is accurately grasped and really influences someone, I think that, even if he does not progress to the finer points of detail, he will have gained an unimaginable maturity compared with the rest of mankind. For he will by himself clear up many of the individual details included in our system, and these same details, being lodged in the memory, will

> be a constant support. They are the kind of things which enable those who already have a sufficiently detailed understanding – or those with a full understanding – to analyse them into applications like this, and so to make a large number of surveys concerning the whole of Nature. But people who are not among those with complete knowledge can get from the others in a mode that does not need the spoken word a survey which they follow in their thoughts of the chief topics with a view to giving tranquillity of mind.[48]

The second of Epicurus' letters quoted by Diogenes Laertius is addressed to Pythocles and is concerned not with general theories of physics and their cosmic consequences but with natural and meteorological phenomena. The start gives quite an illuminating insight into the purposes and uses of this kind of letter: the master is answering questions, replying to correspondence enquiries, coaching and encouraging the students, and supplying a suggestion for further reading :

> Epicurus to Pythocles, greetings.
>
> Cleon brought me a letter from you in which you continue to think as kindly of us as our concern for you deserves and in which you attempted quite persuasively to recall the reasoning which contributes to a happy life and in which you asked me to send you a concise and easy-to-follow rationale concerning meteorological matters so that you could commit it to memory easily. For what we have written in other books is hard to remember even though, as you tell me, you are always picking them up. We were glad to receive your request and it filled us with pleasant expectations. So, having written all the rest, we shall send you the contribution you requested – lines of reasoning which will be of service to many others and especially to those who have recently had a genuine taste of natural philosophy, as also to those who have been involved in more serious pursuits than any to be found in general education. Get a good grasp of them, and, keeping them in your memory, get a clear outline view along with the rest which we sent in the little survey addressed to Herodotus.[49]

There then follows an important methodological point. In spite of the rigorous and detailed understanding of the atomically constituted world which the dedicated Epicurean is expected to acquire, the end-purpose is not scientific but philosophical; appropriate knowledge leads to the possession of a calm, untroubled mind. To this end, when faced with puzzling physical phenomena, it is not always necessary to choose the single correct explanation but only to observe that there may be a number of possible explanations. The important thing is that each of these explanations should have a reasonable basis in purely physical terms; choosing the right one is less important (85–8). The letter ranges comprehensively over the celestial phenomena, starting with the nature of a *cosmos* and the origin of sun, moon and stars, and proceeds through topics like eclipses, the formation of clouds, whirlwinds, hail, snow, rainbows, comets and shooting stars. The section on the waxing and waning of the moon illustrates this methodology of suspending judgement on hypotheses and being satisfied for the moment with that.

> The waning of the moon and again her waxing could happen by the turning of the moon's body and equally by the different configurations of the air; also by interposings, and in any of the ways our perceptions suggest for explanations of this apparition – provided that one is not so satisfied by a single explanation that one ignorantly rejects others without regard to what can and cannot be discovered by man, thus longing to discover what is indiscoverable. It is possible that the moon possesses its own light and it is possible too that the moon gets its light from the sun.[50]

The contrast between the Epicurean attitude and the old Greek view of the world in which superstition played such a large part can be seen clearly in the passage on the thunderbolt. In Greek mythological stories about the gods, the thunderbolt is often Zeus's weapon of choice for punishment and retribution and mortals live in dread of it. Epicurus, on the other hand, offers an alternative:

> It is possible that thunderbolts are caused by numbers of wind-clusters, their being trapped and their violent ignition, and the fragmentation of one part and its more powerful expulsion to the regions below, the fragmentation coming about because the areas adjacent are more dense because of the compression of the clouds; or it is possible that it happens because of the expulsion of the trapped fire, just like the thunder. For the fire accumulates and is more violently inflated and breaks the cloud because it cannot escape to adjacent spaces because of the continual compression. And it is possible that thunderbolts come about in many other ways – only let myth keep out! And it will be kept out if one makes good theories about what cannot be seen, following the track of the phenomena.[51]

The end of the letter reinforces the general view Epicurus is recommending:

> Remember all these things, Pythocles. For then you will escape the reaches of myth and you will be able to see the cognate connections

> between these matters. Most of all, apply yourself to the study of first principles and the notion of infinity and kindred matters – also to criteria and the feelings, and to why we reason these things out. The keen and unified study of this will make it easy for you to get a coherent view of the causes of particulars. Those people who get no satisfaction from doing this could not claim to be studying these things well nor to have an idea of the purpose of studying them.[52]

The third letter quoted by Diogenes Laertius is much shorter and is about philosophy – the end-purpose of all the studies of the physical world. The letter includes some of the cardinal features of the Epicurean world-view and begins with an all-age recommendation:

> Epicurus to Menoiceus, greetings.
>
> Let no-one who is young delay the study of philosophy, nor let the old grow tired of it; for no-one is too immature or too mature when it comes to the well-being of the soul. Saying that the right time for philosophizing has not yet arrived or has passed by is like saying that it is not yet the right time for happiness or that time is no more. So philosophy is for both young and old; for the former, so that as someone grows old he may yet be young in good things because of the pleasure of what has happened to him, and for the latter, so that he can be both young and old because he is fearless for the future. Therefore we must practise the things which make for happiness since, if that is present, we have everything, and, if it is not, we go to all lengths to have it.[53]

One of the great claims of Epicurean philosophy was that it freed humanity from the dominion of death and from fears about the after-life. This is one of the first points made to Menoiceus after the introductory paragraphs.

> Get used to the conviction that death is nothing to us, for all good and evil resides in sense-perception and death deprives us of sense-perception. So a correct understanding of the fact that death is nothing to us makes our mortality a source of pleasure, since it gives us a span which is not boundless and removes a longing for immortality. For there is nothing fearful in life for the person who has genuinely grasped that there is nothing fearful in not living. Therefore that person is foolish who says he is afraid of death, not because it will cause pain when it comes but because the prospect of it causes pain now. For what does not trouble by its presence causes needless pain in its anticipation. So death, the most fearful of evils, is nothing to us, since, when we exist, death is not with us, and when death is with us, we do not exist.[54]

The pursuit of true pleasure through tranquillity of mind was the final aim of the Epicurean and this was the source of much subsequent misrepresentation and caricature. The founder of the school was quite sure what he meant and explained it clearly to Menoiceus:

> One ought to make judgements on all these matters by calculating and examining the advantages and disadvantages. For on different occasions we treat the good as an evil and, conversely, the evil as a good. We regard self-sufficiency as a great good, not in order to make do with little on all occasions, but so that, if we do not have much, we can be satisfied with little, being genuinely convinced that it is those who least need it who get the greatest delight from luxury, and that all natural things are easy to get hold of whereas the intangible is not. For simple tastes give as much pleasure as a luxurious life-style when once the pain of desire is removed, and barley-bread and water can give the utmost pleasure when someone who is hungry is led to them. Getting used to a simple and not luxurious way of life is therefore all one needs for health; it gives people no anxieties in the necessary business of life and, when we do on occasion encounter prosperity, it enables us to take it better and makes us unfearful of chance. So when we say that pleasure is the goal, we are not talking of the pleasures of the dissolute and those that derive from acquisition – this is what some believe, the ignorant, the inconsistent and those who deliberately misrepresent – but we mean the absence of bodily pain and a lack of stress in the soul. For it is not drinking-sessions and constant parties nor the delights of boys, women, fish-dishes and all the other things which accompany a luxurious table which produce a pleasurable life but sober reckoning and tracking down the reasons for each choice and refusal and driving out the thoughts which cause the greatest turmoil in people's souls.[55]

The end of the letter is again a general exhortation to study and a promise of what will result expressed in a confident paradox:

> So practise these things and their relative connections day and night both by yourself and with someone of like mind and you will never be distressed, either awake or in dreams, but you will live like a god among men. Someone who lives in the midst of immortal good is quite unlike a mortal being.[56]

With these three letters a new genre has emerged; the letter-form is being used not only to expand and clarify the details of a philosophical system but to recommend and encourage what is in the end a way of life. There is an evangelical ring, and the correspondence is addressed to communities of like-minded thinkers who are seeking further enlightenment and who may and should draw others into the circle. The letters might without too much distortion be said to be pastoral epistles and to be describing the Way, the Truth, and the Life. In Plato's letter the personal was never very far away; for Epicurus it is the message which is all-important.

The adherents of other philosophical systems were not slow to see the importance of letters as a means to disseminate and popularize their views and to define the thinking of their founders. Plato's Academy was the stimulus to several new directions in philosophy and in one of them, Cynicism, the letter seems to have become an established part of the tradition. The chief founder of Cynicism, the famous Diogenes, was a prolific writer and left a letter-collection, and his pupil Crates certainly used the letter-form for philosophical writing also. Cynicism, 'the behaviour of the dog', is quite hard to define, for it was not so much a coherent system as a way of life based on a very rigorous understanding of living according to nature. Its followers adopted it with varying degrees of strictness, but it developed certain unmistakeable characteristics and was widely influential.[57] The way of life was of course exemplified by Diogenes and consisted in a primitive, utterly basic life-style which actively and confrontationally rejected all social and cultural convention and all intellectualism (apart from an interest in ethics). The resulting freedom and self-sufficiency for the Cynic was, however, to be accompanied by a vigorous, missionary zeal embodied in the Cynic slogan-phrase 'defacing the common coin'. The Greek word for 'common coin' – *nomisma* – is rooted in the idea of *nomos* – 'custom, convention, law'. The Cynic was therefore always to be a zealously uncomfortable critic of conventional life and a deliberately rude challenger of commonly accepted norms.[58] Diogenes Laertius' 'Life' of Diogenes contains much apocryphal material but one thing is clear: letters became an essential part of Cynic tradition, as did the *Sayings*, the collection of maxims, and the so-called diatribes.[59] The famous story of Diogenes taking up residence in a barrel (actually a *pithos*) is, for instance, vouched for by the phrase 'as he himself explains clearly in his letters'. The list of Diogenes' writings included a collection of letters, and his pupil Crates is credited with a book of letters 'in which there is some excellent philosophy, while the style is very akin to that of Plato'.[60] Unfortunately we possess no genuine complete letters from either Diogenes or Crates, but the letter continued as a way of conveying Cynic attitudes and ideas, albeit by somewhat fanciful means, and in the first century AD there was a remarkable revival of Cynic letter-writing.[61] These later letters are made up but purport to be from Diogenes himself (fifty-one letters) and from Crates (thirty-six letters). They are hardly the stuff of very serious philosophy and there is more than a whiff of the rhetorical exercise of writing in character about many of them. However, they were written to promote and recommend a way of life, and, even if it was a much-diluted and derivative vision compared with that of Diogenes, it is a little unkind to dismiss the letters as 'an hereditary collection of well-worn gramophone records'.[62] Two examples from the imaginary letters written in the name of Crates may give a taste of the genre:

> To the rich.
>
> Hang yourselves, because although with your lupin-flowers, dried figs, water and Megarian shirts you sail and cultivate large estates, you are also traitors and tyrants and murderers and all the other things you do – when one ought to live quietly. We, however, keep perfect peace, freed from all ill by Diogenes of Sinope, and, having nothing, we have everything, while you, having everything, have nothing because of quarrelsomeness, envy, fear and vainglory.[63]

There are also more extended praises of the founder with literary allusions and mention of the cloak – one of the defiant badges of the Cynic:

> To Patrocles.
>
> Do not call Odysseus the father of Cynicism because he once donned a Cynic's cloak; he was the most effeminate of all his companions and respected pleasure above everything. For it is not the cloak that makes the Cynic but the Cynic the cloak. This was not the case with Odysseus, who was constantly overcome by sleep and wanting food and praised the sweet life, never doing anything without the help of God and luck, and begged from everyone even from the poorest, taking whatever anyone was good enough to give him. But call Diogenes the father of Cynicism who put on the Cynic's cloak not once but for his whole life, superior to both toil and pleasure; he begged, but not from the poorest, he gave up all the necessities, he was self-confident, he never asked to win honours out of pity but out of pride, and he trusted in reason, not in trickery and the bow. He had strength at the moment of death and was brave in the practice of virtue. You must not strive to be like Odysseus but like Diogenes, who both when he was alive and after his death brought many from vice to virtue through the writings he has left to us.[64]

The letters which claim to be written by Diogenes himself fall into two or three groups and it is likely that there are three or four authors at work. The first group (1–29) was probably written in the first century BC or earlier, the others considerably later. Many are dull, but there is the occasional spark of imagination as when Diogenes is supposed to be writing to Hipparchia, Crates' wife.

> To Hipparchia.
>
> I am delighted by your enthusiasm in that you have really wanted to study philosophy and have become one of our select group (which has astonished even men because of its austerity). But make sure that you bring what you have begun to an enthusiastic conclusion. You will do that, I know, if you are not left standing by your partner, Crates, and if you write regularly to me, your philosophical benefactor, For letters can do a lot, and are not inferior to conversations with people who are actually there.[65]

Odysseus crops up again in the letters and was obviously regarded as a not-very-satisfactory proto-Cynic, and in the following letter Diogenes is supposed to be writing to his father, Hicetas, to explain and justify his 'conversion'. Along with the cloak, the wallet and the staff were traditional signs of the Cynic adherent.

> To Hicetas.
>
> Do not be sad, Father, that I am called a dog [the Greek word became used for a Cynic too] and am clad in a double cloak, carry a wallet over my shoulder and have a staff in my hand. There is no need to be sad about such things, but rather be glad because your son is satisfied with little and is free of public opinion – something which enslaves all men, both Greeks and barbarians. For the name. although it does not fit my deeds, in a way carries a reputation. For I am called heaven's dog, not earth's, because that is how I see myself, living not by public opinion but according to Nature, a free man under Zeus, ascribing to him what is good and not to my neighbour. As for my clothing, Homer himself writes that Odysseus, the wisest of the Greeks, was wearing that kind of thing when he was returning home from Troy with Athena's support, and it was so splendid that it was agreed to be no human invention but divine:
>
> > Then she put another vile rag on him, and a tunic
> > tattered, squalid, blackened with the foul smoke, and over it
> > gave him the big hide of a fast-running deer, with the hairs rubbed
> > off, to wear, and she gave him a staff, and an ugly wallet
> > that was full of holes, with a twist of rope attached, to dangle it.
>
> So be cheerful, Father, at the name by which they call us and at my clothing, since the dog is under divine protection and the clothing is a god's invention.[66]

This mode of philosophizing – hints and tips from everyday life with a touch of humour – which derived originally from more serious accounts of how one ought to live one's life was given a new direction in Latin literature by being turned into verse. Lucilius, the father of satire, wrote verse letters, and Horace, following in his footsteps, wrote two books of verse epistles – lightly and beautifully entertaining (apart from the much more searching and demanding discussions of poetry). The use of the letter-form was continued in Latin by the elder Seneca in his prose *Moral Letters* – pieces containing advice nominally addressed to Lucilius but in reality vehicles for imparting aspects of Stoic wisdom in accessible and persuasive form. The tone is much more serious and sober than that of Horace, but the line of descent from 'philosophic letters' such as those of the later Epicureans and Cynics is clear. However, in the first century AD the idea of the Greek letter as a mode of promoting and defining a way of life and also as a means of keeping scattered communities in touch with their founder received a radically different focus which left the notions of civilized amusement and gentle moralizing far behind and rediscovered strains of evangelism and salvation alongside the nurture of the faithful – the letters written by the founders of the early Christian Church.

6

GREEK LETTERS IN THE EARLY CHRISTIAN CHURCH

The importance of letters in the development of the early Christian Church can hardly be overestimated. Once new communities had been founded, church leaders could by means of their letters continue to keep in touch with them, instruct them, answer their queries, chide them, encourage them and try to sort out their problems – not all of which were religious. In the New Testament twenty-one of the twenty-seven 'books' are in the form of letters and they contain a greater variety of subject-matter than is often appreciated, ranging from complicated theology in the making to quite individual domestic matters, and including not a little advice on community management. The dominant figure is of course Paul, who was probably born at about the same time as Jesus. For someone who was enormously influential little is known of his early life, but his background was clearly that of a Greek-speaking Jew brought up in a Hellenistic/Roman culture and to some extent acquainted with the ideas of Greek philosophical schools including the Stoics, Epicureans and Cynics; as he says himself, 'I am a debtor both to Greeks and barbarians' (Romans 1.14).[1] Tarsus, his birthplace, was the capital of the Roman province of Cilicia and was a typical Hellenistic city with a mixed population. It had become an influential centre of Stoicism and its most renowned citizen was the Stoic Athenodorus, who moved in the highest circles at Rome, being a friend and correspondent of Cicero and a close associate of Augustus himself. Just how far Paul was himself influenced by Stoic ideas is much debated; he quotes handy Greek aphorisms from well-known collections – 'Bad company ruins good morals' – and just before he delivered his famous sermon on the Areopagus in Athens he had provoked curiosity among Epicurean and Stoic philosophers who wanted to know more about his novel ideas; traces of Cynic thinking too have been detected.[2] There is no doubt, though, that Jewish ideas and customs were the bedrock of his early upbringing and a proud part of his heritage – 'I myself am an Israelite, a descendant of Abraham, a member of the tribe of Benjamin' (Romans 11.1). At some point he left Tarsus to complete his Jewish education under the Rabbi Gamaliel in Jerusalem and became a vigorous part of the Jewish opposition to the early spread of Christian groups – until, that is, an errand of persecution turned into a life-changing revelation on the road to Damascus. But Jewish though he was, Paul lived and worked in a Greek-speaking world and Greek was his natural means of communication; so too were the conventions of Greek correspondence, and in Paul's post-conversion evangelical fervour fusion between Greek and Jewish elements is a feature of his letters to young Christian communities.[3]

Of the twenty-one letters in the New Testament, thirteen are attributed to Paul. The first and second letters to Timothy and the letter to Titus – the so-called 'pastoral letters' – are probably not by him, and some doubts have been expressed about his authorship of the letters to the Ephesians and Colossians and the second letter to the Thessalonians. The form of Paul's letters is recognizably Greek. They begin with the conventional formula – 'A to B, greetings' – but the formula has normally been extended and Christianized, and in place of 'greetings' there is a version of what came to be known as the Peace. In the letter to the Romans, for instance the opening is florid and elaborated:

> I, Paul, a servant of Jesus Christ, called to be an apostle, set apart for the gospel of God, which he promised beforehand through his prophets in the holy scriptures, the gospel concerning his Son, who was descended from David according to the flesh and was declared to be Son of God with power according to the spirit of holiness by resurrection from the dead, Jesus Christ our Lord, through whom we have received grace and apostleship to bring about the obedience of faith among all the Gentiles for the sake of his name, including yourselves who are called to belong to Jesus Christ, to all God's beloved in Rome who are called to be saints: grace to you and peace from God our father and the Lord Jesus Christ.[4]

Elsewhere a more simple opening address nevertheless contains a reminder of the apostle's own Christian credentials and a reassuring identification of the community to which he is writing. In the body of the letter there are sometimes echoes of familiar Greek components like the prayer for good health and thanks to the recipient or to the gods, but often the matters Paul addresses are felt to be too urgent and he plunges straight in with his message. The end of the Greek letter was traditionally the place for remembrances to family and friends, and this Paul uses as a regular means of keeping in touch with members of the Christian communities who were especially close to him or who were particularly influential. He had a remarkable memory and the list at the end of the letter to the Romans, for instance, is a tribute to his wide acquaintance.[5]

He obviously dictated his letters, as can be seen from the touching little aside by Tertius who took down the letter to the Romans: 'Timothy, my co-worker, greets you: so do Lucius and Jason and Sosipater, my relatives. I,

Tertius, the writer of this letter, greet you in the Lord' (Romans 16.21–22). Elsewhere there are unmistakable signs of dictation too, moments when the secretary wrote the words as the thoughts came:

> I thank God that I baptized none of you except Crispus and Gaius, so that no-one can say that you were baptized in my name. (I did baptize also the household of Stephanas; beyond that I do not know whether I baptized anyone else.)[6]

Sometimes too Paul added his own personal hand-written greeting as a tail-piece, much as today a businessman may add a hand-written postscript to a typed letter. He even ruefully acknowledges the clumsiness of his own hand-writing as compared with the compact uniformity of the professional scribe: 'See what large letters I make when I am writing in my own hand!' (Galatians 6.11).

All Paul's letters were written to particular communities for particular purposes with a number of issues uppermost in his mind – matters some-times arising from reports reaching him or from enquiries directly addressed to him. The letter to the Galatians, for instance, is written to counter a development which Paul had heard of and conceived to be a serious danger. The letter has a two-fold background: some had begun to promote narrowly Judaizing influences among the Galatian Christians, and then there was the position of Paul himself in regard to other apostles in Jerusalem who had their own views about Gentiles. The letter was probably written about AD 50. Paul begins with the usual extended greeting formula and then straight away launches into a torrent of criticism:

> I am astonished that you are so quickly deserting the one who called you in the grace of Christ and are turning to a different gospel – not that there is another gospel, but there are some who are confusing you and want to pervert the gospel of Christ. But even if we or an angel from heaven should proclaim to you a gospel contrary to what we proclaimed to you, let that one be accursed! As we have said before, so now I repeat, if anyone proclaims to you a gospel contrary to what you received, let that one be accursed![7]

The problem with which Paul was so concerned was one which dogged him to the end of his life: tension between the strict requirements of Jewish law (to which many Jewish Christians adhered) and the more open message which he preached of justification by faith. The Gentile community in Galatia had obviously come under considerable pressure since Paul left to include more Jewish observance as a necessary part of Christian practice (even including compulsory circumcision). This 'gospel contrary to what you received' is what Paul so vehemently rejects, along with those who had introduced it. He is desperately convinced of his mission to Gentile Christians and goes to great lengths to explain the history of his struggle to have this mission recognized. He begins with the early years after his conversion, even feeling it necessary to swear an affidavit to the truth:

> You have heard, no doubt, of my earlier life in Judaism. I was violently persecuting the church of God and was trying to destroy it. I advanced in Judaism beyond many among my people of the same age, for I was far more zealous for the traditions of my ancestors. But when God, who had set me apart before I was born and called me through his grace, was pleased to reveal his Son to me, so that I might proclaim him among the Gentiles, I did not confer with any human being, nor did I go up to Jerusalem to those who were already apostles before me, but I went away at once into Arabia, and afterwards I returned to Damascus. Then after three years I did go up to Jerusalem to visit Cephas [Peter] and stayed with him for fifteen days; but I did not see any other apostle except James the Lord's brother. In what I am writing to you, before God I do not lie![8]

Then he tells the story of how, fourteen years later, he, Barnabas and Titus had had considerable arguments in Jerusalem before James, Peter and John, the acknowledged Christian leaders there, who had finally agreed to his responsibility for a Gentile mission. The opposition had not been negligible – Paul's frustration is obvious: 'false brothers secretly brought in to spy on the freedom we have in Christ Jesus, so that they might enslave us' and 'those who were supposed to be acknowledged leaders (what they actually were makes no difference to me; God shows no partiality)'. Moreover, the Jerusalem agreement proved to be by no means watertight, for later, when Peter was visiting Antioch, he received a deputation from James in Jerusalem – perhaps inspired by the growth of Jewish nationalism – which made Peter much more cautious and even affected Paul's close companion, Barnabas. This provoked an open row:

> But when Cephas [Peter] came to Antioch, I opposed him to his face, because he stood self-condemned; for until certain people came from James, he used to eat with the Gentiles. But after they came, he drew back and kept himself separate for fear of the circumcision faction. And the other Jews joined him in this hypocrisy, so that even Barnabas was led astray by their hypocrisy. But when I saw that they were not acting consistently with the truth of the gospel, I said to Cephas before them all, 'If you, though a Jew, live like a Gentile and not like a Jew, how can you compel the Gentiles to live like Jews?' We ourselves are Jews by birth and not Gentile sinners:

> yet we know that a person is justified not by the works of the law but through faith in Jesus Christ. And we have come to believe in Christ Jesus, so that we might be justified by faith in Christ, and not by doing the works of the law, because no-one will be justified by the works of the law.[9]

Paul, having now established his credentials, once again returns to the attack in vigorous rhetorical style:

> You foolish Galatians! Who has bewitched you? It was before your eyes that Jesus Christ was publicly exhibited as crucified! The only thing I want to learn from you is this: did you receive the Spirit by doing the works of the law or by believing what you heard? Are you so foolish? Having started with the Spirit are you now ending with the flesh?[10]

The bulk of the letter is on this theme – the law being overtaken by faith – and the message is brought home by argument, by analogy, by Old Testament quotation and by a remarkable appeal to an inclusive vision:

> As many of you as were baptized into Christ have clothed yourselves with Christ. There is no longer Jew or Greek, there is no longer slave or free, there is no longer male and female; for all of you are one in Christ Jesus. And if you belong to Christ, then you are Abraham's offspring, heirs according to the promise.[11]

There is even the odd note of pleading, but when it comes to the tricky question of circumcision which had obviously been the cause of divisions, Paul draws the only conclusion possible for him – but cannot resist a vicious sideswipe at his unknown opponents:

> For in Christ Jesus neither circumcision nor uncircumcision counts for anything; the only thing that counts is faith working through love. You were running well; who prevented you from obeying the truth? Such persuasion does not come from the one who calls you. A little yeast leavens the whole batch of dough. I am confident about you in the Lord that you will not think otherwise. But whoever it is that is confusing you will pay the penalty. But my friends, why am I still being persecuted if I am still preaching circumcision? In that case the offence of the cross has been removed. I wish those who unsettle you would castrate themselves![12]

The end of the letter is calmer with the beautiful list of the fruits of the Spirit: 'love, joy, peace, patience, kindness, generosity, faithfulness, gentleness, and self-control'. But Paul adds a postscript triggered by taking to his own hand-writing:

> See what large letters I make when I am writing with my own hand! It is those who want to make a good showing in the flesh that try to compel you to be circumcised – only that they may not be persecuted for the cross of Christ. Even the circumcised do not themselves obey the law, but they want you to be circumcised so that they may boast about your flesh. May I never boast of anything except the cross of our Lord Jesus Christ, by which the world has been crucified to me and I to the world. For neither circumcision nor uncircumcision is anything; but a new creation is everything! As for those who will follow this rule – peace be upon them, and mercy, and upon the Israel of God. From now on, let no-one trouble me; for I carry the marks of Jesus branded on my body. May the grace of our Lord Jesus Christ be with your spirit, brothers and sisters. Amen.[13]

Paul's letters to the church community in Corinth illustrate not only the variety of matters which Paul felt he must address as a result of what he had heard about the development of the community, but also the awkward relationships which could arise between a pretty authoritarian leader and an enthusiastic and diverse group which was evolving in its own way. The first letter (which refers to an earlier one we do not possess) was written when Paul was at Ephesus, probably in the early 50s AD, and comes from a leader who is fairly sure of his own ground but who recognizes the need to tread carefully on occasion. It begins with the conventional greeting and Paul gives thanks for the strength of the Corinthian Christians. In the first section of the letter he then addresses two problems: the dangers of an incipient 'personality-cult' among the faithful, and the need to put both Jewish tradition and Greek intellectualism into proper perspective. The personality-cult seems easily explicable in an enthusiastic band of new devotees who were eagerly adopting their particular baptizer as their mentor, but Paul will have none of it:

> For it has been reported to me by Chloe's people that there are quarrels among you, my brothers and sisters. What I mean is that each of you says, 'I belong to Paul', or 'I belong to Apollos', or 'I belong to Cephas', or 'I belong to Christ.' Has Christ been divided? Was Paul crucified for you? Or were you baptized in the name of Paul?[14]

He is just as definite in his insistence that his Christian message supersedes Jewish and Greek conventions, however lowly the believer:

> Where is the one who is wise? Where is the scribe? Where is the debater of this age? Has not God made foolish the wisdom of the world? For since, in the wisdom of God, the world did not know God through wisdom, God decided, through the foolishness of our proclamation, to save those who believe. For Jews demand signs and Greeks desire wisdom, but we proclaim Christ crucified, a stumbling-block to Jews and foolishness to Gentiles, but to those who are called, both Jews and Greeks, Christ the power of God and the wisdom of God. For God's foolishness is wiser than human wisdom, and God's weakness is stronger than human strength.[15]

And at the end of Chapter 3 he rounds off the argument, bringing together the two themes mentioned earlier and clinching the points with quotations from the Old Testament:

> For the wisdom of this world is foolishness with God, For it is written,
>
> > He catches the wise in their craftiness
>
> and again,
>
> > The Lord knows the thoughts of the wise,
> > That they are futile.
>
> So let no-one boast about human leaders. For all things are yours, whether Paul or Apollos or Cephas or the world of life or death or the present or the future – all belong to you, and you belong to Christ, and Christ belongs to God.[16]

Paul's strong character and claims to leadership emerge in many places in the letters and, after reminding the Corinthians that the work of an apostle is pretty thankless – 'We have become like the rubbish of the world, the dregs of all things, to this very day' (4.13) – he asserts his own authority and issues what amounts to a threat to those who have presumed to question it:

> I appeal to you, then, be imitators of me. For this reason I sent you Timothy, who is my beloved and faithful child in the Lord, to remind you of my ways in Christ Jesus, as I teach them everywhere in every church. But some of you, thinking that I am not coming to you, have become arrogant. But I will come to you soon, if the Lord wills, and I will find out not the talk of these arrogant people but their power. For the kingdom of God depends not on talk but on power. What would you prefer? Am I to come to you with a stick, or with love in a spirit of gentleness?[17]

Corinth, where Paul had lived for some eighteen months, was a place with a notorious reputation. It had always been an important trading city and the constant traffic via the Isthmus meant that its adjacent port was a centre for the facilities which frequently accompany professional seafarers. Corinth had even been commemorated in the Greek language – the verb *corinthiazomai* meant 'I fornicate'. Paul was therefore under no illusions about the moral climate in which the Corinthian Christian community lived and had no hesitation about assuming the role of implacable judge in particular circumstances. Moreover, he was conscious that even among the faithful there were likely to be undesirable characters who were best avoided:

> I wrote to you in my letter not to associate with sexually immoral persons – not at all meaning the immoral of this world, or the greedy and robbers, or idolaters, since you would then need to go out of the world. But now I am writing to you not to associate with anyone who bears the name of brother or sister who is sexually immoral or greedy, or is an idolater, reviler, drunkard, or robber. Do not even eat with such a one.[18]

And he is not afraid of reminding his flock of the colourful past some of them had enjoyed:

> Do you not know that wrongdoers will not inherit the kingdom of God? Do not be deceived! Fornicators, idolaters, adulterers, male prostitutes, sodomites, thieves, the greedy, drunkards, revilers, robbers – none of these will inherit the kingdom of God. And this is what some of you used to be.[19]

The next section of the letter is a reply to written queries from the Corinthians and begins with advice on marriage (Paul as a bachelor cannot resist an unrealistic claim for privileged status):

> Now concerning the matters about which you wrote: 'It is well for a man not to touch a woman.' But because of cases of sexual immorality, each man should have his own wife and each woman her own husband. The husband should give to his wife her conjugal rights, and likewise the wife to her husband. For the wife does not have authority over her own body, but the husband does; likewise the husband does not have authority over his own body, but the wife does. Do not deprive one another except perhaps by agreement for a set time, to devote yourselves to prayer, and then come together again, so that Satan may not tempt you because of your lack of self-control. This I say by way of concession, not of command. I wish

> that all were as I myself am. But each has a particular gift from God, one having one kind and another a different kind.[20]

The thorny question of married couples where one is a believer and one is not is settled sensibly – no radical solutions, since 'Wife, for all you know, you might save your husband. Husband, for all you know, you might save your wife' (7.16). Above all, Paul seems anxious to avoid tendencies to hectic, dramatic revolution: the circumcised should accept their state and so should slaves, for true freedom is to be found elsewhere. Likewise the question of where to eat is dealt with cautiously; Greek and Roman temples customarily offered opportunities for rare meals of choice meat from the sacrificial animals and there had been some doubt about whether the faithful should take advantage of them. Paul replies that in principle there is no problem since 'we know that no idol in the world really exists', but public perception is another thing:

> For if others see you, who possess knowledge, eating in the temple of an idol, might they not, since their conscience is weak, be encouraged to the point of eating food sacrificed to idols?[21]

Then follows a hint of trouble which surfaces even more in the second letter to the Corinthians; Paul goes on the defensive to 'those who would examine me'. The matter at issue seems to be Paul's entitlement to support and maintenance by the Christian community. This seems to have been questioned but Paul is sure of what he should expect:

> Who at any time pays the expenses for doing military service? Who plants a vineyard and does not eat any of its fruit? Or who tends a flock and does not get any of its milk? Do I say this on human authority? Does not the law say also the same? For it is written in the law of Moses, 'You shall not muzzle an ox while it is treading out the grain.'[22]

All the same, he assures the community that, although he deserves their support, he has made no claim on it and feels awkward to be writing in this way. The criticisms have plainly hurt him. However, he returns to two matters relating to the conduct of worship: whether women should veil their heads, and the proper observance of dignity at the Lord's supper. On the first, he ties an unequivocal instruction to veiling with a typically Pauline (and Greek) view of male superiority (11.3–16). The second reveals a very different and surprising view of what later became the communion service or the mass. At this time the celebration of the Lord's supper had no definitive liturgical form and it is plain that sometimes the eating and drinking went beyond the symbolic and indeed could get out of hand:

> When you come together, it is not really to eat the Lord's supper. For when the time comes to eat, each of you goes ahead with your own supper, and one goes hungry and another becomes drunk. What! Do you not have homes to eat and drink in?[23]

Paul replies with what Jesus himself did at the Last Supper, quoting the words which have become enshrined in the prayer of consecration: 'This is my body that is given for you. Do this in remembrance of me.' And Paul ends with a summing up:

> So then, my brothers and sisters, when you come together to eat, wait for one another. If you are hungry, eat at home so that when you come together, it will not be for your condemnation. About the other things I will give instructions when I come.[24]

Now a new thought occurs and one close to Paul's heart: the variety of characters and talents to be found in the Christian community and the basic unity which underlies it. He uses and greatly extends the analogy with the separate parts of the human body which have different functions yet form an organic whole; the result is a genuinely inclusive group:

> For just as the body is one and has many members, and all the members of the body, though many, are one body, so it is with Christ. For in the one Spirit we were all baptized into one body – Jews or Greeks, slaves or free – and we were all made to drink of one Spirit.[25]

This analogy takes off in almost rhetorical style and concludes with an oft-quoted and inspired piece of prophecy which Paul describes as 'a still more excellent way':

> If I speak in the tongues of mortals and of angels, but do not have love, I am a noisy gong or a clanging cymbal. And if I have prophetic powers, and understand all mysteries and all knowledge, and if I have all faith, so as to remove mountains, but do not have love, I am nothing. If I give away all my possessions, and if I hand over my body so that I may boast, but do not have love, I gain nothing.
>
> Love is patient; love is kind; love is not envious or boastful or arrogant or rude. It does not insist on its own way; it does not rejoice in wrongdoing, but rejoices in the truth. It bears all things, believes all things, endures all things.
>
> Love never ends. But as for prophecies, they will come to an end; as for tongues, they will cease; as for knowledge, it will come to an

> end. For we know only in part, and we prophesy only in part; but when the complete comes, the partial will come to an end. When I was a child, I spoke like a child, I thought like a child, I reasoned like a child; when I became an adult, I put an end to childish ways. For now we see in a mirror dimly, but then we will see face to face. Now I know only in part; then I will know fully, even as I have been fully known. And now faith, hope and love abide, these three, and the greatest of these is love.[26]

One of the discoveries made by the Corinthians was the practice of ecstatic utterance – speaking in tongues. The phenomenon, still to be found quite often today in evangelical communities, was plainly threatening to get out of hand in Corinth. It was a practice with which Paul himself was acquainted; apart from the incident at Pentecost when 'tongues of fire' descended and prompted the faithful to speak in most of the languages of the Middle East, one of Peter's audiences in Caesarea received the Holy Spirit and then spoke in tongues, and twelve of Paul's converts at Ephesus did the same (Acts 2.1–13; 10.46; 19.6). At Corinth, however, Paul felt it necessary to explain that the mind was an essential ingredient in Christian life too, not just ecstatic experience. Moreover, visitors and would-be sympathizers could easily be put off: 'If therefore the whole church comes together and all speak in tongues, and outsiders or unbelievers enter, will they not say that you are out of your mind?' (14.23). Paul lays down a pretty strict but sensible rule which cannot have pleased everyone; 'If anyone speaks in a tongue, let there be only two or at the most three, and each in turn; and let one interpret. But if there is no-one to interpret, let them be silent in church and speak to themselves and to God' (14.27–28). It is in this context that he adds his notorious advice on the position of women in worship, betraying both his Jewish and his Hellenistic background: 'As in all the churches of the saints, women should be silent in the churches. For they are not permitted to speak, but should be subordinate, as the law also says' (14.33–34). Obviously, at Corinth women *had* been speaking.

Paul's last main point in the letter is one central to the Christian faith: the reality and consequences of Christ's resurrection. He begins with a statement of that, mentioning all the corroborative witnesses who can guarantee its truth, and he then faces the first of two big questions which have been asked: some have said there is no resurrection of the dead. Paul's reply is firm, logical and simple: if there is no resurrection, that must apply to Christ too, and then the whole edifice of Christian belief as expounded by Paul crumbles. There can be no redemption of human sin, no victory over death and no hope of an after-life. The second big question is posed as hypothetical but it is a fair guess that it is one Paul had frequently encountered: how exactly are the dead raised and what will they be like? By now the apostle's patience is wearing thin and he replies with what seems an awkward analogy between the seed and what grows from it; 'Fool! What you sow does not come to life unless it dies … ' He then develops his argument in terms of the human body being liable to decay and death but the resurrected body being imperishable and partaking of heavenly glory. Here there is not so much argument as a prophecy or vision, and it is one whose words have comforted countless numbers over the centuries:

> What I am saying, brothers and sisters, is this: flesh and blood cannot inherit the kingdom of God, nor does the perishable inherit the imperishable. Listen, I will tell you a mystery! We will not all die, but we will all be changed, in a moment, in the twinkling of an eye, at the last trumpet. For the trumpet will sound, and the dead will be raised imperishable, and we will be changed. For this perishable body must put on imperishability, and this mortal body must put on immortality. When this perishable body puts on imperishability and this mortal body puts on immortality, then the saying that is written will be fulfilled:
>
> Death has been swallowed up in victory.
> Where, O death, is your victory?
> Where, O death is your sting?[27]

After the exaltation of this vision, Paul comes back to earth with a bump and goes straight into housekeeping details and arrangements for a collection for the Christian community in Jerusalem. He then tells the Corinthians of his own plans. He will stay in Ephesus and travel through Macedonia to visit Corinth again, if possible for more than a fleeting visit. Timothy may pass through Corinth on his way to join Paul, but Apollos is not keen at the moment to come there. Finally Paul signs off with greetings from the local Christians in Ephesus and his special friends, Aquila and Prisca; there is then a postscript in his own hand:

> I, Paul, write this greeting with my own hand. Let anyone be accursed who has no love for the Lord. Our Lord, come. The grace of the Lord Jesus be with you. My love be with all of you in Christ Jesus.[28]

There seems little doubt that this first letter to the Corinthians is self-contained and complete. The same cannot be said with certainty about the second letter to Corinth. It has for instance been suggested that Chapters 10–12 may have been written later than the rest of the letter. Certainly these chapters show Paul in a particularly prickly relationship with the Corinthians. There has for one thing been personal criticism, contrasting the paper tiger of the letters with Paul's apparently disappointing public-speaking appearances:

> For they say 'His letters are weighty and strong, but his bodily presence is weak and his speech is contemptible.' Let such people understand that what we say by letter when absent, we will also do when present.[29]

Then there are plainly rival leaders on the scene whose views diverge from Paul's. He is very anxious to re-establish his authority (not forgetting a hint of pique at the criticism of his speaking):

> For if someone comes and proclaims another Jesus than the one we proclaimed, or if you receive a different spirit from the one you received, or a different gospel from the one you accepted, you submit to it readily enough. I think that I am not in the least inferior to these super-apostles. I may be untrained in speech, but not in knowledge; certainly in every way and in all things we have made this evident to you.[30]

The rivals come in for quite as much criticism as Paul's Greek philosophical predecessors bestowed on their opponents – 'Even Satan disguises himself as an angel of light' – and the taunt about Paul's oratory produces a heartfelt and florid piece of rhetoric in self-justification:

> But whatever anyone dares to boast of – I am speaking as a fool – I also dare to boast of that. Are they Hebrews? So am I. Are they Israelites? So am I. Are they descendants of Abraham? So am I. Are they ministers of Christ? I am talking like a madman – I am a better one: with far greater labours, far more imprisonments, with countless floggings, and often near death. Five times I have received from the Jews the forty lashes minus one. Three times I was beaten with rods. Once I received a stoning. Three times I was shipwrecked; for a night and a day I was adrift at sea; on frequent journeys, in danger from rivers, danger from bandits, danger from my own people, danger from Gentiles, danger in the city, danger in the wilderness, danger at sea, danger from false brothers and sisters; in toil and hardship, through many a sleepless night, hungry and thirsty, often without food, cold and naked. And besides other things, I am under daily pressure because of my anxiety for all the churches. Who is weak and I am not weak? Who is made to stumble, and I am not indignant?[31]

Another theme which comes through unmistakably in these chapters is the suspicion that Paul has in some way taken material advantage of the community in Corinth; he again mounts a vigorous defence:

> I will most gladly spend and be spent for you. If I love you more, am I to be loved less? Let it be assumed that I did not burden you.

> Nevertheless (you say) since I was crafty, I took you in by deceit. Did I take advantage of you through any of those whom I sent to you? I urged Titus to go, and sent the brother with him. Titus did not take advantage of you, did he? Did we not conduct ourselves with the same spirit? Did we not take the same steps? Have you been thinking all along that we have been defending ourselves before you?[32]

The end of the letter offers the usual warm Christian greetings but also tells the Corinthians to get things straight. Whether or not these concluding chapters are a later addition, the start of the letter already gives hints of serious differences, and it appears that, apart from misunderstandings about Paul's intention to visit Corinth, the cause of friction was an earlier and rather critical letter from Paul which was threatening to provoke a rift. He tries to explain that he wrote with the best of intentions and with the interests of the Corinthians at heart, but he obviously feels that a fresh start is needed and refers to the convention of the letter of introduction to indicate his feelings:

> Are we beginning to commend ourselves again? Surely we do not need, as some do, letters of recommendation to you or from you, do we? You yourselves are our letter, written on our hearts, to be known and read by all; and you show that you are a letter of Christ, prepared by us, written not with ink but with the Spirit of the living God, not on tablets of stone but on tablets of human hearts.[33]

He reiterates his unshakable personal confidence and what he believes is its source and uses that as a door to open the Christian message of hope for the future and the expectation of a more glorious life beyond this one. He makes use of the Old Testament and various analogies, including one which was particularly apt for someone who spent part of his time in Corinth working as a tent-maker:

> For we know that if the earthly tent we live in is destroyed, we have a building from God, a house not made with hands, eternal in the heavens. For in this tent we groan, longing to be clothed with our heavenly dwelling – if indeed, when we have taken it off we will not be found naked. For while we are still in this tent, we groan under our burden, because we wish not to be unclothed but to be further clothed, so that what is mortal may be swallowed up in life.[34]

The plea to the Corinthians is heartfelt and urgent and it ends in relief, for Titus had evidently reported that Paul's letter had been accepted by the Corinthians and had not caused the division that he feared.

There is then an abrupt change of subject, and in spite of the previous difficulties Paul plunges straight into fund-raising. In 'making the ask' he uses the familiar strategy of comparing the generosity of others with the anticipated generosity of his addressees:

> We want you to know, brothers and sisters, about the grace of God that has been granted to the churches of Macedonia; for during a severe ordeal of affliction, their abundant joy and their extreme poverty have overflowed in a wealth of generosity on their part. For, as I can testify, they voluntarily gave according to their means, and even beyond their means, begging us earnestly for the privilege of sharing in this ministry to the saints – and this, not merely as we expected; they gave themselves first to the Lord and, by the will of God, to us, so that we might urge Titus that, as he had already made a beginning, so he should also complete this generous undertaking among you. Now as you excel in everything – in faith, in speech, in utmost eagerness, and in our love for you – so we want you to excel also in this generous undertaking.[35]

And to keep things up to the mark Titus and an assistant are to be dispatched to Corinth; the plea is quite an extended one and the Corinthians are put under some pressure.

In both his letters to Corinth Paul seems to be a little on edge – sure of his mission but rather less sure of his reception and standing with the community and uncertain how far he can go with instruction and hectoring. In the letter he wrote to the Christian communities in Rome the feeling is quite different. Although he had not visited the people in Rome at this point, he is confident that they are solidly with him and looks forward one day to sharing their enthusiasm. The letter is unusually long and, in contrast to other letters where particular circumstances and questions are obviously in the background, it seems to be a general essay for the converted, summarizing and reinforcing central features of Paul's belief for public consumption. In that respect it is more akin to Greek philosophical letters like those of Epicurus, though the personal warmth, the many individual greetings and the use of Old Testament quotations set it in a category of its own. The letter begins with sin and the judgement of God, but quite soon it is into the familiar territory of the function of Jewish law and the place of Jew and non-Jew in the new order; this was a theme which was of crucial importance in the early Christian communities:

> For we hold that a person is justified by faith apart from works prescribed by the law. Or is God the God of Jews only? Is he not the God of Gentiles also? Yes, of Gentiles also, since God is one; and he will justify the circumcised on the ground of faith and the

> uncircumcised through that same faith. Do we then overthrow the law by faith? By no means! On the contrary, we uphold the law.[36]

Paul goes on to considerable elaboration of the doctrine of justification by faith and what follows from it, and then returns to the question of the Jewish law and its proper place in the scheme of things. The Christian community at Rome must have included many Jews, for in Chapters 9–11 there are frequent quotations from the Old Testament in a way that seems to assume the reader will be quite familiar with them. Then, almost as if to redress the balance, Paul reminds the congregation of the need for individuals to develop their own gifts and goes into a list of maxims for living, recalling the collections of moral sentences which most educated Greeks and Romans would remember from their schooling:

> Let love be genuine; hate what is evil; hold fast to what is good; love one another with mutual affection; outdo one another in showing honour. Do not lag in zeal, be ardent in spirit, serve the Lord. Rejoice in hope, be patient in suffering, persevere in prayer. Contribute to the needs of the saints; extend hospitality to strangers.[37]

What was Paul actually doing in writing the letter and (as he admits) preaching to the converted? His own account is that of a *primus inter pares* issuing minor corrections of course:

> I myself feel confident about you, my brothers and sisters, that you yourselves are full of goodness, filled with all knowledge, and able to instruct one another. Nevertheless on some points I have written to you rather boldly by way of reminder, because of the grace given me by God to be a minister of Christ Jesus to the Gentiles in the priestly service of the gospel of God, so that the offering of the Gentiles may be acceptable, sanctified by the Holy Spirit.[38]

He feels a little guilty that he has not visited such a committed centre, but somehow the needs of evangelism elsewhere have always been more pressing. He does, however, promise to come after he has taken to Jerusalem the results of his fund-raising in Macedonia and Corinth. The letter ends with greetings to a long list of friends and relatives, both Greek and Roman.

The letter to the Christians at Philippi shows Paul in another light, writing not as a free evangelist but as a prisoner dangerously close to death. It is not known where he was being imprisoned when he wrote – Rome or Caesarea are among the possible places – nor is the date at all certain, though it is likely to have been in the late fifties or early sixties AD. It is not even clear that what we have is a single letter, for there are some abrupt transitions, though it can be argued that the exigencies of prison life and the likelihood of interrupted composition may account for this lack of continuity. The letter begins with a simple formulaic greeting to the community, which seems by now to have appointed senior members (though 'bishops and deacons' is probably too grandly anachronistic a translation). Although the letter is said to be from both Paul and Timothy, it is clear that Paul is the writer and thinker behind it. The opening is warm and confident – in spirit like the beginning of the letter to the Romans:

> Paul and Timothy, servants of Christ Jesus, to all the saints in Christ Jesus who are in Philippi, with the bishops and deacons: grace to you and peace from God our Father and the Lord Jesus Christ.
>
> I thank my God every time I remember you, constantly praying with joy in every one of my prayers for all of you, because of your sharing in the gospel from the first day until now. I am confident of this, that the one who began a good work among you will bring it to completion by the day of Jesus Christ. It is right for me to think this way about all of you, because you hold me in your heart, for all of you share in God's grace with me, both in my imprisonment and in the defence and confirmation of the gospel.[39]

Paul refers to his imprisonment almost in passing and goes on to say that it has actually had some good results:

> I want you to know, beloved, that what has happened to me has actually helped to spread the gospel, so that it has become known throughout the whole imperial guard [*praetorium*] and to everyone else that my imprisonment is for Christ; and most of the brothers, having been made confident in the Lord by my imprisonment, dare to speak the word with greater boldness and without fear.[40]

He hopes that he will be released but knows he is on a knife-edge. Either way, he is supremely confident of his message and assures the Philippians that, if they continue on the right path, he will hear of it and be glad. He then turns to the question of humility and urges them to imitate Jesus in that virtue, quoting what some scholars believe is an example or version of an early Christian hymn:

> Let the same mind be in you that was in Christ Jesus
> Who, though he was in the form of God,
> did not regard equality with God
> as something to be exploited,
> but emptied himself,
> taking the form of a slave,
> being born in human likeness.

And being found in human form
  he humbled himself
  and became obedient to the point of death –
  even death on a cross.
Therefore God also highly exalted him
  and gave him the name
  that is above every name,
so that at the name of Jesus
  every knee should bend
  in heaven and on earth and under the earth,
and every tongue should confess
  that Jesus Christ is Lord,
  to the glory of God the Father.[41]

Paul cannot have been the easiest person to work with and he was not always prepared to listen to views which differed from his own. This comes over in several places in the letters, and from the isolation of prison life he seems particularly distrustful of his close associates. He tells the community in Philippi that he is sending to them the co-author of this letter, Timothy, but he is not sure of anyone else (though in the next breath he actually sends Epaphroditus as well):

> I hope in the Lord Jesus to send Timothy to you soon, so that I may be cheered by news of you. I have no-one like him who will be genuinely concerned for your welfare. All of them are seeking their own interests, not those of Jesus Christ. But Timothy's worth you know, how like a son with a father he has served with me in the work of the gospel. I hope therefore to send him as soon as I see how things go with me; and I trust in the Lord that I will also come soon.[42]

He returns to what, in spite of his personal circumstances, is a joyful message and makes no apology for repeating himself; the Philippians are asked to join him in striving hard to live as Christians and to reach the goal of eternal life. They are to keep their minds focused on the good life, its virtues and rewards and to enjoy their happiness: 'Rejoice in the Lord always; again I will say, rejoice' (3.4). Paul obviously had a soft spot for the Philippians, and, like all good fund-raisers, he does not forget to thank them for their present and past generosity:

> You Philippians indeed know that in the early days of the gospel, when I left Macedonia, no church shared with me in the matter of giving and receiving, except you alone. For even when I was in Thessalonica, you sent me help for my needs more than once. Not that I seek the gift, but I seek the profit that accumulates to your

> account. I have been paid in full and have more than enough; I am fully satisfied, now that I have received from Epaphroditus the gifts you sent, a fragrant offering, a sacrifice acceptable and pleasing to God.[43]

The letter ends with simple Christian good wishes and, of course, the Peace; it is interesting to see that converts are already to be found in Roman official circles (is Paul a little proud of them?):

> Greet every saint in Christ Jesus. The friends [Greek – brothers] who are with me greet you. All the saints greet you, especially those of the emperor's household. The grace of the Lord Jesus Christ be with your spirit.[44]

Paul's first letter to the Christians in Thessalonica was probably written from Corinth, and although it purports to come from Paul, Silvanus and Timothy, it was again written by Paul himself, the other two being included out of courtesy. Paul was rather proud of the Thessalonians – 'you became an example to all the believers in Macedonia and in Achaia' (1.7) – and the opening shows his pleasure. Nevertheless he soon adopts a curiously defensive, self-justifying tone and it may be that news of some critical comments had reached him via Timothy:

> As you know and as God is our witness, we never came with words of flattery or with a pretext for greed; nor did we seek praise from mortals, whether from you or from others, though we might have made demands as apostles of Christ. But we were gentle among you, like a nurse tenderly caring for her own children. So deeply do we care for you that we are determined to share with you not only the gospel of God but also our own selves, because you have become very dear to us.[45]

The passage testifies again to Paul's Greek background, for the image of the nurse caring for her children has very plausibly been shown to come from one of the familiar analogies used by Greek Cynic philosophers.[46] Paul goes on to explain that he really wanted to pay a second visit 'but Satan blocked the way' and Timothy was sent instead; he has now returned with an encouraging report which has delighted Paul and provokes an outpouring of good wishes. He then repeats and intensifies some of his earlier instructions on sexual morality, mutual affection and a quiet, workmanlike approach to life before coming to a section which seems like an answer to further queries connected with resurrection, and in particular to what will happen to those believers who may still be alive at the second coming of Jesus. Not easy, and Paul replies with a rather speculative vision:

> For the Lord himself, with a cry of command, with the archangel's call and with the sound of God's trumpet, will descend from heaven, and the dead in Christ will rise first. Then we who are alive, who are left, will be caught up in the clouds together with them to meet the Lord in the air; and so we will be with the Lord for ever.[47]

The 'day of the Lord' will be unexpected and he urges the community to remain alert, dedicated and encouraged. Then, as if he has been distracted from what he meant to do, he fires off a final list of further gnomic instructions:

> And we urge you, beloved, to admonish the idlers, encourage the faint-hearted, help the weak, be patient with all of them. See that none of you repays evil for evil, but always seek to do good one to another and to all. Rejoice always, pray without ceasing, give thanks in all circumstances; for this is the will of God in Christ Jesus for you. Do not quench the Spirit. Do not despise the words of prophets, but test everything; hold fast to what is good; abstain from every form of evil.[48]

The signing-off shows how Paul expected his letter to be used when it reached Thessalonica:

> Greet all the brothers and sisters with a holy kiss. I solemnly command you by the Lord that this letter be read to all of them. The grace of our Lord Jesus Christ be with you.[49]

Paul intended his letters to be dispatches read aloud to the community in public meetings, and this may account for what some have seen as patterns of rhetoric and traces of the habits of public speaking in some of the letters – the Greek background again.[50]

The second letter to the Thessalonians may be taken as an example of a problem which affects a number of letters attributed to various writers in the New Testament – authenticity. It has been seriously doubted that Paul was the author of this second letter to Thessaly. The evidence is all internal and not by any means conclusive: there are demonstrable differences in language and thought (especially with regard to the second coming), there are odd repetitions of phraseology from the first letter, and there are none of the personal or concrete allusions to be found in the first letter. A small example of the disputable nature of the evidence can be found in the signing-off:

> Now may the Lord of peace himself give you peace at all times and in all ways. The Lord be with all of you. I, Paul, write this greeting with my own hand. This is the mark in every letter of mine; it is the way I write. The grace of the Lord Jesus Christ be with all of you.[51]

It can be argued that this personal touch of hand-writing at the end is a typical Pauline habit and therefore an indication of authenticity (cf. Galatians 6.11), and perhaps another writer would hardly have had the nerve to flaunt an impersonation trick so brazenly. On the other hand, it can be plausibly argued too that this is an example of an imitator trying just a little too hard – would the real Paul have needed to tell his readers that this was his trade-mark?

Doubts about authenticity of authorship have also touched the letters to the Ephesians and the Colossians. The letter to the Ephesians, for instance, was probably written later than the other New Testament letters, for the Jew/Gentile question seems by then to have been settled and it also looks as though the letter has been to some extent modelled on the earlier letter to the Colossians. The two letters to Timothy and the letter to Titus, which since the eighteenth century have been known as the 'Pastoral Letters', are attributed to Paul, but many scholars believe they were written by someone who may have used parts of Pauline letters but who was writing for a later situation in which the Church was already more structured and in need of orderly rules. The first letter to Timothy, for instance, contains a fairly comprehensive person-specification for a bishop:

> The saying is sure: whoever aspires to the office of bishop desires a noble task. Now a bishop must be above reproach, married only once, temperate, sensible, respectable, hospitable, an apt teacher, not a drunkard, not violent but gentle, not quarrelsome, and not a lover of money. He must manage his own household well, keeping his children submissive and respectful in every way – for if someone does not know how to manage his own household, how can he take care of God's church? He must not be a recent convert, or he may be puffed up with conceit and fall into the condemnation of the devil. Moreover, he must be well thought of by outsiders, so that he may not fall into disgrace and the snare of the devil.[52]

The personal instructions to Timothy as pastor even include some dietary advice for his precarious health: 'No longer drink only water, but take a little wine for the sake of your stomach and your frequent ailments' (5.23). However valuable and sometimes curious the advice and instructions in these three letters may be, they do not read like the work or thinking of Paul and it is hard to believe they were written by him.

The two letters attributed to Simon Peter have likewise been called in question and it is pretty well certain that the second of them was written by someone else after Peter's death in the form of a 'testament' or farewell message from the supposed author. Peter's first letter has difficulties too, for it is written in good, educated Greek – not the language of an illiterate fisherman – and it also uses the Greek translation of Old Testament writings.

Peter was of course an immensely forceful and central character and may well have had the services of a quality Greek secretary, but even so doubts remain.

A letter from one of Jesus' brothers would be of uncommon interest and that is what the letter of James claims to be. It begins with a short, if grand, greeting:

> James, a servant of God and of the Lord Jesus Christ, to the twelve tribes in the Dispersion, greetings.

It is written in good Greek and seems to show little or no acquaintance with the ideas Paul was promoting. The Greek can be explained by a good secretary, but even with careful reading, it is hard to take the letter as a coherent, thought-through, connected piece of writing. Rather it seems to be a collection of passages, some short giving pithy instruction, others quite extended and elaborately rhetorical which sometimes break off abruptly. Thus religion is given a strangely limited definition:

> If any think they are religious, and do not bridle their tongues but deceive their hearts, their religion is worthless. Religion that is pure and undefiled before God, the Father, is this: to care for orphans and widows in their distress, and to keep oneself unstained by the world.[53]

James' views do not sit easily with Paul's elaborated doctrine of justification by faith, though apologists have tried hard to lessen the apparent contradictions:

> What good is it, my brothers and sisters, if you say you have faith but do not have works? Can faith save you? If a brother or sister is naked and lacks daily food, and one of you says to them, 'Go in peace; keep warm and eat your fill', and yet you do not supply their bodily needs, what is the good of that? So faith by itself, if it has no works, is dead.[54]

One theme which is the subject of two extended passages is that of the unfair privileges often accorded to the wealthy and the retribution which such violations of social justice can expect:

> My brothers and sisters, do you with your acts of favouritism really believe in our glorious Lord Jesus Christ? For if a person with gold rings and in fine clothes comes into your assembly, and if a poor person in dirty clothes also comes in. and if you take notice of the one wearing the fine clothes and say, 'Have a seat here, please', while to the one who is poor you say, 'Stand there', or 'Sit at my feet', have you not made distinctions among yourselves, and become

> judges with evil thoughts? Listen, my beloved brothers and sisters. Has not God chosen the poor in the world to be rich in faith and to be heirs of the kingdom he has promised to those who love him? But you have dishonoured the poor. Is it not the rich who oppress you? Is it not they who drag you into court? Is it not they who blaspheme the excellent name that was invoked over you?[55]

The theme is pursued again later with almost Ruskinian (or Cynic) fervour and the author is deeply convinced of the evils of social inequality:

> Come now, you rich people, weep and wail for the miseries that are coming to you. Your riches have rotted, and your clothes are moth-eaten. Your gold and silver have rusted, and their rust will be evidence against you, and it will eat your flesh like fire. You have laid up treasure for the last days. Listen! The wages of the labourers who mowed your fields, which you kept back by fraud, cry out, and the cries of the harvesters have reached the ears of the Lord of hosts. You have lived on the earth in luxury and in pleasure; you have fattened your hearts on a day of slaughter. You have condemned and murdered the righteous one, who does not resist you.[56]

The letter has no closing formula and it is impossible to know whether it was a compilation edited from parts of addresses given by James, whether he himself assembled some familiar themes from different occasions, or whether it was written by someone else in his name.

The three letters attributed to the apostle and gospel-writer John clearly come from a common context. The themes and phraseology are related, and it has been suggested that they were written to the members of a community which took its foundation and original inspiration from John the apostle. It was, however, by the time the letters were written, a community mature enough to be influenced by divergent ideas and by at least one leader who was thought to be dangerous enough to imperil the essential message of the gospel. The letters were almost certainly not written by the apostle John – he would hardly have referred to himself as 'the elder' – but the writer or writers were very aware of and close to his teaching. The first letter has no opening or closing formula but is addressed to the community and is probably the letter referred to at the end of the third – 'I have written something to the church' (John 3.9). The opening makes much use of the imagery of light and darkness to characterize the states of believers and unbelievers, and the first of the two main themes of the letter is dramatically introduced in the middle of the second chapter:

> Children, it is the last hour! As you have heard that antichrist is coming, so now many antichrists have come. From this we know

> that it is the last hour. They went out from us, but they did not belong to us; for if they had belonged to us, they would have remained with us. But by going out they made it plain that none of them belongs to us. But you have been anointed by the Holy One, and all of you have knowledge. I write to you, not because you do not know the truth, but because you know it, and you know that no lie comes from the truth. Who is the liar but the one who denies that Jesus is the Christ? This is the antichrist, the one who denies the Father and the Son. No-one who denies the Son has the Father; everyone who confesses the Son has the Father also. Let what you heard from the beginning abide in you. If what you heard from the beginning abides in you, then you will abide in the Son and in the Father. And this is what he has promised us, eternal life.[57]

The situation to which this refers has been much disputed, but there has obviously been a breakaway group and the issue at stake seems to be rival views about the claim of Jesus to be the Messiah, the Christ. The author is anxious to prevent doubt spreading further and to strengthen the belief which he regards as essential and argues his case relentlessly. In the middle of Chapter 3 the second main theme of the letter is introduced: 'For this is the message you have heard from the beginning, that we should love one another' (3.11). The two themes of Jesus, the true Son of God, and the practice of love are interwoven and summarized at the end of the chapter: 'And this is his commandment, that we should believe in the name of his Son Jesus Christ and love one another, just as he commanded us' (3.23). The writer then returns to his first theme with another dramatic warning:

> Beloved, do not believe every spirit, but test the spirits to see whether they are from God; for many false prophets have gone out into the world. By this you know the Spirit of God: every spirit that confesses that Jesus Christ has come in the flesh is from God, and every spirit that does not confess Jesus is not from God. And this is the spirit of the antichrist, of which you have heard that it is coming; and now it is already in the world.[58]

The theme of love returns and once again belief in Jesus as the Son of God and all that flows from it is united with the command to love: we are to love one another as God has loved us by sending his Son. The argument is closed with an either/or choice: 'whoever has the Son has life; whoever does not have the Son of God does not have life' (5.11–12).

The second letter attributed to John shares some of the same thoughts but is quite different in scale and in its tone. It begins with a conventional Christian formulaic greeting to a lady and her family and has an intimate, affectionate note. The original was apparently written by the author himself rather than by a scribe, and it is a very personal slant on the situation addressed in the first letter:

> The elder to the elect lady and her children, whom I love in the truth, and not only I but also all who know the truth, because of the truth that abides in us and will be with us for ever: grace, mercy and peace will be with us from God the Father and from Jesus Christ, the Father's Son, in truth and love.
>
> I was overjoyed to find some of your children walking in the truth, just as we have been commanded by the Father. But now, dear lady, I ask you, not as though I were writing you a new commandment, but one we have had from the beginning, let us love one another. And this is love, that we walk according to his commandments; this is the commandment just as you have heard it from the beginning – you must walk in it.
>
> Many deceivers have gone out into the world, those who do not confess that Jesus Christ has come in the flesh, any such person is the deceiver and the antichrist! Be on your guard so that you do not lose what we have worked for, but may receive a full reward. Everyone who does not abide in the teaching of Christ, but goes beyond it, does not have God; whoever abides in the teaching has both the Father and the Son. Do not receive into the house or welcome anyone who comes to you and does not bring this teaching; for to welcome is to participate in the evil deeds of such a person.
>
> Although I have much to write to you, I would rather not use paper [papyrus] and ink; instead I hope to come to you and talk with you face to face, so that our joy may be complete.
>
> The children of your elect sister send you their greetings.[59]

The third letter is also very short and quite similar in tone to the second; it is addressed simply to one Gaius and combines the usual Greek health-wish at the start with approval for the state of Gaius' soul:

> The elder to the beloved Gaius, whom I love in truth.
>
> Beloved, I pray that all may go well with you and that you may be in good health, just as it is well with your soul. I was overjoyed when some of the friends [brothers] arrived and testified to your faithfulness to the truth, namely, how you walk in the truth.[60]

The rest of the letter is quite businesslike; Gaius is praised for his hospitality to some Christian visitors, and then the anonymity of the first letter is broken and we learn who is the ring-leader of the trouble in the religious community:

> I have written something to the church; but Diotrephes, who likes to put himself first, does not acknowledge our authority. So if I come, I will call attention to what he is doing in spreading false charges against us. And not content with those charges, he refuses to welcome the friends [brothers], and even prevents those who want to do so and expels them from the church.[61]

The author identifies himself as the writer of the second letter by repeating a version of his polite hope to see the addressee soon: ' I have much to write to you, but I would rather not write with pen and ink … ' (13–14). As before, a personal greeting ends the letter.

The letter attributed to Jude – or more accurately Judas, another of Jesus' brothers, not of course Judas Iscariot – has been defended as authentic but has also been thought to be the work of a later writer. It is addressed to an unspecified community and may come from a context of Jewish Christianity in Palestine, for the author is familiar with the Hebrew text of the Old Testament rather than the Septuagint, and some similarities in method have been observed between this letter and the writers of the Dead Sea scrolls. The main purpose of the letter is to urge members of the community to hold steady to the faith they have been taught, and not to believe some persuasive newcomers who are conveying dangerously false messages and condoning loose moral standards.

> For certain intruders have stolen in among you, people who long ago were designated for this condemnation as ungodly, who pervert the grace of God into licentiousness and deny our only master and Lord, Jesus Christ.[62]

They are denounced as comparable to the citizens of Sodom and Gomorrah and the denunciation becomes quite poetic:

> They are waterless clouds carried along by the winds; autumn trees without fruit, twice dead, uprooted; wild waves of the sea, casting up the foam of their own shame; wandering stars for whom the deepest darkness has been reserved for ever.[63]

Nevertheless, they seem to have had some success and – to judge by the criticism – some rhetorical gifts: 'These are grumblers and malcontents; they indulge their own lusts; they are bombastic in speech, flattering people to their own advantage' (16). The remedy is simple and direct:

> But you, beloved, build yourselves up on your most holy faith; pray in the Holy Spirit; keep yourselves in the love of God; look forward to the mercy of our Lord Jesus Christ that leads to eternal life. And

> have mercy on some who are wavering; save others by snatching them out of the fire; and have mercy on still others with fear, hating even the tunic defiled by their bodies.[64]

The letter to the Hebrews was, as the title suggests, probably written to a community of Jewish Christians, but their location is unknown. Jerome in his translation attributed the letter to Paul but it is pretty certain that it is not by him. The style is quite different and the writer claims to have come to a belief in Jesus through 'those who heard him' – not Paul's experience. Of the names which crop up in Paul's correspondence, Apollos and Barnabas have been suggested among others as likely authors, but there is no firm evidence. The letter probably pre-dates the destruction of Jerusalem and the Temple in AD 70 since the Levitical priesthood appears still to be at work. It is much the longest of the New Testament letters (although the writer claims 'I have written to you briefly' [13.22]), and, though it has a short farewell greeting, there is no opening formula and it is again much more like Epicurus' letters – a treatise with a nod to the letter-form – than a letter which was sent to a particular person or persons in order to address special circumstances. It is also directed at a very restricted readership, and most of the contemporary Gentile world would surely have regarded it as a rather parochial document – arguing for the supremacy of Jesus, to be sure, but with many details and ample Old Testament quotation which was largely irrelevant to them.

It is by now obvious that the true authorship of a number of letters in the New Testament is open to question, and it is certain that some are not written by the authors identified by tradition. In the art market in the modern world the discovery that a work is not genuine has dire consequences, and critical writing on artistic matters seems to have a tendency to mirror financial valuation. The same is obviously not true with regard to letters. Many of the 'unauthentic' New Testament letters are an accepted part of the canon, contain fine writing and argument, and have made essential contributions to the development of Christian theology; whoever the authors were, they deserve respect. In fact, as can be seen from the previous chapter, the phenomenon of authors writing in the name of a prominent thinker was by no means new and was familiar to all followers of Greek philosophy, and whether they were Platonists, Aristotelians, Epicureans or Cynics, they were used to a body of correspondence amplifying and extending the thought and original works of the founder and helping to interpret them for future generations. Such letters had often been conceived as a means of contact with communities geographically separated but sharing a common vision which had constantly to be tested against and verified from what was believed to be the thought and practice of the founder. The first century AD was particularly notable for a proliferation of letters written in the names of others which, in terms of intent, ran the gamut from serious philosophizing to cultivated literary entertainment. It is therefore not altogether surprising to find that a vigorous and growing religious movement like Christianity, and in particular a driven and charismatic leader like Paul, should use letters for very detailed instruction and communication but should also stimulate the creation of correspondence which was maybe not authentic, but was the next best thing and undeniably useful.

The New Testament letters may fit into a recognizable context, but it is certain that they also mark the beginnings of a new genre; they are at the start of a tradition in which church leaders, a little like the Hellenistic kings before them, used more or less public letters to dispense important advice on community management, doctrine, instruction, exhortation and discipline, as well as more mundane matters of administration. The continuation of this process can be clearly seen in some of the early Christian letters which did not claim to be apostolic, like the first letter of Clement (there is no second letter) or the seven letters of Ignatius of Antioch. The letter of Clement is a good example because it deals with a problem Paul too had faced – trouble in the Church at Corinth. Though the manuscript tradition assigns the letter to Clement, it is by no means certain that he was the author or that he was the third bishop of Rome after Peter. What is certain is that the writer spoke and wrote good Greek, knew the Septuagint very thoroughly, and felt himself to have the authority to write on behalf of the Church in Rome to the congregation in Corinth; the letter can probably be dated to the middle-90s AD. It starts with an institutional rather than a personal address, but the formula follows the style of Paul's openings:

> The church of God which has its lodging in Rome to the church of God which has its lodging in Corinth, to those called, to those blest in the will of God through our Lord Jesus Christ. May grace and peace abound for you from the omnipotent God through Jesus Christ.[65]

The trouble in the Corinthian Church appears once more to concern faction politics, and the author is not slow to introduce the main theme:

> Because of the sudden disasters and misfortunes which have come one upon another, we think we have been rather slow to turn to the matters which have been found wanting among you, beloved people – that strife, alien and foreign to those chosen of God, foul and unholy, which a few over-eager and brash characters have fired to such a point that your respected and much-talked-of reputation, deservedly loved by all men, has been seriously traduced.[66]

He tactfully reminds them of their past good works at some length but, when it comes to the heart of the matter, he again minces no words:

> All glory and sufficiency was given to you, and then what was written was fulfilled: 'The beloved ate and drank, became bloated and fat, and kicked.' From this came envy and grudging, strife and quarrelling, harassment and anarchy, war and capture. Thus the dishonourable were roused up against the honourable, bad reputations against good, the mad against the sane, the young against the old.[67]

The adaptation of the verse from Deuteronomy is typical and the letter is shot through with echoes and quotations from the Old Testament – more in the manner of the writer of the letter to the Hebrews. However, it is Paul who is in the background, and the Corinthians are told to remember him and what he had written to them:

> Take up the letter of the blessed Paul, the apostle. What was the first thing he wrote to you in proclaiming the good news? Assuredly, acting with the Spirit, he sent you word of himself, Cephas and Apollos because even then you were supporting factions. But that business of factions involved you in lesser sin, for you were supporting apostles who were vouched for, and a man they had tested.[68]

Though the pattern of the letter is Pauline, there are some marked differences. Most obviously the letter is very long – too long, perhaps, for its rather limited aim. It takes nearly an hour and a half to read, and if, like Paul's letters, it was intended to be read to the congregation in Corinth, the attention of some probably strayed well before the end. Nevertheless, it shows unmistakably the loose template which Paul had established and which was the source and example for a great deal of subsequent ecclesiastical communication between church leaders and their flocks.

7

LETTERS IN GREEK LITERATURE[1]

European literature begins with Homer, and Book vi of the *Iliad* contains the first Greek fictional letter – or more properly, message in writing – which is the only one to be found in the Homeric poems. In a much-discussed passage, the Trojan warrior Glaucos is explaining his ancestry to the Greek Diomedes, whom he has encountered on the battlefield. In typical epic fashion his account of his ancestry spills over into a story: Glaucos' grandfather, Bellerophon, had been an unusually handsome man and Anteia, the wife of King Proitos of Argos, had fallen madly in love with him. When Bellerophon rejected her passionate advances, she tried to take her revenge:

> So she went to Proitos the king and uttered her falsehood:
> 'Would you be killed, O Proitos? Then murder Bellerophontes
> who tried to lie with me in love, though I was unwilling.'
> He shrank from killing him, since his heart was awed by such action,
> but sent him away to Lycia, and handed him murderous symbols,
> which he inscribed in a folding tablet, enough to destroy life,
> and told him to show it to his wife's father, that he might perish.[2]

In the event the king of Lycia observed the customs of hospitality and entertained his guest, Bellerophon, for nine days before opening the tablet. Then, instead of accomplishing the murderous intent of the message, he set Bellerophon a series of tasks and contrived an ambush, all of which Bellerophon triumphantly survived, living to become the king's son-in-law and a partner in the Lycian kingdom. The written message on a folded tablet sits oddly in the Homeric world in which oral communication is universal, and the murderous symbols are a puzzle. From the literary point of view there has perhaps been an understandable tendency to overload this proto-letter with significance.[3] A written message certainly introduces something new and probably suspect into an oral culture, and it begins to offer new possibilities to the story-teller: a written message is fixed and unresponsive, not subject to the subtleties and adjustments of oral exchange, and once sent, it passes out of the control of the sender and may be misused or misunderstood or ignored, with results that the sender did not foresee or wish. This is the source of an unease which lasts quite a long time in the Greek world; it is the essence of Socrates' celebrated warnings in Plato's *Phaedrus* about the limitations of writing:

> For writing, I guess, Phaedrus, has this shortcoming – and really it is the same as with painting. For the products of painting stand there as if they were living but, if you ask them something, they preserve a total solemn silence. Just so with written word; you would imagine they were saying something on the basis of thought, but if you ask them something about what they are saying because you want to understand, you get only the one, self-same meaning all the time. And every verbal communication, once it is written down, rolls off in all directions, indiscriminately both among those who understand it and among those for whom it is not at all suitable, and it does not know to whom it should and should not address itself. When it is taken wrongly and unjustifiably insulted, it always needs its father to come to its aid, for it cannot on its own defend or help itself.[4]

Likewise, not only is a written communication fixed in its message but it is also a tangible physical object; it can therefore be carried about and the carrier can know or not know its contents. The Homeric story of Bellerophon makes use of all these possibilities: Proitos loses control of the message, and does not know that his brother king will delay reading it and not act on the contents as instructed; there is no herald or message-carrier to report back. Moreover, we have also the dramatic irony of Bellerophon carrying his own death-warrant quite unawares. Yet in two very long epics this is the only hint of what a letter can be or do in the telling of a story.

Homer was the inspiration for much that went into classical Greek tragedy, but the device of the letter as an important ingredient in a story-line or as an opportunity for special theatrical moments does not seem to have been taken up by either Aeschylus or Sophocles so far as we know.[5] Whether they felt that letters were incongruous or anachronistic in the situations they were constructing, or whether letter-writing was still not that much a part of the world in which they were living, neither tragedian chose to introduce letters or written messages as part of their plots. With Euripides the situation changes – though since we only possess nineteen of his ninety-two or so plays, some caution is necessary. The introduction of the device of a letter turned a play which had been a failure into one of his relatively few conspicuous successes during his lifetime, and at the end of his working life he was still experimenting with the dramatic uses of letters. The failure was the first version of his play *Hippolytos.* This was probably set in Athens and represented Phaedra, wife of Theseus, so desperately in love with her step-son, Hippolytos, that she finally swore him to secrecy, offered herself passionately to him, and promised him the throne. Hippolytos covered his head in shame and refused (hence the title of this first play, *Hippolytos Calyptomenos* – 'Hippolytos of the covered head'). Phaedra, disappointed, in fury accused Hippolytos of assault, producing false evidence, and made out that she was going to kill herself with Hippolytos' sword. Theseus therefore cursed and banished Hippolytos, whose death ensued; revelation of the truth then shamed Phaedra into committing suicide herself.[6] The extent of the play's 'failure' is unknown; we are simply told in the confused hypothesis attached to the text that 'the unseemly element deserving criticism' was corrected in the second, rewritten play. In this surviving play a letter is made to play a crucial role. The plot is quite radically recast so that Phaedra's passion has a believable beginning and carries in itself nothing openly blameworthy. She and Theseus have come from Athens to Trozen where Hippolytos has been living, and it is the renewal of her acquaintanceship with Hippolytos which has awakened a blazing love. However, she is deeply ashamed of it and keeps it absolutely secret until her nurse, persistently troubled by Phaedra's physical and mental state, wrings a confession from her. The nurse then tries to blur the moral boundaries for Phaedra, but Phaedra will not listen, so the nurse decides to act on her own initiative and goes to tell Hippolytos of Phaedra's passion. This unleashes a torrent of disgust from Hippolytos, who in any case has forsworn sex, and Phaedra overhears his outburst aghast. The shame of her passion becoming public becomes unbearable and she hangs herself. Theseus returns to Trozen from visiting an oracle at the moment when her dead body is discovered and is beside himself with grief. In the midst of his lamentation he notices a wooden tablet sealed and hanging by its binding threads from Phaedra's hand. He breaks the seal and opens the tablet expecting a last family message; what he actually finds is a suicide note incriminating Hippolytos for supposedly assaulting her. In a remarkable moment of theatre the writing tablet almost becomes a living thing, taking on Phaedra's identity and speaking for her:

> *Thes.* The tablet cries out, cries out things that can never be forgotten.
> How can I escape
> The heaviness of these troubles? For I go ruined.
> Such, such is the song I realize in misery is uttered by this writing.
> *Chor.* Alas, you reveal a story which presages troubles.
> *Thes.* I shall no longer keep this gated in my mouth, hard to
> Express, a trouble destructive. Oh, my city!
> 'Hippolytus has dared to assault my bed
> with violence, dishonouring the holy eye of Zeus.'[7]

Theseus without further thought curses his son and banishes him. Hippolytos leaves Trozen, but on his journey Poseidon, acting on Theseus' curse, sends a bull from the sea which overturns Hippolytos' chariot and scares his horses so that Hippolytos is mortally injured. A messenger brings the news and the dying Hippolytos is brought back to the palace. At this point Artemis appears and explains the truth of the whole business to Theseus; the final death-scene between him and his son is heart-rending.

The result of reworking the play was to give Euripides first prize at the Dionysia of 428 BC, one of only five first prizes that he ever won. The use of the letter is central to the changes he made and it had dramatic consequences. First, it enabled the playwright to present the audience with a sudden and shocking take on Phaedra's character when part of the letter was read. Up to that point Phaedra had seemed to act with propriety; she may have suffered from a secret passion but she only discussed it with the nurse, and her suicide seemed to be motivated by the fear of shame and dishonour for herself and her family. The letter changed everything, providing visible evidence on the stage of disgraceful slander, and opening the way for tragic events to follow.

In another play of which only fragments survive, the *Palamedes*, Euripides again made use of a letter and it was crucial to the action.[8] The play deals with alleged treachery in the Greek camp before Troy; Odysseus is at odds with a fellow-Greek, Palamedes, and causes a forged letter to be 'found' in Palamedes' tent. The letter is supposed to be from the Trojan king, Priam, and Palamedes' apparent treachery brings about his death at the hands of the Greeks. The details of the story vary a little in the tradition and we do not know enough about Euripides' play to say how he treated it.[9]

In two plays written at the end of his life Euripides deliberately exploited the possibilities of introducing letter-writing to a heroic world where communication at a distance was the proper prerogative of heralds and envoys trusted with oral messages. In *Iphigeneia in Tauris* a letter is part of the climactic recognition-scene in which Orestes and Pylades discover the true identity of the priestess they have met in Tauris.

Iphigeneia has been serving in that capacity for years and is bound by the terms of the cult she serves to arrange the killing of any stranger who comes to the temple; she herself was saved from sacrifice at Aulis by Artemis, who replaced her with a hind under Agamemnon's knife. When Orestes and Pylades arrive at the temple, she is therefore under an obligation to have them killed, but she allows one of them to go free on condition of taking back to Argos a letter she dictated long ago to explain her plight. The letter had been written for her by one of her previous victims, who felt pity for her while acknowledging her religious duty to have his life ended. Orestes insists that Pylades should be the messenger and that he himself should remain to die; as yet no-one knows who is who. Iphigeneia requires an oath from Pylades that he will truly deliver the letter to friends of her choosing: Orestes in turn insists that she should also swear to keep her promise to send Pylades on his way. It then occurs to Pylades that letters can get lost on long and dangerous journeys, and this thought introduces the crucial recognition-scene. Iphigeneia answers that she will recite the contents of the letter so that, if the original is lost at sea, Pylades will have the contents in his memory and can deliver them verbally. She then begins to read the text.[10] Euripides uses the reading of the letter in a masterly way, first to register the passage of Orestes and Pylades from astonishment to convinced realization (Iphigeneia has no inkling of the effect of her reading and in fact is tetchily irritated by Orestes' and Pylades' amazed interruptions), and then to reveal the identity of Orestes by the immediate and dramatic delivery of the letter on stage to its addressee, the voice of the letter thus becoming for a moment a central participant in the action. Aristotle regarded this as one of the most successful recognition-scenes in the dramas that he knew.[11]

Iph. Give this message to Orestes, child of Agamemnon:
'She who was slain at Aulis sends this letter,
Iphigeneia, living, but yet not living to those there.'
Orest. Where is that woman? Has she come back from the dead?
Iph. She is here, the woman you see. Do not distract me with your words.
'Take me to Argos, my brother, before I die
And remove me from this barbarous land and the goddess's
Sacrifices, for which I have the duties of stranger-slaying.'
Orest. Pylades, what shall I say? Wherever have we found ourselves?
Iph. 'Or I shall haunt your home,
Orestes' – so that hearing the name twice you may again understand.
Pyl. Gods!
Iph. Why do you call on the gods in the midst of my words?
Pyl. Nothing. Go on. For I was elsewhere.
Perhaps in questioning I shall come to things incredible.
Iph. Say that 'Substituting a fawn for me, the goddess
Artemis saved me when my father was sacrificing me,
Since he thought it was on me that he struck his sharp dagger,
And settled me in this land.' This is the letter,
This is what is written in the tablets.
Pyl. You who have bound me by oaths easy to keep
And have beautifully sworn, I shall not long delay.
I will fulfil the oath I swore.
See, I bear to you the tablet and I give it up,
Orestes, the one from this your sister.
Orest. I receive it. Putting aside the folds of the letter,
I will first – not in words – seize the delight.[12] [He embraces his sister]

Some years later Euripides again used a letter in a play, but not as an enabling device in the action but as a means of heightening the perception of tension. *Iphigeneia in Aulis* begins with a restless, uneasy Agamemnon talking with an old man he meets near his tent at Aulis just before dawn. The essential point of the scene is what the old man saw before the conversation began: Agamemnon sitting by a lamp drafting and redrafting a letter, sealing it and unsealing it, even sometimes in his frustration throwing the pine-wood writing tablet to the ground. The old man asks what is wrong, and Agamemnon explains at some length, for his benefit and for ours. He has now, after much soul-searching, repented of his decision to summon his daughter to Aulis, and he asks the old man to deliver to Argos this second letter he has been composing with such difficulty; it is short and to the point and tells Clytemnestra that the wedding to Achilles must wait.

> *Agam.* I send to instruct you in addition to my former
> letter, child of Leda;
> do not dispatch your daughter to
> the enfolding wing of Euboia,
> Aulis of the calm waters.
> For to another occasion
> Shall we designate the marriage of our child.[13]

Agamemnon reads the text to the old man and gives him the original letter-seal as a guarantee of authenticity. A chorus intervenes and the next scene opens with violence: Menelaus has unexpectedly intercepted the old man, seized the letter and read it. The old man calls on Agamemnon, who accepts responsibility and has a bitter dispute with Menelaus, but maintains his firm resolve not to kill his daughter. Menelaus accuses him of betraying his country, saying he will take his allegiance elsewhere. But at this point the letters and past intentions suddenly become irrelevant since a messenger announces that Clytemnestra and Iphigeneia are just about to arrive in Aulis and that all the army knows it. The letters have served their dramatic purpose and it is worth asking what they have added. Most obviously they are tangible objects – props – which can be physically seized, read out and summarized as firm evidence. Euripides, however, goes further and invites us to enquire into the state of mind of the letter-writer; we never hear the words of Agamemnon's first letter to Clytemnestra summoning her and Iphigeneia to Aulis for the supposed marriage to Achilles, but, whatever they were, we have markedly different accounts of Agamemnon's motives for writing it. Agamemnon represents himself as initially prepared to dismiss the army rather than contemplate his daughter's sacrifice and only finally agreeing to all the necessary deception under heavy pressure from Menelaus (94–105). Menelaus, on the other hand, paints the picture of an insecure commander-in-chief, desperate to find a way of continuing the expedition and of holding on to his own position, who was delighted when he was offered a way out of the impasse and therefore wrote the necessary letter to Clytemnestra quite willingly (354–62). Who is right? The playwright gives no answer and the audience is left to make up its own mind. We do hear the words of Agamemnon's second short letter, but the words are less significant than the agonies of its composition; Agamemnon is seen wrestling in frustration all night, not only with the decision to recant at the eleventh hour but also with actual words to use in the letter – the result still not satisfactory since his previous deceit compels him to continue with the lie about the marriage to Achilles (34–42; 117–23). All this could have been composed within the old heroic convention: Agamemnon's mental indecision could have been described, the old man could have been given an oral message, and he could have been captured and interrogated by Menelaus so that Agamemnon's secret could be revealed. However, the letter-device sharpens the focus on every occasion: Agamemnon's frustration is the more vivid when in the depths of the night he takes it out on his writing-materials, the old man's vulnerability is emphasized by the fact that the actual letter entrusted to him is violently snatched by Menelaus, and Agamemnon's first letter is the perfect peg on which Menelaus can hang his accusations of betrayal and his denunciations of Agamemnon's character-faults.

Moving on from the tragedians, it might be thought that stage comedy was a natural location for situations involving letters and their secrets, but strangely Aristophanes – to judge from the surviving plays – made no use of the opportunities letters offer to a comic writer. In Aristophanes all depends on direct, instant, earthy communication and the letter seems to have no place, belonging rather to the more sophisticated urban culture which later formed the stuff of New Comedy. One of Aristophanes' older contemporaries, Cratinus, appears to have introduced the reading of a letter into one of his comedies,[14] but the letter as a dramatic device was apparently not a part of the traditions of Old Comedy. In Middle and New Comedy – the genesis of the 'comedy of manners' – things are very different. Letters have clearly become a normal part of the kind of bourgeois social life portrayed on the stage, and although so little survives, there are enough clues to make the situation clear. There are, for instance, three comedies with the title *The Letter* (by Alexis, Euthycles and Machon) and one entitled *The Letters* (by Timocles).[15] We unfortunately do not have the texts, but the Latin descendants of New Comedy, Plautus and Terence, mention and use letters often in their plays.[16]

On the fringes of letter-writing is to be found the idea of sending a gift or making an offering with a consciously artistic passage of writing attached, often in the form of a short poem. Such epigrams are sometimes described as 'letter-poems' but they very rarely use the conventional letter-form and are better described as literary notelets. Their most likely origins lie, not in letters, but in the votive dedications which were put up so frequently in all ancient Greek religious and cult centres. The form of such dedications is instantly recognizable: someone makes a gift to the god and identifies himself or herself as the giver, and perhaps adds the purpose of the dedication – sometimes the gift itself is made to seem to speak.[17] Thus in the sixth century BC an ornamental axe-head was offered to Hera and carried the inscription: 'I am sacred to Hera in the Plain. Cyniscos the butcher dedicated me.'[18] It was quite common for dedications to be not only in poetic form but also to show a conscious artistry in their physical lay-out by the use of symmetry or spacing.[19] So Hippylla at the beginning of the fifth century BC made an offering to Artemis of a bronze mirror in the sanctuary of Brauron in Attica, and her dedication, cut very beautifully into the surrounding inner edge of the mirror, is itself a work of art: 'Hippylla, daughter of Onetor, dedicated this to Artemis in Brauron.'

The Hellenistic poets and their successors took up this custom of dedicatory ornament in verse and turned it into a literary conceit, embellishing it with pretty turns of phrase and sentimental feelings, the skill and taste of the poet thus becoming the focus of attention rather than the supposed object with which and for which the message was sent. An early and elaborate example is the fanciful poem Theocritus ostensibly sent with the gift of an ivory distaff to the wife of his friend, Nicias.[20] The *Greek Anthology*, that Byzantine collection of collections, contains large numbers of less elaborate gift-poems spanning a long period. One favourite theme was the worker or craftsman attaching a little verse note to the tools of his trade as he dedicated them to the god on his retirement. This often rather charming fiction takes us into very much the same imaginary world of sophisticated, elegantly poetic working men which is to be found in the verse letters of Alciphron to be described later in this chapter:

> To you the gardener, Priapus, did Potamon who got prosperity from his trade make this dedication: his hoe, digger of his thirsty garden, his curved sickle, cutter of the stems, his ragged cloak for his back which kept the rain off, his tough, raw-hide boots, his dibber for planting out the cabbage-seedlings which went straight into the well-raked soil, and his spade that never ceased refreshing the thirsty plot from the water-channels in the dryness of summer.[21]

Imaginary messages – almost but not quite letters – could also be sent by bizarre messengers. Meleager's girl-friend may not have been too delighted by the arrival of this one, however much affection is pretended:

> Fly for me, mosquito, swift messenger, and, having touched the tip of Zenophila's ear, whisper this to her: 'He cannot sleep and waits for you. But you are sleeping, lazy and forgetful of those who love you.' Go on, fly off – yes, lover of the Muses, fly off. But speak softly

> lest you rouse the man beside her and provoke painful blows of envy against me. If you bring the girl, I will garland you, mosquito, with the lionskin and give you a club to carry in your hand.[22]

Very occasionally the form of the conventional letter is actually recalled in the wording of an epigram. In the following poem the beginning and the wishes for good health are deliberately introduced, not as a natural part of the structure but as a reference the reader is meant to pick up:

> Rufinus to my sweetest Elpis, many greetings – if greetings [happiness] there can be when I am not there. By your eyes, I can no longer bear the separation of being apart from you and on a lonely bed. Constantly bathed in tears I go either to Coressos or the temple of great Artemis. But tomorrow my home town will have me back. I shall fly to your eyes with a thousand prayers that you are in good health.[23]

The idea of collections of letters put together for predominantly literary purposes (as distinct from those made for the promotion of philosophy or religion) is slow to develop. One of the first examples may be the short collection of the letters of Lysias, the speech-writer and orator who was born in the middle of the fifth century BC. A selection of seven of his letters was put together and published, one being a business letter, the rest love letters, of which five were addressed to young men. Someone who had so many contacts through his legal and political activities must have written a good many letters, and it is a reasonable guess that the selection was made to show off fine examples of his much-admired style and of his colourful private life.[24] A phenomenon which reached its peak in the Greek world of the first to third centuries AD – the period known as the Second Sophistic – was the appearance of collections of imaginary letters, some written in the names of famous historical personalities and some attached to characters from a make-believe world. Many of the collections have been shown to be the work of more than one author and to have grown by accretion, and some of them (the letters of Plato and Demosthenes, for instance) contain letters that are genuine.[25] Sorting out the collections is complicated, and scholarship in this area was long in the shadow of Richard Bentley who in the work which first made his scholarly name in 1697 triumphantly demonstrated that many letters bearing famous names were in fact written by others.[26] With characteristic venom he dismissed the authors as 'little pedants, that have stalked about so long in the apparel of heroes', and in terms of literary and intellectual quality there is some justice, if not mercy, in his verdict. Nevertheless, the letters were in their day popular, and perhaps the attraction of some of them was akin to the appeal of the historical novel or drama today. They seemed to dramatize and amplify the past, to propose the actual words that might have been in the mouths of famous people and or ordinary folk from other days, and the authors – like modern script-writers or novelists – asked readers to accept for the moment the historical imagination as credible personal history, a request easier to make at a time when the line between fact and fiction was less clearly drawn than it is today.

The intentions and reactions of the ancient authors and readers of imaginary letters are inaccessible, but certain background features of their world help to explain the popularity of the genre, One is the educational exercise of trying to enter into another's character and to write and speak accordingly – *prosopopoieia*. This was a feature of Greek oratory almost from its inception and was a necessary skill for early speech-writers like Lysias and Antiphon, who wrote scripts for ordinary citizens to deliver in law-courts. Probably for purposes of training as well as virtuoso display, the 'characters' sometimes assumed by later speech-writers and teachers in their published works were mythological – Gorgias' defences of Palamedes and Helen, for instance. This introduced a potential element of literary fancy and opened a great range of possibilities for educational practice and display as well as provoking an interest in the typology of character. By the second and third centuries AD – the hey-day of the imaginary letter – learning to write and deliver speeches in the character and style of another person had become a regular ingredient in rhetorical education. There was therefore a readership already sensitized to many of the skills and charms of the imaginary letter-writer. Another feature of the background in the time of the Second Sophistic was a keen and nostalgic interest in the great days of Greece from the Persian Wars to Alexander the Great. Writers, uncomfortably aware of what was taken to be a degeneration in the Greek language into the commonness of everyday speech, began to cultivate a conscious imitation of classical Greek and an 'atticizing' style became fashionable among authors. More importantly from the point of view of imaginary letters, the subjects chosen for imaginary composition frequently harked back to this Golden Age. It has, for instance, been estimated that, of the surviving 350 or so historical themes used by writers of speeches for performance in the approximate period of the Second Sophistic, 283 are taken from the fifth and fourth centuries BC.[27] This nostalgia helps to explain why many of the imaginary letters were written in the names of famous (or notorious) historical figures with whom the reader would already be familiar.

Although a large proportion of the imaginary prose letters belong to the period of the Second Sophistic, there were significant precursors. Letters are an essential part of the so-called *Alexander Romance* – a Greek novel or novella – and although in its present form it may have been compiled as late as the third century AD, it has been argued on good grounds that it is probably based on a collection of imaginary letters written around AD 100 which were meant to amplify the legend building up around Alexander the Great by reconstructing his dealings with notable and colourful characters like

Darius and Poros, an Indian king, and by retailing accounts of the wondrous things and people he encountered.[28] The letter which Darius sends on hearing of Alexander's approach is clearly exuberant fiction, much in the spirit of the Dauphin's embassy in Shakespeare's *Henry V*:

> King of Kings, kinsman of the gods, I who rise to heaven with the Sun, a god myself, I Darius to my servant Alexander give these orders:
>
> I instruct you to return to your parents, to be my slave, and to sleep in the lap of your mother, Olympias: that is how old you are – you need to be corrected and nursed. So I have sent you a strap, a ball, and a money box of gold, and you can take whatever you like first. I sent the ball so that you can play with children your own age and not mislead so many young men at such an arrogant age into going around with you, like a brigand chief, and disturbing the peace of the cities: not even if this whole world is brought together by a single man will it be able to overthrow the kingdom of the Persians. I have such huge numbers of troops that, like grains of sand, no one could ever count them; and I have enough gold and silver to fill the whole earth. I have also sent you a money box full of gold so that should you run out of food to give your fellow brigands, you may give them each the wherewithal to go back to their own homeland.
>
> But if you do not obey my instructions, I shall send a force after you, and the result will be that you will be arrested by my soldiers – and you will not be educated as the son of Philip but crucified as a rebel.[29]

Alexander quells the alarm felt by his soldiers (who are assumed to have heard a reading of the letter) by assuring them that Darius is simply a small dog compensating for its size by barking loudly. Alexander then vents his fury by ordering the crucifixion of the messengers who, by some well-placed flattery and a reminder of diplomatic convention, win a pardon. In their gratitude they offer some treacherous hints on how to trap Darius, but Alexander waves them aside with a heroic gesture which wins a standing ovation from the army; this is how heroes ought to be. After his resounding successes against Persia Alexander does not forget to write home to let his mother, Olympias, and his old teacher, Aristotle, know how things have been going:

> King Alexander to my much-beloved mother and to Aristotle, my most-esteemed teacher, greetings.
>
> I thought it necessary to write to you of the battle I had with Darius. Hearing he was at the Gulf of Issos with a mass of soldiers

> and other kings, I took a large number of goats and fastened torches to their horns, then set out and marched by night. They saw the torches in the distance and thought it was an innumerable army, as a result of which their thoughts turned to panic and they were defeated. This was how I gained the victory against them. At that spot I founded a city which I called Aigai; and I founded another city on the Gulf of Issos, calling it Alexandria. Darius was abandoned, captured, and wounded by his own satraps, and I was extremely distressed about him: having defeated him, I did not want to murder him but to have him under my command. I came upon him still alive and took off the cloak I had on and covered him. Then, recognizing the uncertainty of Fortune as displayed in Darius's case, I lamented him. I gave him a royal funeral and ordered the ears and noses of those guarding his tomb to be cut off, following the native custom. And I ordered the killers of Darius to be crucified at Darius's grave. Leaving there, I won control of the kingdom of Ariobarzan and Manazakes; I subjugated Media and Armenia, Iberia and the whole territory of Persia that Darius ruled over.[30]

There are letters from exotic places too. Poros, an Indian king in the Punjab, who has already had from Darius urgent (documented) requests for help, hears that Alexander has designs on his kingdom and writes an arrogant *ad terrorem* note:

> King Poros of India, to Alexander, who plunders cities.
>
> I instruct you to withdraw. What can you, a mere man, achieve against a god? Is it because you have destroyed the good fortune of others by meeting weaker men in battle that you think yourself more mighty than me? But I am invincible: not only am I the king of men, but even of gods – when Dionysus (who they say is a god) came here, the Indians used their own power to drive him away. So not only do I advise you, but also I instruct you, to set off for Greece with all speed. I am not going to be frightened by your battle with Darius or by all the good fortune you had in the face of the weakness of the other nations. But you think you are more mighty. So set off for Greece. Because if we had needed Greece, we Indians would have subjected it long before Xerxes; but as it is, we have paid no attention to it, because it is a useless nation, and there is nothing among them worth the regard of a king – everyone desires what is better.[31]

Alexander sends a suitably robust reply, 'But I am engaging in war with a loudmouthed man and an absolute barbarian.' When it comes to it, he has technological tricks like the red-hot wall of human look-alikes which roasts the attacking elephants and helps to defeat Poros.

And at the end of Alexander's life there is the deathbed letter to his mother, dictated to his secretary:

> King Alexander to my dearest mother, greetings.
>
> When you receive this, my last letter, prepare an expensive meal to thank Providence above for having given you such a son. But if you wish to do me honour, go on your own and collect together all men, great and humble, rich and poor, for the meal, saying to them: 'See the meal is prepared! Come and feast! But no one who now or in the past has experienced suffering should come, as I have prepared a meal not of suffering but of joy.'
>
> Farewell, Mother.[32]

Most of this is pure fantasy, and some of it is an entertaining read for that reason. Some of the 'historical' letter-collections stick more closely to known events and explore in some detail what prominent figures might have been expected to say, think or write in well-known historical contexts. A good example is the letters of Themistocles – twenty-one letters which are supposed to date from the period of his ostracism in the late 470s BC and which also mark the transition from Athenian statesman and hero of the Persian Wars to the appointment as Persian governor of Magnesia-on-the-Maeander.[33] After leaving Athens he had lived first at Argos, and then, suspected by the Spartans of negotiations with Persia, went west to Corcyra and Epirus and finally to Persia via Macedonia. There is no way of dating the composition of the Themistocles letters accurately – the end of the first century AD seems a reasonable guess – and no way of deciding whether or not there was a single author. They do seem to fall into two groups, each taking us from west to east; letters 1–12 go from Argos to Susa and 13–21 from Argos to Magnesia-on-the-Maeander.[34] Whatever sources were used, the author (or authors) plainly had quite a detailed knowledge of the events and personalities involved and a genuine interest in the likely thoughts and feelings of a remarkable man. The author was obviously also a good Greek; at the end of the long *Letter 20* in which Themistocles describes his installation as Persian governor at Magnesia, Themistocles assures his friend, Polygnotos, that in spite of everything he will never take up arms against his mother city and her patron goddess, Athena. The letters explore the plight of a great man exiled: his bitterness, concern for his family, his personal feuds, anxiety about the security of his money, self-justification for what many would see as treachery plus a certain self-confidence and a desire to show how much his abilities are still in demand. The first letter in the collection is written to Aeschylus to explain how his choice of Argos as a domicile was simply a response to requests that could not be refused:

> Themistocles to Aeschylus.
>
> When I left, I had resolved to call at Delphi with a view to living there for as long as the Athenians decided. On the road some of my friends from Argos met up with me, Nicias and Meleagros and the man who had been in Athens not long before, Eucrates. They stood round enquiring, and when they learnt of the ostracism, they were straightway furious and made many accusations against the Athenians. But when they learnt that I was intending to call at Delphi, they stopped accusing the Athenians and attacked me, continually saying that they were being insulted if, friends as they were, they were not thought the right people to take my calamity upon themselves. They instanced Neocles, my father, and his very long stay in Argos and they said, since I loved Argos and my friends there, I was letting myself down; they came pretty near to praising the Athenians for justly punishing me. Finally they begged me not to condemn them for simply being responsible for a meeting between us nor to abuse the happy chance of their encounter with me – they again brought up Neocles and how fitting it would be for me to live in the same house as my father in the same city. Aeschylus, they took me with them and led me off to Argos. And now in Argos I have stopped running away and am suffering greatly because I do not wish to rule over the Argives; they pressure me on the ground that they are being wronged if I do not rule them. Seeming to be a great man gives me no pleasure, not only because it did me harm because it is enough to have enjoyed that sort of thing when it was needed.[35]

When later on Themistocles has arrived in Persia, he is presented as being unable to resist writing (with a few vicious digs) to his old rival at Athens, Aristeides, and assuring him that Persia is actually treating him rather well:

> Themistocles to Aristeides.
>
> I have gone over to the Persians, Aristeides, I have gone over to them and nothing terrible has happened to me at their hands. I know that in your own mind you will wonder at this, but to everyone else you will make out that the news is no surprise to you and at the same time you will use it as proof to the people that the slanderous accusation against me is well-founded, since I have trusted the Persians and they have been kind to me. Well, whenever you keep prattling on about this, the Salamis trophy will fall down on you – it is stone, you know, and seriously big. You would not, I believe, stir up the people any more or be envied by other doers of good deeds if some god, who is just, not by the standards of your

> bragging but truly so, were to hurl that rock on to your cursed and unlovely head.
>
> The Great King is not doing a favour in return by saving me (his answer would have given you ample gratification if you had found out what he had suffered because of me), but he knew that in other respects I was his enemy, yet he admired my worth and pitied my bad luck. So, you are very likely sending a delegation to him about me saying that you wronged me so that he might help me as one being wronged, and that you yourselves made me an object of pity by exiling me and that he properly took pity on an exile. As things now stand I am not an exile who needs pity. So, Aristeides, son of Lysimachos, get stuffed. And let everyone get stuffed who is not happy that things have turned out better for me than he thought.[36]

Moving on from history and the historical imagination to a more philosophical view of the world, probably the earliest surviving example of a truly imaginary letter-collection from an almost mythical figure is the correspondence written in the name of Anacharsis who was, according to Herodotus, the nephew of a Scythian king, Idanthyrsos, and lived in the sixth century BC. Anacharsis was attracted to travel abroad and on his way back from one of his journeys he is said to have called at Cyzicus and was so taken with the celebration of a Greek religious festival there in honour of Hera that he resolved to celebrate a similar ceremony in Scythia if he made a safe return. This was a step too far towards Hellenism for the nationalist Scythians and Anacharsis was executed by arrow-shot – according to Herodotus, because he had visited Greece and adopted foreign ways.[37]

Whatever the truth of the history, Anacharsis became the type of the sympathetic foreign visitor to Greece who died for his philhellenism, and perhaps in the third century BC a series of ten letters was written in his name.[38] The name of the writer is unknown but he certainly used Anacharsis as a peg on which to hang some of his own ideas and there is more than a whiff of Cynic thinking.[39] The first letter is a little essay in multi-culturalism and the importance of foreign languages; it is addressed to the people of Athens:

> Anacharsis to the Athenians.
>
> You laugh at my speech because I do not pronounce Greek letters clearly. So, Anacharsis sounds foreign to the Athenians and Athenians sound foreign to the Scythians. It is not in their speech that people differ from each other in true worth but in their thinking – in that Greek differs from Greek. The Spartans do not speak Attic Greek well but because of their deeds they are conspicuous and renowned. The Scythians do not criticize words which express what is necessary nor do they praise words which do not reach that

> goal. You yourselves make many arrangements without worrying if someone's speech is not fluent. You import Egyptian doctors, you use Phoenician sea-captains, and you buy goods in the marketplace without paying over the odds because the sellers speak Greek. You are not afraid of getting things from non-Greeks if they sell what suits you. Persian monarchs and their friends, when they have some great project, necessarily sound foreign when they want to address delegates from Greece in Greek – and you criticize neither what they think nor what they do. Speech is not poor if good thoughts and fine deeds follow the words. You will be left far behind if you are annoyed by foreign languages and then do not understand what is said. For you will make many people afraid of importing things which are to your advantage. Why do you value foreign fabrics and have no respect for foreign language? You seek out *aulos*-players and singers if their music is tuneful and you criticize the work of poets if their verses are not composed in Greek letters. When people speak, look at what is actually being said. The final outcome of this is to your advantage. If you are sympathetic to foreigners, you will not allow your women and children to pay you no attention if your speech is not perfect. For it is better to be saved by obeying people who do not speak perfectly than to suffer great harm by listening to beautiful speakers of Attic. Men of Athens, this is the behaviour of uneducated people who do not know what is good for them. No sensible person would think in this way.[40]

Granted common Greek views of the barbarian, this is quite a provocative piece and it may be a little exercise in making people think or even 'defacing the common coin', to use Cynic terminology. Whatever modern sympathies might be, the sentiments were probably somewhat at odds with the feelings of many contemporary Greeks, even though the pill was sugared by putting the ideas into the mouth of a foreigner. A shorter cautionary letter is addressed to the Athenian tyrant Hipparchos, and recommends an aspect of that austerity for which Diogenes, the founder of Cynicism, was famous:

> Anacharsis to Hipparchos, the tyrant.
>
> Much unmixed wine does not go with a good disposition of what is proper, for it confuses the mind which is the seat of human reason. It is not easy for someone eager for great deeds to carry out his intentions well unless he adopts a sober and careful life-style. So, abandon dice and drunkenness and turn to the substance of ruling, following the example of your father's good deeds, helping both friends and suppliants. If you do not, in addition to being debauched, you will risk your own life. Then your friends will recall that man from Scythia, Anacharsis.[41]

Anacharsis cheerfully acts as life-style adviser to other nations too. The fifth letter is addressed to a Carthaginian, Hanno, and its simple recipe led Cicero to translate it and use it in his *Tusculan Disputations.*[42]

> Anacharsis to Hanno.
>
> For me, my clothing is a Scythian cloak, my shoes are the skin of my feet, my bed is the whole earth, my best meal is milk, cheese and meat, and my whole diet is hunger. So, since I have time for the things for which most people sacrifice their time, join me if you need anything. As for the gifts in which you luxuriate, I will give others in return. You, give them to the Carthaginians or dedicate your gratitude to the gods.[43]

There is no continuous story in the Anacharsis letters, and in many ways they are quite similar to the much later collection of so-called Cynic letters of the second century AD, where simple tenets of Cynic wisdom are given letter-form as the barest of disguises.

One collection which does tell a story, and does so quite elaborately, is the sequence of letters which dramatizes a meeting between the legendary doctor Hippocrates of Cos and the 'laughing philosopher', Democritus.[44] Here there is a very careful attempt at realism, for the letters establish an elaborate *mise-en-scène* involving visiting delegates, boat-hiring, house-sitting and medical requisitions, together with documentation in the shape of scientific papers, an honorific decree of the Athenians, and the scripts of two speeches. The collection is impossible to date with any accuracy but a papyrus of the early first century AD shows that *Letter 11* was being read at that date and the letters may have been composed at any time in the previous two hundred years. The letters fall into two groups: the first (Letters 1–9) tell of the attempts of the Persian king, Artaxerxes, to get Hippocrates to come and diagnose the nature of an epidemic affecting the Persian army. Hippocrates on high-minded grounds refuses and Artaxerxes threatens the Coan people with shock and awe if they do not persuade him – all to no avail. The second series of letters begins with the Council and people of Abdera writing to Hippocrates with a serious problem which is affecting their most famous son, the philosopher Democritus; in their view he has had a breakdown:

> The Council and people of Abdera to Hippocrates, greetings.
>
> The city is now in the greatest danger, Hippocrates. That man of ours who was expected to be our city's eternal glory, both now and in the future (let there be no envy of this now, all you gods), this man has fallen ill under the weight of his great learning so that there is no idle fear that, if Democritus loses his reason, the city of the Abderites may actually be left deserted. For he, not being concerned

> previously about anything including himself, is continuously awake both day and night, laughing at everything, be it great or small, and thinks the whole of life is worthless. One person gets married, another is in business, another in politics, someone takes office, goes on a delegation, votes, falls ill, is wounded, dies – he laughs at everything, whether he sees people dejected and scowling or happy. The man enquires about people in Hades and writes it down, and he says the air is full of phantoms and he secretly listens to the voices of birds. He gets up in the night and seems to be quietly singing songs on his own. Sometimes he says he pays a visit to the Infinite and that there are innumerable Democrituses like himself. He lives with a complexion as ruined as his mind.[45]

The Abderites follow this with a heartfelt plea to Hippocrates to come to cure Democritus of his 'laughing sickness', and Hippocrates graciously agrees in a reply letter (no. 11) which has little touches of 'authenticity' to captivate the reader, e.g. the emissary who brings the petition from Abdera is given a name, Amelesagoras, and he happens to arrive on Cos at a particularly busy time since a local festival is in progress. All the same, Hippocrates recognizes the urgency of the case and rather sententiously proclaims it as a call from Nature herself – not forgetting to remind the Abderites that he could get much higher fees in Persia. The next five letters construct a quite elaborate context and personality for Hippocrates before he finally meets his 'patient' on Cos. *Letter 12* is an answer to a letter in which a friend, Philopoimen, has offered to put Hippocrates up while he is in Abdera, an offer which Hippocrates gratefully accepts, adding for his friend a little lecture on the pathology of obsessive scholars. *Letter 13* is a request to another friend, Dionysios, to house-sit while Hippocrates is away and to look out for his wife, nipping in the bud any signs of a roving eye. *Letter 14* hires a ship called *The Sun* for the voyage to Abdera and briefs the ship-owner, Damagetos, on the troubles with Democritus. *Letter 15* is to the same friend who is giving Hippocrates lodgings and describes a vivid dream Hippocrates has just experienced. He has had a vision of Asclepius, snakes and all, who introduced him to two ladies, Truth and Opinion.[46] Hippocrates becomes his own dream-interpreter and concludes that Democritus does not after all need a physician. Just in case, however, he also writes a discursive letter to a herbal specialist called Cratenas asking him to collect and send a collection of choice herbs.[47] At long last the stage is set for the crucial encounter between Hippocrates and Democritus, and the very long *Letter 17*, which is – rather surprisingly – written to the ship-owner from whom Hippocrates hired *The Sun*, describes what happened when he reached Abdera. The arrival is melodramatic: men, women and children from the city are waiting for him, all in a state of hysterical depression. He insists on going straight to see Democritus and the crowd of

Abderites accompanies him with cries of 'Save him! Help him! Cure him!' They find Democritus not in a state of madness, but presenting the very picture of the unkempt, dedicated scholar in a setting which is meant discreetly to recall for the educated reader the pleasant spot which Socrates chose for his conversation with Phaedrus in Plato's dialogue of that name.[48]

> Democritus himself was sitting beneath a spreading, low plane tree with a thick vest on, alone, preoccupied, on a stone seat, quite pale and drawn, with stubble on his cheeks. And beside him a little stream murmured gently down the sloping hill, and on that hill there was a sanctuary which at a guess was a seat of the nymphs, covered over with wild vines. He had a book neatly on his knees and others had been put down on both sides. And there was a heap of lots of animals, all dissected. Sometimes he bent over and concentrated on writing, sometimes he paused for a moment quite quietly, thinking hard to himself, and, after a short spell of this, he got up and walked around, examined the entrails of the animals, put them down and returned to his seat.[49]

Hippocrates and Democritus greet each other with the courtesies proper to a meeting of two great men. Hippocrates says who is putting him up (tactfully testing Democritus' sanity by an apparently idle query) and, as scholars do, asks Democritus what he is writing at the moment. Democritus replies that it is a book *On Madness* and enlarges on the contents. At this point Hippocrates tells him how lucky he is to have the time, since he himself is just overcommitted. This produces a worryingly prolonged fit of laughter from Democritus and transports of despair from the Abderan citizens watching nearby. Hippocrates is interested and presses Democritus on the reasons for what seems his often inappropriate laughter, and after a little prompting Democritus launches into the point of the whole encounter – and of the letters – an extended homily on the follies of mankind and the paradoxes of human behaviour:

> He, giving me a keen glance, said 'You think there are two reasons for my laughter – what is good and what is bad. But I laugh at one thing – mankind – full of ignorance, but with regard to right action empty, infantile in all its endeavours, and suffering pointless toils for no benefit, making its way to the ends of the earth and to the measureless depths with unbounded desires, melting gold and silver and never losing its greed for them, constantly clamouring for more so that it can be less. And it is not ashamed to be called fortunate because it digs pits in the earth using the hands of prisoners, some of whom are killed when unstable earth falls in; some,

> in long-term compulsion, living with their punishment as though it were their homeland, search for silver and gold, seeking out traces of dust and gold-dust, collecting different sands from different places and cutting the veins of the earth for prosperity, constantly making spoil-heaps from Mother Earth. This one and the same earth they walk upon in wonder. How one laughs! They fall in love with the earth that demands toil and lies hidden: they ruin the one that is before their eyes. They buy dogs and horses, they fence off great tracts of land and make it officially their own and, wanting to be masters of much, they cannot even master themselves. They rush to marry the women they shortly divorce. They love, then they hate. Their desire produces children and then they throw them out when they grow up. What is this hollow, senseless energy, no different from madness? They make war on their fellows and, instead of choosing peacefulness, set traps for each other and slaughter kings. They look for silver by digging the land and when they have found silver, they want to purchase land, and when they have bought the land, they put its produce on the market, and when they have sold the produce, they get the silver back again. All this barter! All this evil! When they have no possessions, they desire them; when they have them, they hide them and put them out of sight. I laugh at their failures, I keep laughing at their misfortunes, for they have passed the bounds of truth in their competitive hatred for each other.[50]

Hippocrates tactfully agrees that this is a fitting account of human misery but points out that some of what Democritus describes is a necessary consequence of the world as it is. Democritus will have none of it:

> This is the reason for my laughter: men without minds, paying penalties for their wickedness, greed, insatiability, hostility, opportunism, plotting and malice. It is painful to describe the deviousness of their sins, for these sins are limitless. Vying with each other in trickery, with twisted minds, their version of virtue is depravity … In no circumstance do they have a stable mind. Rulers and kings bless the life of the common man, the common man longs for royal power, the politician envies the workman for his security, the workman envies the politician for his all-embracing confidence. For they do not contemplate the straight path of peacefulness, pure and smooth where no-one trips and on which none of them has dared to set foot. They are carried over a treacherous, twisted path, rough going, borne downwards and stumbling; most of them fall by the wayside, gasping as if they were being pursued, fighting, falling behind, pushing ahead.[51]

The torrent flows unabated and in the end Hippocrates is quite won over, convinced that Democritus, so far from being mad, is preaching a doctrine of wisdom and has seen to the heart of human reality.

> Saying this he smiled and to me, Damagetos, he seemed like a god; I forgot the previous impression he had made and I said, 'Renowned Democritus, I shall take back with me to Cos great gifts from all your generosity as a host. You have filled me with great amazement at your wisdom. I go back to proclaim you as someone who has investigated and understood the truth about human nature, and I leave you now – time and the needs of the body require it – having received healing for my mind. Tomorrow and the day after we shall meet at the same place.' I said this, stood up, and he was ready to go with me. Someone appeared from nowhere and he gave him his books. I accordingly hurried over to the true Abderans who were waiting for me at their vantage point. 'Gentlemen,' I said, 'many thanks for the delegation you sent to me. For I have seen Democritus, the wisest of men and the only one capable of bringing men to their senses.' That is the very good news I have to tell you, Damagetos, about Democritus.
>
> Farewell.[52]

One purpose of this fictitious letter-collection is simply to intrigue and entertain the reader – and it does. The scene-setting with its domestic details, the hysterical population of Abdera, the dignified personality of the great physician, and the careful faking of records all contribute to the effect, but there is no doubt that the end purpose of the letters is to give a lesson in moral philosophy; Democritus' apparently eccentric perceptions receive the blessing of a patently sane, wise, famous and reliable man. From the literary point of view the collection is important because it demonstrates that a sequence of letters (admittedly with supporting evidence) could bear the weight of coherent story-telling. It is a significant part of the background to the introduction of a new genre in European literature – the novel in letters, the so-called *Briefroman.* Before that, however, it is worth looking at how some of the earliest Greek novelists used letters as a part of romantic story-telling.

The first surviving example of what may be called a Greek novel is *The Story of Callirhoe* by Chariton, probably written at some time between 25 BC and AD 50. It is a work of light romantic fiction and as such not regarded as serious literature by ancient critics; it was, however, a popular work and the Roman satirist Persius recommended it as a good early afternoon read.[53] The plot, which is set in a semi-historical context, is complicated and involves the beautiful Callirhoe being finally re-united with her husband and the love of her life, Chaireas, after a series of exotic adventures. Before this happens Callirhoe is taken for dead (having been kicked by her husband in a fit of affectionate jealousy), miraculously saved by a tomb-robbing pirate, and eventually married to a rich and prominent citizen of Miletus, Dionysios, in spite of being pregnant. Chaireas too has his moments, being captured, sold into slavery to the Persian governor of Caria, having a spectacular military success at the head of a company of Greek mercenaries, and finally being re-united with Callirhoe. Letters play an important part at some crucial turning points in the action and they are essential to the structure of the novel. One example is the letter which Chaireas writes to Callirhoe to tell her that, in spite of perilous adventures, he is after all alive and safe, having been rescued from the clutches of pirates by Mithridates; it also expresses his understandable disappointment at learning that Callirhoe has married again after believing him dead, and he pours out a husband's passion for a dearly loved wife:

> To Callirhoe from Chaireas.
>
> I am alive, and I am alive because of Mithridates, my benefactor and yours too, I hope. For I was sold in Caria by barbarians who burnt that lovely trireme, your father's flagship; on board the city had dispatched a mission for you. As for the other citizens, I do not know what happened, but the mercy of my master saved me and my friend, Polycharmos, when we were on the very point of being killed. But although Mithridates has been my benefactor in everything, in this he has grieved me by telling me of your marriage. For death I anticipated, being human, but I never expected your marriage. I beg you, change your mind. I pour out my tears and kisses over my words. I am your Chaireas, the man whom you saw when as a maiden you made your way to Aphrodite's temple – the man for whom you lay awake. Remember our marriage bedroom and that magical night when you had your first experience of a man and I of a woman. But I was jealous, you said; that is what lovers are. I have paid the penalty: I was sold, enslaved, bound. Do not hold a hasty kick against me, for I have gone on the cross because of you, accusing you of nothing. If you should still remember me, my suffering is nothing; but if you think otherwise, you will hand me my death-warrant.[54]

This letter never reaches Callirhoe (who actually only hears its contents for the first time in a dramatic court-room scene at the end), but falls into the hands of some dissolute slaves. They and the letter are apprehended by the chief magistrate of Priene and sent with a covering note to Dionysios, Callirhoe's present husband. At this point the Persian satrap of Lydia and Ionia, Pharnaces, makes an appearance. He happens to be a personal friend of the wealthy Dionysios and is persuaded to write to the Great King with a complaint against Mithridates who, as Dionysios believes, has been making inappropriate advances to Callirhoe (unknown to Callirhoe, Mithridates is the saviour of her Chaireas!). Pharnaces sends his complaint to the Great King and, just to assure the reader the letter must be authentic, uses the typical lord/slave vocabulary of Persian royal communication so abhorrent to Greeks: 'Dionysios, the Milesian, is your slave and there has been loyalty and goodwill towards your house from the time of his ancestors … '[55] At the end of the story Callirhoe is of course re-united with Chaireas, but Dionysios, her second husband, is left distinctly out in the cold and Callirhoe has to write him a rather awkward letter, promising to be with him henceforth in spirit if not in person, and rather surprisingly leaving her son in his well-endowed care and even arranging her son's future marriage.

> Callirhoe to her benefactor Dionysios, greetings.
>
> You are the one who released me from the pirates and slavery. I beg you, don't be angry. For I am with you in spirit through the son we share; I hand him over to you so that you can bring him up and educate him in a way worthy of us. Don't let him experience a stepmother. You not only have a son but a daughter too; two children are enough for you. When he becomes a man, unite them in marriage and send him to Syracuse so that he can see his grandfather too. I send best wishes to you, Plangon. I have written this with my own hand. Farewell, good Dionysios, and remember your Callirhoe.[56]

Later Greek novels like the popular *Leucippe and Cleitophon* by Achilles Tatius, probably dating from the last quarter of the second century AD, also made use of letters, and in one place in that work the reader is even made to hear the emotional thoughts of Cleitophon as he reads a vital letter from Leucippe.[57] Lucian, whose *True Stories* certainly lie in the realm of light fiction, if not of the novel, plays with the idea of letters from the famous purely for the purposes of amusement.[58] Here Odysseus, who happened to be sitting next to Lucian at dinner on the Island of the Blest, asked him to take the following letter to Calypso in her island home, Ogygia:

> Odysseus to Calypso, greetings.
>
> Know that, immediately after I built my raft and sailed away from you, I was shipwrecked and was brought by Leucothea safely but with some difficulty to the country of the Phaeacians. I was sent back to my homeland by them and I found my wife had many suitors who were living a life of luxury at my expense. I killed them all and was afterwards murdered by Telegonos, the son I had by Circe. Now I am on the Island of the Blest, much regretting having abandoned life with you and the immortality which you offered. So, if I get an opportunity, I shall run away and come back to you.[59]

The letter is duly delivered and, over the knitting, Calypso asks some affectionately curious questions about her old flame. We are on the wilder shores of the imagination and a cultivated chuckle is the desired response.

The first example of what can truly be called a new literary form – a story told entirely through the medium of letters with no supporting detail – is the work which goes under the title of its main character, *Chion of Heraclea*. The author's name is not known and the work can only be dated roughly to the late Hellenistic period or the early first century AD.[60] It is the story of a young man, Chion, who decides to go to Athens for a serious course of philosophical study with Plato (encouraged in this by Xenophon, whom he meets in Byzantium). After five years he decides to return to his home city, Heraclea, where he has heard that the tyrant Clearchos is acting violently and outrageously. His resolution to do something about the situation is strengthened when the tyrant sends an agent to murder him – he thwarts the assassin and brings him to justice. Chion thereupon decides that there is no other option for a true philosopher than to kill the hated tyrant – an action which will certainly entail his own death. His last letter is addressed to his old teacher, Plato, and is written just before he sets off on his tyrant-slaying suicide mission. The work is quite closely based on real history: there was an exceedingly cruel tyrant of Heraclea called Clearchos in the mid-fourth century BC and he was killed as a result of a conspiracy led by a young man called Chion.[61] What the novel of seventeen letters does is to recreate a character for Chion and to outline or suggest the progress of a young man from innocent student of philosophy to committed political assassin in the cause of freedom. All the letters in the collection save three are addressed to Chion's father, Matris, and although the first starts with the conventional 'Chion to Matris, greetings', the others to his father are simply headed 'To the same'. We first meet Chion as a considerate son writing from Byzantium to console worried parents who are missing him; he then meets Xenophon, who encourages the young man to study philosophy in Athens, and this news too goes home in a letter. In *Letter 5* we see Chion as the eager young university student just arrived in Athens and writing a typically enthusiastic letter to his father about his new teacher, Plato, and showing off some of the lessons he has learnt. Intellectual pleasures there may be, but students are also grateful for food-parcels and money (even if philosophy makes them feel a little guilty about them):

> To the same.
>
> Phaidimos brought me a box[?] of pickled fish, five amphoras of honey, and twenty jars of myrtle-flavoured wine, and in addition three talents of silver. I am delighted with his reliability and conscious of your thoughtfulness. I have been wishing for some time that you would send me the first-fruits, as it were, of your local produce if the opportunity arose. For with these I can give pleasure

> to my friends and be a little clever with Plato who refuses gifts. I have not the slightest desire for money, particularly as I am in Athens and studying with Plato, for it would perhaps be odd, when I have sailed to Greece in order to become less in love with money, that love of money should nevertheless sail to me from Pontus. So you would do me a greater favour by sending things reminding me not of wealth, but of my native land.[62]

Five years later Chion is happily embedded in academic (and other) life at Athens and rather resistant to a father who plainly feels that his son has now spent quite enough time in higher education and who has written to tell him so. In *Letter 11* Chion puts up a robust defence: study takes time, no-one benefits from stopping too soon, and in fact another five years in Athens are needed. Father cannot have been too pleased, but only a short time later everything has changed; Chion has heard about the dreadful tyranny of Clearchos in his home city and philosophical calm has been shattered:

> To the same.
>
> Previously, as I wrote to you, I wanted to come back to you when I had completed my ten years here, but now, having heard about the tyranny, I could not bear any more to be in a safer place than my fellow-citizens, but when spring comes, I shall set sail if God preserves me (I couldn't do it now when it is still mid-winter). It would be completely wrong if I were to be like those who run off in any direction whenever there is some trouble in their native land, and are not on hand then most of all when there is a need of men to help. If helping is altogether in the realm of impossibility, at least taking a voluntary share in the injury seems to me to border on virtue, though perhaps as a favour it is a little deficient. I have been quite daring in writing to you since it is Lysis who is delivering this letter.[63]

This marks the turning point for the reader; henceforth Chion is the man of action and the first challenge comes quickly. The news that a determined young intellectual has vowed enmity reaches the tyrant, Clearchos, almost at once and he sends one of his bodyguards, the Thracian Cotys, to Athens to kill Chion. In *Letter 13* Chion tells his father how he was surprised by the assassin and gives a graphic account of his commando-like response and victory. Hostilities have now commenced, and the next letter is sent to his father from Byzantium on Chion's journey back to Heraclea. *Letter 16* is a copy of a letter actually written to Clearchos himself by Chion and is a deliberate attempt at disinformation; it is long, wordy and sententious and assures Clearchos he has nothing to fear. The last letter (17) is Chion's farewell letter to his old teacher, Plato. It is a proud and touching suicide note and says all that philosophically trained tyrant-slayers should say and feel on such occasions. The reader is left to assume (as he should already know and as the letter prophesies) that the assassination is successful and that Chion does indeed sacrifice his life for freedom and for his fellows:

> Chion to Plato, greetings.
>
> Two days before the Festival of Dionysus I sent you the most reliable of my servants, Pylades and Philocalos, for at the Festival I intend to make my attempt on the tyrant, having plotted for a long time not to be suspected by him. On that day there is a procession for Dionysus and because of that the bodyguards are likely to be somewhat lax; if not, I shall not shrink from the task, even if I have to go through fire, nor will I bring disgrace on myself or on your philosophy. The details of the conspiracy are firmly set, more so by mutual trust than by our numbers. I know that I shall be killed, and I only pray that I shall have accomplished the tyrant's murder before that happens to me. For I would leave this life with a hymn to Apollo and victory celebrations if I can take my departure from mankind after destroying the tyranny. Religion and bird-signs and every kind of prophecy point to my dying after I have set these matters to rights. I myself have seen a vision more clearly than in a dream; for it seemed to me that a woman, a thing of wondrous beauty and stature, was wreathing me with wild olive and headbands, and after a while showed me a very beautiful memorial saying, 'When you have done your work, Chion, go to this memorial and rest.' As a result of this dream I have every hope of a good death, for I think a prophecy of the soul is no counterfeit coin – as you too recognize. If the prophecy proves true, I shall think myself more blest than if, after killing the tyrant, I had been granted a life stretching to old age. For, having done great deeds, it is a fine thing to depart from one's fellows rather than get the benefit of a little time, and whatever I do will be considered far greater than what I suffer, and I shall be held in greater honour by those who have been advantaged if I have bought freedom for them at the price of my own death. The benefit to the recipients of generous deeds is greater if the doer takes no profit from them. So I am truly optimistic with regard to the prophecy of my death. Farewell, Plato, and may you prosper till a ripe old age. I shall now be speaking to you for the last time, as I believe.[64]

So the story ends – a self-contained narrative deliberately constructed only in letters and with it the birth of a minor genre in European literature. The reader is certainly encouraged to reflect on the virtues of a philosophical education and the wickedness of tyranny, and odd snippets of Platonic doctrine are hinted at, but the main purpose of the story-in-letters is the creation of a little historical novel with a noble, human young hero at its centre – not just history, not just philosophy, but a dramatic mixture of those two and edifying entertainment.[65]

Cultured entertainment and literary virtuosity are also the prime purposes of another category of Greek literary letters. These purport to be letters from everyday life, not written by famous historical characters deliberately harking back to great moments or great thoughts from the past, but representing moments of ordinary living observed by ordinary people. They are not, however, ordinary at all on closer inspection because, unlike the private letters of Chapter 2, they portray a literary construct of an imagined world which frequently looks back to the fourth century BC and especially to the world of Menander and New Comedy. In them the rude mechanicals and the parasites all happen to be literate and rather articulate; they sometimes have quaintly made-up names, they live in an affluent society, even if they themselves are in its bottom ranks, and they often do their best to write good Attic Greek. The letters they are supposed to have written are little imagined picture-postcards from an artificial society; what gives some of them their charm is the impression that behind the literary and precious veneer there are echoes of genuine feelings and relics of real family situations – a curious hovering between successful *prosopopoieia* and real life.[66] Most of the letters belong to the period of the Second Sophistic and date from the second or third century AD, though the genre continued to at least the sixth century AD with the letters of Aristainetos. Alciphron was one of the most prolific letter-writers in this style and left a collection of 123 letters in four groups, the pretend writers being fishermen, farmers, parasites and *hetairai*.[67] The first letter of Alciphron's collection is from 'Fairweather' to 'Boatlover' and the reader is given a happy, idealized picture of the fisherman's trade.

> Fairweather to Boatlover.
>
> It was useful for us that the sea became smooth and calm today. For when the storm continued into the third day, the north winds blowing furiously from the headlands over the sea, the deep rippling and turning black, and the foam flowering on the water's surface, as the waves of the sea broke against each other – here they dashed against the rocks, there they swelled up within themselves before breaking in spray – there was no possibility of work at all. We took over the little huts along the shore, and collecting a few chips of wood which the shipwrights had recently left after cutting down the oaks, we lit a fire with them and relieved ourselves of the bitter cold. This fourth day that has come is a 'halcyon', I think (you can judge by the clear sky), and it has given us a wealth of good things all at once. For when the sun appeared and the first beam shone on the sea, we eagerly launched our boat, which had recently been beached;

then stowing our nets on board we set to work. A short distance offshore we let out the nets, and, my goodness, what a catch of good food! What masses of fish we hauled in! – the bulging net almost dragged the cork-floats under the water.

Well, the fishmongers were right on the spot: they lifted up their yokes on their shoulders, hung their baskets from each end and, paying us cash in return, hurried away from Phalerum to the city. We had enough to satisfy them all, and in addition we took away for our wives and children a fair load of the smaller fry, enough for them to have their fill not just for one day, but for several if bad weather comes.[68]

Boatmen sometimes catered for pleasure-cruising and parties, and in the next letter from one fisherman to another it is possible to imagine that one catches just an edge of real envy and resentment at the excesses of gilded youth – even if the hire-fee in the end makes it worthwhile for the event-organizer.

Boatlife to Stern.

I had no idea how delicate and effeminate are the rich men's boys at Athens. But recently Pamphilus and his pals hired my little boat, so that they could sail about while the sea was calm, and at the same time take part in our fishing. Then I learnt what extraordinary luxuries they are provided with from land and sea. For he couldn't bear the planks of my fishing boat, and lay down on some imported rugs and cloaks, saying he couldn't lie on the decks like the others – I suppose he imagined that the timbers were rougher than rock. Then he asked us to organize some shade for him by stretching a sail over him like an awning, since he absolutely couldn't bear the rays of the sun. For the likes of us, however – not just those working at this trade, but all those in general who do not have or aim at abundance – it is possible sometimes to get warm by sunning ourselves: for cold and sea go together.

So we sailed around together, and Pamphilus wasn't alone, nor accompanied by his friends only, for a bunch of extremely attractive girls had joined him, all musicians. There was one called Kroumation, who played the pipes; another one, Erato, plucked the harp; and another was Euepis, and she clashed the cymbals. So my little boat was full of music, the sea echoed with melody, and everywhere delight filled the heart. But I wasn't too pleased myself at all this; for several of my colleagues were looking at me enviously – especially that spiteful Glaucias, who is more overbearing than a Telchis. But since Pamphilus paid me well, the silver cheered me up and now I rather like his nautical revels, and even long to come across another such lavish and extravagant man.[69]

Farmers come in for the full pastoral treatment, charming their herds of goats with sweet song, delivering their produce, and in the following letter succumbing to the tricks of a conjuror with appealing innocence.

> Woody to Fountainson.
>
> You know that I loaded my donkey with figs and fruit cakes. Well, I stabled him until I was due to deliver the stuff to one of my friends, and then somebody got hold of me and took me off to the theatre. He found me a good seat and entertained me with all kinds of shows. I can't remember the others, as I'm no good at keeping in mind and reporting such things; but let me tell you I saw one thing that made my jaw drop and I was almost speechless. A man came among us, set down a three-legged table, and put three little bowls on it. Then under these bowls he hid some little round white pebbles – the sort we find on the banks of fast-flowing streams. Sometimes he would hide one of these under each bowl; sometimes, goodness knows how, he would reveal them all under one bowl; then again he would make them completely vanish from the bowls and produce them in his mouth. Next, he would swallow them, and then, drawing forward the bystanders near to him, he would take a pebble from one man's nose, another from another man's ear, another from another man's head; and then, gathering them up, he would make them disappear again. A most dexterous thief! – superior even to the notorious Eurybates of Oechalia. I hope such a creature doesn't appear on my farm: nobody could catch him, and he would filch all my household goods and do his vanishing trick with everything I have on the farm.[70]

Farmers also have their family problems and the despair of a father whose son has undergone sudden 'conversion' and joined a contemporary cult (the Cynics again) might strike a chord with some present-day parents.

> Righteous to Friend.
>
> I sent my son to the city to sell wood and barley, charging him to come back the same day with the cash. But some emotional fit seized him, sent by who knows what evil spirit, which altered his whole being and drove him out of his wits. What happened was that he was watching one of those lunatics who, as they suffer from a frenzy like rabies, are usually called Cynics, and through imitation he has surpassed even the founder of that wicked sect. And now he presents a revolting and horrible sight – tossing back his filthy hair, staring around him insolently, half-naked in a tattered cloak, a pouch hanging by his side, a pear-wood stick in his hands, barefoot, dirty, idle, not knowing the farm or us his parents, but denying us and saying that all things come about through nature, and that the

> cause of birth is not parents but a combination of the elements. And it's pretty obvious that he despises money and hates farming. What is more he has no sense of shame and he has wiped modesty from his countenance. Alas, O Farming, how has the thinking-shop of these rogues perverted you! I blame Solon and Draco, who thought fit to give the death penalty to men who steal grapes, but let off scot-free men who deprive the young of their wits and enslave them.[71]

Not all is easy-going, however, in this never-never land; there are signs of social stirrings and occasional outbreaks of surprising independence. The *hetaira* Petale has become fed up with her sighing, conventional, superficial lover, Simalion, and in the second letter of a pair (another revealing pair has an imaginary exchange between Menander and his *hetaira* Glycera) she tells him some remarkably frank home-truths about her profession and puts romantic passion firmly in its place:

> Petale to Simalion.
>
> I wish that a courtesan's house could be maintained on tears, for I would be doing marvellously, with the endless supply I have of them from you. But, as it is, I must have money, clothes, finery, maids: running my life depends entirely on these. I have no inherited estate in Myrrhinus, nor a share in the silver mines – just my paltry fees and these wretched thank-offerings I get from my stupid lovers, covered in their sighs. I've been your mistress for a year and I'm fed up. My hair is all dry and horrible, as I've not seen any unguent for it all that year, and I'm wearing tatty old Tarentine cloaks that – so help me! – make me ashamed to meet my girl-friends. Where do you think I'm going to find a living if I only stay by your side? So you're weeping? You'll soon get over it. But if I can't find a generous man, I'll well and truly starve. As for your tears, I do wonder: they're not convincing. By our lady Aphrodite, you say you're in love, sir, and you want your mistress to take you to bed, for you can't live without her. Well – haven't you men got any goblets at home? Don't come near me unless you are bringing me your mother's jewels or money borrowed from your father. Lucky Philotis! The Graces looked on her with kindlier eyes. What a lover she has in Menecleides, who brings her a gift every day. That's better than weeping and wailing. Poor me: I have a dirge-singer, not a lover. He sends wreaths and roses as if to the grave of someone untimely dead, and says he cries all night long. If you are bringing something, then come without crying, or else you'll cause not me but yourself to suffer.[72]

Aelian who probably lived and worked round about the same time as Alciphron (the beginning of the third century AD) left twenty *Farmers'*

Letters. He was a Roman who claimed never to have left Italy, but he was well schooled in Attic oratory as well as being familiar with much New Comedy.[73] His letters are more self-consciously literary than Alciphron's and seem rather more remote from real, direct feeling. The farmer who writes to a friend to lament the loss of a swarm of bees is quite sweet but his sentiments are pure Arcadian – and he happens to have read Virgil's fourth *Georgic*:

> Baiton to Anthemion.
>
> My hives are deserted by the bees: they have left hearth and home, though they weren't runaways before. In fact they used to remain loyal and lived in their hives as their very own homes. They had a dewy meadow too, one that was rich in flowers, and we used to feast them on the richest of banquets. They, in turn, with excessive industry would feed us on lots of lovely honey, and never failed to produce this sweet fruit of their labours. But now they have gone off and away, though we did nothing to annoy them: I swear it by Aristaeus and by Apollo himself. So they have fled, and their home is bereft, and the meadow flowers are deserted and wasting away.
>
> As for me, whenever I think of their flights and their graceful dancing I can only consider that I have lost my daughters. I am indeed angry with them (why did they desert their foster-father – quite simply their guardian, and their keeper, who was not unwelcome to them?), but I must track down their wanderings, and find out where the fugitives have settled, and who has taken them over – that too must be found out. For he is keeping bees that don't belong to him. Then, when I've found them, I shall scold them mightily for being ungrateful and disloyal.[74]

Flavius Philostratus, an approximate contemporary of Alciphron and Aelian, was a prolific author with a genuine and catholic interest in philosophical ideas and the personalities responsible for them; his *Lives of the Sophists* is an important, though wayward, source for the history of the original sophistic movement, and he also wrote a life of the mysterious Cappadocian holy man, Apollonius of Tyana.[75] His seventy-three imaginary *Letters of Love*, however, are more the products of fancy or even playful literary experiment. In fact only fifty-five letters have to do with love, very broadly defined, the rest dealing with a variety of other subjects. All of them, unlike those of Alciphron and Aelian, are written as from Philostratus himself and the 'letters of love' are addressed both to boys and girls. Two characteristics are noticeable: an obsessiveness, almost amounting to fetishism, with some of the accompaniments and symbols of love (e.g. roses, the eyes, bare feet), and a tendency to strain the letter-form to points it can hardly bear (e.g. in *Letter 25* Philostratus advises his addressee to look at herself in a mirror and then congratulates her for having immediately done what he has suggested).

Roses are the messengers and symbols of love, and the first letter in Philostratus' collection elaborately accompanies a bunch sent to an attractive boy. This and similar poems actually belong to the genre of poems sent with gifts, even though Philostratus includes them in his *Letters of Love.*

> [To a boy]
> These roses, carried on their leaves as on wings, have made haste to come to you. Receive them kindly either as reminders of Adonis or as the dye of Aphrodite or as treasures of the earth. The wild olive suits the athlete, the upright tiara suits the Great King, the helmet's crest the soldier, but roses suit a lovely boy, both through the kinship of their fragrance and the likeness of their complexion. You will not wear these roses; they will wear you.[76]

A delicate conceit, but the boy has to work quite hard for his compliment. To appreciate it he must know that roses sprang from the blood of Adonis and that their colour came from Aphrodite's blood when she pricked her feet on rose thorns after Adonis's death; he must also know that the Persian king alone had the privilege of wearing his tiara upright.

Roses are also used without the clever allusions to pay a courteous and refined compliment to a lady, a compliment which had a well-known resurrection in Elizabethan times, having caught the attention of Ben Jonson:

> [To a woman]
> I have sent you a garland of roses, not to do you honour – though that too – but as a favour to the roses themselves so that they may not wither.[77]

A little adjustment and the rose can be deployed in cultured flattery of a lady of slightly mature years:

> To Cleonide.
> Sappho loves the rose and always crowns it with praise, comparing lovely girls to it; and she also compares it to the arms of the Graces, when she describes their bare forearms. Now the rose, though indeed the most beautiful of flowers, has a short season of perfection; for in common with other flowers it has its youth in the spring. But your beauty is a perpetual bloom, so that the autumn of your loveliness, as if it were still spring, goes on smiling in your eyes and cheeks.[78]

Philostratus had some curious enthusiasms, though, and the ancient reader may well have been as disconcerted as the modern one to discover the admiration bestowed on a boy's bare feet, and feel that Philostratus is here going over the top, not to mention his over-generous helping of mythology:

> To a young man with no shoes.
>
> You are rather unwell and I'm sure it's because your sandal is pinching you: new leather is terribly apt to cut into delicate skin. For that reason Asclepius is willing to heal wounds received in fighting and hunting and all that sort of mishap; but he ignores those arising from voluntary acts, since they are due to folly rather than God's abusive treatment. So why don't you walk barefoot? Do you bear the earth some ill will? Slippers and sandals and boots and shoes are for invalids and old people to wear. At any rate Philoctetes is described having such protective wear, as he was lame and diseased; whereas the philosopher from Sinope and Theban Crates and Ajax and Achilles are barefoot, and Jason has only one shoe. According to the legend, when Jason was crossing the river Anaurus one of his boots was caught by the stream when it stuck fast in the mud; so he had one bare foot, not through his own choice, but the accident taught him what he had to do; and he continued on his way most luckily stripped of his shoe. Let there be nothing between the earth and your foot. Don't be afraid: the dust will receive your step as it would grass, and we shall all kiss your footprint. O beautifully formed beloved feet! O exotic flowers, sprung from the earth! O kiss cast upon the ground![79]

The imaginary Greek letters written during the second and third centuries AD were a development of earlier essays in letter-writing of various kinds and constitute a self-conscious literary genre which had a surprising continuity. Aristainetos, writing in the fifth century AD, and even Theophylact of Simocatta, in the seventh, follow the same imaginary patterns, and Aristainetos went to the extent of making Alciphron the writer of one of his letters. One mystery is that this was such a peculiarly Greek phenomenon: Latin writers followed and modified Greek examples in so many ways, but, with the exception of Ovid's elaborate and inventive verse letters, the *Heroides*, in which famous heroines write to well-known addressees,[80] and the letters which occur in Latin comedies, there are no Latin literary conceits parallel with the Greek tradition. The existence of Cicero's massive collection of letters, carefully filleted and published by his secretary, Tiro, has been tentatively suggested as a kind of blockage against the development of imaginary Latin letter-writing, and the fact that literary giants like Horace and Ovid in his *Letters from Pontus* played with the convention of letters may have been somewhat intimidating, not to mention Seneca's later *Moral Letters*. Part of the explanation for the lack of Latin experimentation with imaginary letter-writing may be that Latin writers simply did not feel the same sense of ownership or the same kind of nostalgia as their Greek counterparts, either for a legendary past peopled with mythological and historical heroes, or for a culture that boasted so many unquestionably great writers and thinkers, or for the experience – however idealized and romanticized – of civilized city-state life. Linguistically too there was no comparison: Latin writers, however respectful of their predecessors, felt little temptation to return to writing in the manner of Ennius or Cato, and there was no fashion akin to Atticism – the Greek style harking back to the fifth and fourth centuries BC – until very much later. In its way the imaginary Greek letter was an expression of and a contribution to that phenomenon which has constantly defied description, which has over the centuries been threatened and assaulted in many ways, but has emerged in different forms and still persists today – the Hellenic consciousness.

NOTES

1 GREEK LETTERS: AN INTRODUCTION

1 Trapp (2003), 1 who also has an excellent introduction to Greek and Roman letter-writing, 1–46. See also Sykutris (1931); Schneider (1954); White (1986) 3–20 and 189–220; van den Hout (1949); Parsons (1980); Stowers (1989); Stirewalt (1993).
2 Vinogradov (1971); Chadwick (1973); Miller (1975); Merkelbach (1975); Wilson (1998). The circumstances are not at all clear – Trapp (2003), 195–8.
3 Hdt. i.124; vii.128; 8.22. Thuc. i.128; i.137; vii.8–15.
4 Suidas (Adler) iv.793–4 s.v. *chairein*; Lucian, *Pro lapsu* 3.
5 Xen. *Cyr.* 4.5.27–33.
6 *SIG*[3] 1259; Reinach (1910), 312–13; Crönert (1910), 157–60.
7 On the difficult question of brother/sister marriage in Egypt, see Thierfelder (1960) and Hopkins (1980).
8 *P. Ent.* 25.
9 *P. Tebt.* 56.
10 1 Corinthians 1–3.
11 Plut. *Phocion* 17.6 (quoting the authority of two other historians, one of whom, Chares, was a member of Alexander's staff).
12 Latin letter-writers recognized and took over the convention, often abbreviating it to a string of initial letters: SVBEEQV (*si vales bene est, ego quidem valeo*).
13 Keyes (1935), 28–44.
14 Turner (1980), 141, n. 32.
15 Theophr., *Characters* 24.13.
16 Ariston in Wehrli (1952), vi.36 *fr.* 14.ii.
17 Bradford Welles (1934), xxxvii–xlvi.
18 Diog. Laert. x.35.
19 For a list with bibliographies, see Holzberg (1994), 172–90; Rosenmeyer (2006), 97–129; the Euripides letter in Costa (2001), 84–9; for Socrates, see Sykutris (1933).
20 For an admirable survey of the 'Second Sophistic' in all its aspects, see Whitmarsh (2005); for literary letter-writing, see Rosenmeyer (2006), 130–60; Costa (2001), xi–xxiii.
21 See especially Koskenniemi (1956), 35–147; Thraede (1970).
22 Homer, *Iliad* vi.166–70.
23 Rosenmeyer (2001), 39–97.
24 Chapa (1998), 15–47.
25 These matters deserve more attention. See especially Montserrat (1996), 6–10.

26 Rowlandson, (1998); Bagnall and Cribiore (2006); Cribiore (2001), 223–39.
27 For a very thorough survey of the development of the *koine* and changes to the language, see Horrocks (1997), 32–127.
28 Harris (1989) *passim* and especially 3–24.
29 Lewis (1983a), 81–2, n. 17.
30 Galatians 6.11; 1 Corinthians 21.
31 See p. 67 and 106.
32 For a survey of these conventions, see White (1986), 215–18.
33 Rosenmeyer (2001), 206–7.
34 *BGU* 1079 = *SP* i.107.
35 *P. Oxy.* 1678.
36 *P. Oxy.* 292 = *SP* i.106.
37 Hdt. viii.98.1–2.
38 *BGU* 1232 = *SP* ii.366.
39 *P. Hib.* 110.ll.51–114 = (in part only) *SP* ii.397.
40 Plutarch, *Lys.* 19 cf. Aulus Gellius 17.9. Thucydides mentions it (i.131.1) but not as a *secret* device.
41 Hdt. v.35.3.
42 Hdt. vii.239.3.
43 Text Bettalli (1990); trans. Whitehead (1990).
44 Burkert (1984), 32. For tablets in the Semitic world, see Diringer (1982), 79–112.
45 *Iliad* vi.169.
46 Bowman (1994); Bowman and Thomas (1994) and (1996).
47 With picture, Schubart (1961), 41.
48 Dio Cassius 72.8.2; Herodian i.17.1.
49 Eur. *Hipp.* 862–5; *Iph. at Aulis* 112, 307, 325; *Iph. in Tauris* 38–9.
50 See n. 2.
51 See n. 6.
52 Sanmarti and Santiago (1987).
53 Parthenius ix.3; Dio Cassius xlvi.36; Plutarch *De mul. virtut.* 254d; Frontinus *Strateg.* iii.13.7.
54 Curse tablets: Gager (1992), 3–41. Questions to oracles: Parke (1967), 100–14 and 259–73.
55 Wilcken (1899) contains a massive collection. See also *SB* vi.9017. Lang (1990) catalogued the variety of *ostraca* found in the Athenian Agora.
56 *O. Tait* 1704.
57 Bingen *et al.* (1992).
58 *O. Claud.* 138, ll. 9–10.
59 Bagnall (1976). *O. Flor.*
60 *O. Flor.* 14, ll. 13–15.
61 Diog. Laert. vii.174.
62 For general surveys of the use and nature of papyrus as a writing material, see Parkinson and Quirke (1995) and Lewis (1974).
63 Pliny *Nat. Hist.* xiii.74–80; for a very detailed analysis of Pliny's account of papyrus manufacture, see Lewis (1974), 34–69.
64 Lewis (1974), 131, n. 19.
65 Turner (1980), 1.
66 Lewis (1974), 87; Turner (1980), 2.
67 Lewis (1974), 129–34; Harris (1989), 95.
68 Parkinson and Quirke (1995), 44.
69 Parássoglou (1985), 273–5.
70 See in general Turner (1980), 8–16; Reed (1972), 118–73.

71 Eur. *fr.* 627 in Nauck²; Galen vii.890 in Kühn (1965); 2 Timothy 4.13.
72 Diodorus Siculus ii.32.4; Devréesse (1954), 3; for the use of parchment for Persian administrative correspondence in Egypt, see Reed (1972), 260–1.
73 Strabo xv.1.73 mentions an Indian delegation presenting a letter written on leather to the emperor Augustus.
74 Innes (1995), 312–21; other dates have been proposed for Demetrius from the third century BC to the first century AD. See also Grube (1961) and Schenkeveld (1964).
75 Text: Weichert (1910); trans. Malherbe (1988), 30–41, 4. For the dating, see Koskenniemi (1956), 54–5.
76 Bradford Welles (1934), xlii, perhaps thinking of this section, regarded the whole work as Hellenistic and purporting to be 'a guide for state secretaries'. Secretaries working in Hellenistic chanceries, however, probably had a much more sophisticated training.
77 Text – Föerster (1921–2); trans. Malherbe (1988), 66–81, see also 10, n. 43.
78 E.g. White (1986), 189–90; Trapp (2003), 37–8.
79 *P. Par.* 63; Koskenniemi (1956), 57–9.
80 *P. Bon.* col. iii.3–13; trans. Malherbe (1988).
81 *P. Oxy.* 724 = *SP* i.15.
82 *OCD* s.v. tachygraphy.
83 For an excellent introduction, see Reynolds and Wilson (1991).
84 The following section owes a great deal to Turner (1980), 16–41, where much additional detail can be found.
85 Cicero *In Pisonem* 28–9; Horace, *Sat.* i.2.121.
86 See especially Bagnall (1995).
87 The names of Grenfell and Hunt are now legendary. Scholars working on papyri in the Sackler Library in Oxford often have the pleasure of using Hunt's own books which contain many pencilled editorial suggestions in his own hand.
88 For a most readable account from a leading papyrologist of the life in that city which the papyrus finds have revealed, see Parsons (2007).
89 Quoted from Turner (1980), 30.
90 Skeat (1974).
91 Pestman *et al.* (1981).
92 *PECS* s.v. Pergamum, Miletus, Priene, Magnesia-on-the-Maeander.

2 PERSONAL AND FAMILY LETTERS

1 For a more detailed general introduction, see Lewis (1983a); Bowman (1986).
2 For a thorough archaeological summary and description of the region, see Bagnall and Rathbone (2004), 127–54.
3 Timon of Phlios *fr.* 12 in Diels (1901).
4 *PSI* 1080.
5 *P. Oxy.* 744 = *SP* i.105.
6 *BGU* i.332.
7 *P. Athen.* 60.
8 *P. Oxy.* 130 = *SP* i.130.
9 *SP* i.133.
10 *P. Oxy.* 119.
11 *BGU* 846 = *SP* i.120.
12 *BGU* 1680 = *SP* i.134.
13 *BGU* 423 = *SP* i.112.
14 *BGU* 632. Krebs, the editor of 632, examined the writing of 423 carefully and was convinced that both letters were written by the same hand.

15 *P. Mich.* viii.490.
16 *P. Mich.* viii.491.
17 *P. Oxy.* 1481.
18 *P. Mich.* viii.464.
19 *BGU* 33.
20 *BGU* 27 = *SP* i.113.
21 *P. Giess.* 17 = *SP* i.115.
22 *P. Par.* 43 = *SP* i.99.
23 *P. Oxy.* 524; *P. Oxy.* 1487 = *SP* i.174.
24 *P. Oxy.* 3313. For the *Rhodophoria*, see notes 8 and 9, p. 103 *ad loc.*
25 *P. Ant.* 93.
26 *P. Hib.* 54 = *SP* i.95.
27 *P. Oxy.* 300; Suet. *Life of Domitian* 13.
28 *P. Mil. Vogliano* = Trapp (2003), no. 56.
29 *C. P. Jud.* 446.
30 *P. Ryl.* ii.229.
31 *P. Ryl.* ii.231. Soter may be a month-name left over from Ptolemaic times; it is probably an alternative for Thoth or Phaophi – see *P. Ryl.* ii.147–8.
32 *BGU* i.33.
33 *P. Oxy.* 938.
34 *P. Tebt.* 56 = *SP* i.102.
35 *P. Oxy.* 2680.
36 *P. Oxy.* 299 = *SP* i.108.
37 For accounts of both Memphis and the cult of Serapis, see Bagnall and Derow (2004), 94–105; Lewis (1986), 69–72.
38 *P. Lond.* 42 = *SP* i.97.
39 *UPZ* 78.
40 *P. Par.* 47 = *SP* i.100
41 *P. Oxy.* 1493
42 *P. Oxy.* 115.

3 BUSINESS LETTERS

1 For general histories, see Turner (1984); Bowman (1986); Bowman (1996); Hölbl (2001a); Hölbl (2001b).
2 Plut. *Mor.* 790A–B.
3 Turner (1980), 6 and 181, n. 2.
4 Isoc. *Letter* 4.
5 *P. Lond.* 2026 = *PZA* 176–7.
6 *P. Lond.* 2027 = *PZA* 177–8.
7 His boss, Apollonios, used to receive even more valuable gifts: on one occasion in 257 BC a Jew called Tobias sent him a eunuch and four slaves (with full descriptions attached) – *C.P. Jud.* i.4.
8 *P. Cair. Zen.* 59.192 = *SP* i.92.
9 *P. Petrie* ii.11.(1); *GPE* 38.
10 Paul to Philemon.
11 *P. Petrie* ii.13.5; *GPE* 43.
12 *P. Petrie* ii.4.8; *GPE* 43 (the general sense is clear although the text has many gaps).
13 *P. Petrie* ii.13.1 = *GPE* 43.
14 *P. Cair. Zen.* 59.451; Austin (1981), no. 246.
15 *P. Lond.* 1948 = *PZA* 36–7.

16 *P. Oxy.* 3854.
17 *P. Cair. Zen.* 59.015
18 *P. Lond.* 2052 = *PZA* 198–201.
19 *P. Ent.* 25 = *GPE* 66–7.
20 For a good survey of this topic, see Bowman (1996), 121–64. On a wider front, see the essays in Goldhill (2001).
21 *P. Ent.* 79 = *GPE* 61.
22 *P. Ent.* 11 = *GPE* 60.
23 *P. Hal.* I. col. viii, 166–85 = *SP* ii.207.
24 *P. Lond.* 1976 = *PZA* 70–2.
25 *P. Ent.* 26 = *SP* ii.268.
26 *P. Lond.* 2045 = *PZA* 193.
27 *PSI.* 328 = *SP* ii.411.
28 *P. Cair.* 59.107.
29 *PSI* 530.
30 *P. Lond.* 2059 = *PZA* 208–9.
31 *PSI.* 414.
32 *P. Lond.* 2041 = *PZA* 189.
33 *P. Cair. Zen.* 59.029.
34 U. Wilcken, *Chrestomathie* 52 = *SP* ii.301.
35 *P. Lond.* 1973 = *PZA* 62–6.
36 *P. Lond.* 2056 = *PZA* 205–7.
37 *P. Grenf.* ii.14 (b) = *SP* ii.414.
38 *P. Tebt.* 33 = *SP* ii.416.
39 *P. Lond.* 1941 = *PZA* 26–8.
40 *P. Lond.* 2017 = *PZA* 169–72.
41 *GPE* 46–9; *OCD*[3] s.v. banks.
42 *P. Hamb.* 173 = *GPE* 52.
43 *P. Cair. Zen.* 59.253.
44 *P. Lond.* 2033 = *PZA* 180–1.
45 *P. Beatty Panop.* i.389–91.
46 See, for example, the petition translated in Bowman (1986), 80.
47 *P. Lond.* 1350 = *SP* ii.433.

4 LETTERS OF STATE

1 Bradford Welles (1934) – henceforth BW – is the standard collection of royal letters from the Hellenistic period. It has an excellent introduction and gives a text, translation and commentary for each letter. In detail it has sometimes been overtaken by more recent scholarship but it is still indispensable. For the Letter-Writer, see p. xxxviii.
2 Xen. *Oec.* iv.8. Also Holland (2005), 212–13.
3 *SIG*[3] 22; Meiggs and Lewis (1988), 12; van den Hout (1949), 144–52. The authenticity of the letter has been questioned and the inscription found near the site of ancient Magnesia is a copy, probably made in the second century AD. However, historians have generally accepted the text as genuine and the juxtaposition of two such unlikely pieces of subject-matter surely implies an unbelievably bizarre imagination on the part of a supposed fabricator. However, van den Hout makes a good case for saying some wording may have been changed. The gardeners may have found some sympathetic ears: there is evidence for Greeks being involved in higher administration in Persia – see Lewis (1977), 3 and 13–14.
4 Hdt. i.123–24; iii.40; iii.122; v.14; v.35; vii.239; viii.128.

5 Westlake (1977), 103.
6 Hdt. iii.40.
7 Rosenmeyer (2001), 53 insists, however, that it should be read as a letter. See West (1985), 286 and Harris (1989), 59–60.
8 Thuc. i.22.
9 Thuc. iv.50.
10 Thuc. i.128.
11 Thuc. i.129.
12 Thuc. i.137.
13 Most historians are sceptical about the authenticity of the three letters, though the letters still have some defenders. Hornblower (1991), 291 points out that they occur in a part of the history which is marked by 'easy narrative Greek' and is 'in a different style from the rest of Bk i and indeed from the rest of Thucydides'; he too is very doubtful about the letters. See further Westlake (1977), 102–3; Cawkwell (1971), 50–1; Sykutris (1931). 209–10.
14 Thuc. vii.8.
15 Thuc. vii.11. Nicias' dispatch was sometimes regarded as a true letter in antiquity and actually published separately; it was also regarded as a speech. See van den Hout (1949), 36–8. Rosenmeyer (2001), 59, using a category she elsewhere rejected, classed it as an 'epistle'.
16 Thuc. vii.14.
17 Thuc. viii.33; viii.38; viii.50. 2,4 and 5.
18 Xen. *Hell.* i.1.23.
19 Demosth. *De cor.* 157.
20 For a forthright demonstration of the spuriousness of the documents quoted in Demosthenes' speech, see Yunis (2001), 29–31.
21 *SIG*[3] 283; Tod (1948), no. 192.
22 In the fifth century BC Lebedos had been optimistically assessed at a three-talent subscription to the Delian League but this had been swiftly reduced to one talent. Teos, on the other hand, paid a regular six talents. *PECS* 492–3 and 893–4.
23 BW no. 4; *SIG*[3] 344; Austin no. 40.
24 Fontenrose (1988), 63–7.
25 BW no. 5; *SIG*[1] 170; *OGIS* 214.
26 *PECS*, 317.
27 BW no. 15; *OGIS* 223; Austin no. 183. The reference to 'the Galatian business' is unclear; there must have been a special tax raised to pay the costs of dealing with trouble from the Galatians, who were often uncomfortable neighbours.
28 BW no. 23; *OGIS* 267.1; Austin no. 195.
29 Polybius 36, 15.3.
30 BW no. 25; *SIG*[3] 456.
31 It had been presented to the renegade Themistocles by Artaxerxes and some of Themistocles' female relatives had served as priestesses at the shrine of Artemis – *PECS* 544.
32 *PECS* 481, s.v. Laodicea.
33 *OGIS* 233; Austin no. 190.
34 BW no. 31; *OGIS* 231; Austin no. 184.
35 For the pay and conditions of mercenary service in the Greek world, see Griffith (1935), 264–316.
36 Maier (1959), no. 76; Austin no. 202.
37 BW no. 24; *SIG*[3] 1018
38 BW no. 67; *OGIS* 331; Austin, no. 210. The other two letters are BW nos 65 and 66 and all three are translated in Austin no. 310.

39 *I. Cret.* iv. pp. 230–2, no. 168; Hands (1968), no. D64, pp. 133 and 203. For the letter from Cnossos, *I. Cret.* i. p. 62, no. 7; *SIG*[3] 528; Austin no. 124. For the method of choosing doctors and for Hermias' service at Halicarnassus, see Sherwin-White (1978), 267–8. For the history of the Cos medical school, *ibid.* 278–89.
40 For this policy dating from the time of Alexander the Great and frequently employed, see Lane Fox (1973), 140–1.
41 *Didyma II: Die Inschriften*, ed. A. Rehm and R. Harder (Berlin: n.p., 1958), 492 A–C; BW no. 18; *OGIS* 225; Austin no. 185 (B).
42 For more detailed background, see *CAH*[2] vii. 715–20; Cary (1972), 395–9.
43 BW nos 55–61. The letters came to light on marble blocks found in the Armenian cemetery at Sivrihissar at some time between 1836 and 1859, and the texts were then copied. In 1883 an Austrian archaeologist took a set of 'squeezes' which are now in the Archaeological Institute in Vienna (two are missing). The marble blocks, which may have been part of the temple at Cybele at Pessinos where the priest-king Attis presided, have since disappeared.
44 For more detail, see Mitchell (1993), 42–58.
45 BW no. 56; *OGIS* 315.
46 BW no. 61; *OGIS* 315.
47 For detail of the events, see Hammond and Walbank (1988), 429–32; Habicht (1970), 273–9.
48 *SIG*[3] 543; Austin, no. 60.
49 *ibid.*
50 Gruen (1984), 576.
51 BW no. 52; *OGIS* 763; Austin no. 203.
52 For a fuller account of these events, see *CAH*[2] ix (1994), 129–64.
53 BW no. 73; *SIG*[3] 741.
54 BW no. 74; *SIG*[3] 741.
55 Reynolds (1982), no. 12; Trapp (2003), no. 64.

5 THE LETTER AS TRACT

1 Demetr. *On Style* 228.
2 For a brief summary of the debate and a list of the chief contributors, see *CHCL* i.480–1 and 744; also Gulley (1971), 105–30; Skemp (1976), 9–11.
3 *Plato: Phaedrus and Letters vii and viii*, trans. W. Hamilton (Harmondsworth: Penguin, 1973).
4 Plato *Letter vii*, 323d–326b.
5 *ibid.* 326b.
6 *ibid.* 337e.
7 *ibid.* 340b–341a.
8 *ibid.* 341c. This sounds more like Socrates in Plato *Phaedr.* 275c–e and is particularly inappropriate coming from Plato. Was Plato using the word *suggramma* to mean something like 'explanatory commentary'? It is the word also used by Demetrius in the passage referred to in n. 1.
9 Plato *Letter vii*, 347e–348a.
10 *ibid.* 352a.
11 For studies of all the Platonic letters, see Harward (1932) and Morrow (1962).
12 For a thorough survey of Isocrates' work and its context, see Usher (1999), 118–26 and 296–323.
13 Usher (1976), 37–9.
14 Cic. *De orat.* ii.22.94.
15 Isoc. *To Philip* 21.

16 Texts of the letters in Van Hook (1945), 372–485. For a bibliography on the authenticity of the letters, see Kennedy (1963), 191, n. 97.
17 Isocrates' real opinion of Dionysius was not flattering – *To Philip* 65.
18 Isoc. *Letter iv*, 1–4.
19 For Philip's pugnacious habits, see Dem. *De cor.* 67.
20 Isoc. *Letter ii*, 1–4.
21 *ibid.* 13.
22 Isoc. *Letter vi*, 8.
23 *ibid.* 4.
24 Text and translation in DeWitt (1949). For a detailed introduction to the letters with translation and commentary, see Goldstein (1968); in his view only Letters i–iv are likely to be by Demosthenes. Demosthenes' letters were appreciated in antiquity – Cic. *Brutus* 121; *Orator* 15; Plut. *Life of Dem.* 20; Quintil. x.1.7.
25 Demosth. *Letter iii*, 1.
26 *ibid.* 5–7.
27 *ibid.* 37–8.
28 Demosth. *Letter ii*, 1–2.
29 *ibid.* 3–8.
30 *ibid.* 17–19.
31 Demosth. *Letter iv*, 1–2.
32 *ibid.* 10–12.
33 Demosth. *Letter i*, 1–2.
34 *ibid.* 8–9.
35 *ibid.* 15–16.
36 For a brief introduction, see *CHCL* i.625–30. Also Rist (1972) and *The Cambridge History of Hellenistic Philosophy*, ed. K. Algra, J. Barnes. J. Mansfield and M. Scholefield (Cambridge: Cambridge University Press, 1999) – topic-based but contains much about Epicureanism.
37 Lucr. *De rer. nat.* i.62–9.
38 Hor. *Epist.* i.4.16.
39 Diog. Laert. x.26; x.30.
40 Diog. Laert. x.27. For the texts and commentaries on the surviving works, see Arrighetti (1973); Diano (1974). Also Long and Sedley (1987), 18–162 and (for translations) Inwood and Gerson (1994).
41 Diog. Laert. x.5.
42 *ibid.* x.11.
43 Aristot. *Eud. Eth.* i.1217b 22.
44 Diog. Laert. x.35.
45 *ibid.* 38–9.
46 *ibid.* 45.
47 *ibid.* 61.
48 *ibid.* 82–3.
49 *ibid.* 84–5.
50 *ibid.* 94.
51 *ibid.* 103–4.
52 *ibid.* 116.
53 *ibid.* 122.
54 *ibid.* 124–5.
55 *ibid.* 130–2.
56 *ibid.* 135.
57 For a general account, see Moles (2000). For more detail, see Dudley (1937). Navia (1996), 193–213 has an extensive bibliography.

58 There was a story that, when Plato was asked what sort of man Diogenes was, he replied, 'Socrates gone mad' – Diog. Laert. vi.54. The caricatures of Diogenes may often have been overdone – see Long (1999).
59 A diatribe was a short moral lecture; it is thought to have had some influence on the development of the Christian sermon – *OCD*[3] s.v. diatribe; Dudley (1937), 111.
60 Diog. Laert. vi.95.
61 For the complete collection edited and translated, see Malherbe (1977b).
62 Dudley (1937), 124.
63 'Crates' *Letter vii* (the numbers refer to Malherbe's edition).
64 *ibid. Letter xix.*
65 'Diogenes' *Letter iii.*
66 *ibid. Letter vii.* Quotation from Hom. *Od.* xiii.43–8, trans. Lattimore.

6 GREEK LETTERS IN THE EARLY CHRISTIAN CHURCH

1 For a scholarly general introduction to Paul and his work, see Hooker (2003). For more general surveys, see Doty (1973); White (1986). I have not attempted to enter the considerable discussion which has resulted from the distinction between 'Brief' and 'Epistel' first drawn by Deissmann (1927); the distinction now seems unsatisfactory on both literary and theological grounds.
2 The quotation is from the *Sayings of Menander*, 808 (Jaekel 1964). For the philosophers' interest, Acts 17.18–21. For Cynic influence, see Malherbe (1970).
3 For a detailed survey, see Aune (1987), chs 5 and 6. Also Stowers (1989), esp. 42–7.
4 Romans 1.1–7. All the Scripture quotations contained herein are from the New Revised Standard Version of the Holy Bible (Anglicized Edition).
5 Romans 16.1.
6 1 Corinthians 1.13–16.
7 Galatians 1.6–9.
8 Galatians 1.13–20.
9 Galatians 2.11–16.
10 Galatians 3.1–3.
11 Galatians 3.27–29.
12 Galatians 5.6–12.
13 Galatians 6.11–18. It should be noted that the New Revised Standard version of the Bible translates the Greek *adelphoi* as 'brothers and sisters'.
14 1 Corinthians 1.11–13.
15 1 Corinthians 1.20–25.
16 1 Corinthians 3.19–23.
17 1 Corinthians 4.16–21.
18 1 Corinthians 5.9–11.
19 1 Corinthians 6.9–11.
20 1 Corinthians 7.1–7.
21 1 Corinthians 8.10.
22 1 Corinthians 9.7–9.
23 1 Corinthians 11.20–22.
24 1 Corinthians 11.33.
25 1 Corinthians 12.12–13.
26 1 Corinthians 13.1–13.
27 1 Corinthians 15.50–55.
28 1 Corinthians 16.21–24.
29 2 Corinthians 10.10–11.
30 2 Corinthians 11.4–6.

31 2 Corinthians 11.21–29.
32 2 Corinthians 12.15–19.
33 2 Corinthians 3.1–3.
34 2 Corinthians 5.1–4.
35 2 Corinthians 8.1–7.
36 Romans 3.28–31.
37 Romans 12.9–12.
38 Romans 15.14–16.
39 Philippians 1.1–7.
40 Philippians 1.12–14.
41 Philippians 2.5–11.
42 Philippians 2.19–24.
43 Philippians 4.15–18.
44 Philippians 4.21–23.
45 1 Thessalonians 2.5–8.
46 Malherbe (1970).
47 1 Thessalonians 4.16–17.
48 1 Thessalonians 5.14–23.
49 1 Thessalonians 5.26–28.
50 See for example Betz (1979) on the letter to the Galatians.
51 2 Thessalonians 3. 16–18.
52 1 Timothy 3.1–7.
53 James 1.26–27.
54 James 2.14–17.
55 James 2.1–7.
56 James 5.1–6.
57 1 John 2.18–25.
58 1 John 4.1–3.
59 2 John (complete) = Trapp (2003), 39.
60 3 John 1–3.
61 3 John 9–10.
62 Jude 4.
63 Jude 12–13.
64 Jude 20–23.
65 Preface to *1 Clement*. Text and translation of the letter in Ehrman (2003).
66 *1 Clem.* 1.1.
67 *1 Clem.* 3.1–3. The quotation is adapted from Deuteronomy 32.15.
68 *1 Clem.* 47.1–4.

7 LETTERS IN GREEK LITERATURE

1 This chapter is mightily in debt to what I have learnt from two scholars, Professor Patricia Rosenmeyer and the late Professor C.D.N. Costa; their work has done so much to interpret and illuminate some rather forgotten corners of Greek literature.
2 Hom. *Iliad* vi.163–70, trans. Lattimore.
3 For instance, Rosenmeyer (2001), 42–4, sees it as prefiguring later themes of fictional letter-writing: the connection of letters with treachery, their association with women, and the functions of introduction, recommendation and the carrying of news.
4 Plato *Phaedr.* 275d–e.
5 Rosenmeyer (2001), 62, n. 6 lists passages in Aeschylus, Sophocles and Euripides which contain 'early metaphors of writing suggestive of letters'.

6 For what is known or can be guessed about this first play, see Halleran (1995), 25–37; Barrett (1964), 10–45.
7 Eur. *Hipp.* 877–86.
8 Eur. *Palamedes fr.* 578.1–9 (Nauck²).
9 For a thorough treatment of the various versions of the story, see Woodford (1994), 164–9.
10 But does she read? It is logically correct to suggest that Iphigeneia could not read and write since she originally had to dictate her letter to a sympathetic prisoner. However, it surely makes little dramatic sense for her to be holding a letter-tablet on stage and then recite the contents as from memory; in any case it was common practice to dictate letters *and* to be able to read. The audience could surely have been relied upon to suspend its disbelief. For the strictly logical view, see Rosenmeyer (2001), 76, n. 36.
11 Aristot. *Poetics* 1455a.
12 Eur. *Iph. in Tauris* 769–94.
13 Eur. *Iph. in Aulis* 117–23.
14 A sentence survives: 'Now listen to this letter too'; Cratinus (Kassel-Austin), 316.
15 Kassel-Austin *fr.* 2; Koskenniemi (1956), 185, n. 1.
16 In Plautus, for instance, letters are everyday occurrences and sometimes integral parts of the plot: *Asinaria* iv.1.16–19; *Bacchides* ii.1.7, ii.6.32, iv.3.97, iv.8. 11ff.; *Epidicus* i.1.56, ii.2.68; *Miles Gloriosus* ii.1.51–55; *Persa* ii.2.13–14; *Trinummus* ii.3.45–8, ii.3.66–7.
17 For the typical patterns and formulas of such dedications, see Guarducci (1974), 9–11.
18 *ibid.* 44–5.
19 Woodhead (1981), 41–2.
20 Theoc. *Idyll* 28.
21 *AP.* vi.21.
22 *AP.* v.152.
23 *AP.* v.9.
24 Suidas (Adler) s.v. Lysias. It is dangerous to assume too much about texts we do not have, e.g. Blass (1887), 423: 'Nicht der Redner sprach hier … sondern der heitere Privatmann.'
25 For a bibliography to each of the collections, see Holzberg (1994), 172–90.
26 R. Bentley, *A Dissertation upon the Epistles of Phalaris, Themistocles, Socrates, Euripides and the Fables of Aesop* (London, 1697).
27 Russell (1983), 107.
28 Trans. and introduction by K. Dowden in Reardon *et al.* (1989), 650ff. I am very grateful to Professor Dowden and to the University of California Press for permission to use these stylish translations.
29 *Alexander Romance* i.36, trans. K. Dowden.
30 *ibid.* ii.31, trans. Dowden.
31 *ibid.* iii.2, trans. Dowden.
32 *ibid.* iii.33, trans. Dowden.
33 Text and trans. in Doenges (1981).
34 See Penwill (1978), 83–103.
35 *Letter 1* (Doenges 1981).
36 *Letter 12* (Doenges 1981).
37 Hdt. iv.76.
38 Reuters (1963); Kindstrand (1981).
39 Malherbe (1977), 6.
40 *Letter 1* (Kindstrand 1981).

41 *Letter 3.*
42 Cic. *Disp. Tusc.* 5.90.
43 *Letter 5.*
44 Text and trans. in Smith (1990).
45 *Letter* 10.321–2.
46 Smith (1990), 69, n. 2, refers to the popular moral fable of the Choice of Heracles (Xen. *Mem.* 2.1.21–34); there is also an obvious allusion to the fundamental Platonic distinction between knowledge and opinion.
47 There was a herb specialist who was physician to the famous Mithridates; perhaps readers are to believe he had an ancestor in the same trade – Smith (1990), 71, n. 1.
48 Plato *Phaedr.* 230b. The coincidences of wording are unmistakable.
49 *Letter 17*.351–2.
50 *ibid.* 360–4.
51 *ibid.* 368–70.
52 *ibid.* 378–80.
53 Text and trans. in Goold (1995); Persius i.134. For detailed discussion and interpretation, see Rosenmeyer (2001), 137–47. For a concise survey of the development of the Greek novel, see Bowie (1985). There is a collection of essays in Swain (1999).
54 *The Story of Callirhoe* 4.4.7–10.
55 *ibid.* 4.6.3–4.
56 *ibid.* 8.4.5–6.
57 Text in Gaselee (1947); trans. by J.J. Winkler in Reardon *et al.* (1989). Detailed discussion in Rosenmeyer (2001), 147–54.
58 For a good short introduction to Lucian and the *True Stories*, see Reardon *et al.* (1989), 619–20.
59 Lucian *True Stories* ii.35. Trans. in Reardon *et al.* (1989), 645.
60 Text and trans. in Düring (1951); for the date, see pp. 14–16. See also Konstam and Mitsis (1990).
61 For a survey of the historical evidence, see Düring (1951), 9–12.
62 *Letter 6.*
63 *Letter 12.*
64 *Letter 16.*
65 For more detailed comment on the work and its nature, see Rosenmeyer (2001), 234–52.
66 Russell (1983), 21–39, wryly constructed an imaginary world, Sophistopolis, from the situations and people conjured up in Greek declamations; it would be possible to construct a rather similar world from the imaginary letters.
67 Text and trans. in Benner and Fobes (1949). For a most perceptive study of Alciphron's collection and his modes of writing, see Rosenmeyer (2001), 255–307. There is an excellent selection of Greek fictional letters, including letters of Alciphron, edited and translated in Costa (2001); I am grateful to the Oxford University Press and the late Professor Costa's wife for her kind readiness to allow me to use his exemplary translations.
68 Alciphron 1.1, trans. Costa.
69 *ibid.* 1.15, trans. Costa.
70 *ibid.* 2.17, trans. Costa.
71 *ibid.* 2.38, trans. Costa.
72 *ibid.* 4.9, trans. Costa.
73 Text and trans. in Benner and Fobes (1949). There has been debate about whether Aelian was influenced by Alciphron – also about the quality of his work: see Rosenmeyer (2001), 308–21; *CHCL* i.680–2.

74 Aelian *Letter 5*, trans. Costa.

75 Text and trans. in Benner and Fobes (1949). For the likely identification of Philostratus (there are four Philostrati), see Rosenmeyer (2001), 322, n. 2. He was born on Lemnos, educated in Athens, and was a member of the philosophical group patronized by the Syrian empress, Julia Domna (to whom the last of his letters is addressed) – *CHCL* i.655–8. See also Anderson (1986).

76 Philostr. *Letter 1*.

77 Philostr. *Letter 2*. This is one of four letters by Alciphron (2; 32; 33; 46) which (perhaps via a Latin translation) gave Ben Jonson phrases and ideas for 'To Celia' ('Drink to me only …).See Herford *et al.* (1925), i.251 and ii.386; Fitton Brown (1959); Donaldson (1985), 293.

78 *ibid. Letter 51*, trans. Costa

79 *ibid. Letter 18*, trans. Costa

80 In *Heroides* 16–21 Ovid made use of paired letters in the same way as some Greek authors of imaginary letters. He claimed in *Ars Amat.* iii.346 that he had invented a new literary form in the *Heroides.*

BIBLIOGRAPHY OF WORKS CITED

Alston, R. (1995) *Soldier and Society in Roman Egypt* (London: Routledge).

Anderson, G. (1986) *Philostratus* (London: Croom Helm).

Arrighetti, G. (1973) *Epicuro: Opere*, second edition (Turin: Einaudi).

Aune, D. (1987) *The New Testament in its Literary Environment* (Philadelphia: Westminster Press).

Austin, M.M. (1981) *The Hellenistic World from Alexander to the Roman Conquest* (Cambridge: Cambridge University Press).

Bagnall, R.S. (1976) *The Florida Ostraka* (Durham, NC: Duke University Press).

Bagnall, R.S. (1995) *Reading Papyri, Writing Ancient History* (London and New York: Routledge).

Bagnall, R.S. and Cribiore, R. (2006) *Women's Letters from Ancient Egypt* (Ann Arbor, Michigan: University of Michigan Press).

Bagnall, R.S. and Derow, P. (2004) *Sources: The Hellenistic Period* (Oxford: Scholars' Press).

Bagnall, R.S. and Rathbone, D.W. (2004) *Egypt from Alexander to the Copts* (London: British Museum Press).

Barrett, W.S. (1964) *Euripides Hippolytos* (Oxford: Clarendon Press).

Benner, A.R. and Fobes, F.H. (1949) *Alciphron, Aelian and Philostratus: The Letters*, Loeb Classical Library (Cambridge, Mass., and London: Harvard University Press).

Bettalli, M. (1990) *Aenea Tattico: La difesa di una Città Assediata* (Pisa: ETS Editrice).

Betz, H.D. (1979) *Galatians: A Commentary on Paul's Letter to the Churches in Galatia* (Philadelphia, Penn.: Fortress Press).

Bingen, J., Bülow-Jacobsen, A., Cockle, W.E.H., Cuvigny, H., Kayser, F., Rubenstein, I. and Rengen, W. van (1992) *Mons Claudianus: ostraca graeca et latina* (Cairo: Institut français d'archéologie du Caire).

Blass, F. (1887) *Die attische Beredsamkeit* (Leipzig: Teubner).

Bowie, E.L. (1985) 'The Greek novel' in P.E. Easterling and B.M.W. Knox (eds) *The Cambridge History of Classical Literature*, Vol. 1 (Cambridge: Cambridge University Press), 683–99.

Bowman, A.K. (1986) *Egypt after the Pharoahs*, second edition (London: University of California Press).

Bowman, A.K. (1994) *Life and Letters on the Roman Frontier* (London: British Museum Press).

Bowman, A.K. (1996) 'Egypt' in *The Cambridge Ancient History*, second edition, Vol. 10, *The Augustan Empire: 43 BC–AD 69* (Cambridge: Cambridge University Press).

Bowman, A.K. and Thomas, J.D. (1994) *Vindolanda: The Latin Writing Tablets* (London: British Museum Press).
Bradford Welles, C. (1934) *Royal Correspondence in the Hellenistic Period* (New Haven, Conn.: Yale University Press).
Burkert, W. (1984) *Die orientalisierende Epoche in der griechischen Religion und Literatur* (Heidelberg: Winter).
Cary, M. (1972) *A History of the Greek World 323 to 146 BC* (London: Methuen).
Casson, L. (1974) *Travel in the Ancient World* (London: Edgar Kent).
Cawkwell, G.L. (1971) 'The fall of Themistocles' in *Auckland Classical Studies presented to E.M. Blaiklock* (London: Oxford University Press).
Chadwick, J. (1973) 'The Berezan lead letter', *Proceedings of the Cambridge Philological Society*, n.s. 19, 35–7.
Chapa, J. (1998) *Letters of Condolence in Greek Papyri* (Firenze: Gonelli).
Costa, C.D.N. (2001) *Greek Fictional Letters* (Oxford: Oxford University Press).
Cribiore, R. (2001) 'Windows on a woman's world: some letters from Roman Egypt' in A. Lardinois and L. McClure (eds) *Making Silence Speak: Women's Voices in Greek Literature and Society* (Princeton, NJ: Princeton University Press), 223–39.
Crönert, W. (1910) 'Die beiden ältesten griechischen Briefe', *Rheinisches Museum für Philologie* 65, 157–80.
Deissmann, G.A. (1927) *Light from the Ancient East*, trans. L. Strachan (London: Baker Book House).
Devréesse, R. (1954) *Introduction à l'étude des manuscrits grecs* (Paris: Klincksieck).
DeWitt, N.W. and DeWitt, N.J. (1949) *Demosthenes VII*, Loeb Classical Library (Cambridge, Mass., and London: Harvard University Press).
Diano, C. (1974) *Epicuri Ethica et Epistulae* (Florence: Sansoni).
Diels, H. (1901) *Poetarum Philosophorum Fragmenta* (Berlin: Weidmann).
Diringer, D. (1982) *The Book before Printing* (New York: Dover Press).
Doenges, N.A. (1981) *The Letters of Themistocles* (New York: Arno Press).
Donaldson, I. (ed.) (1985) *Ben Jonson* (Oxford: Oxford University Press).
Doty, W.G. (1973) *Letters in Primitive Christianity* (Philadelphia, Penn.: Fortress Press).
Dudley, D.R. (1937) *A History of Cynicism* (London: Ares Press).
Düring, I. (1951) *Chion of Heraclea: A Novel in Letters* (Göteborg: Wettergren and Kerber).
Ehrman, B.D. (2003) *The Apostolic Fathers*, Loeb Classical Library (Cambridge, Mass., and London: Harvard University Press).
Exler, F.X.J. (1923) *The Form of the Ancient Greek Letter* (Washington, DC: Ares Press).
Fitton Brown, A.D. (1959) 'Drink to me, Celia', *Modern Language Review*, 54, 554–7.
Foerster, R. (ed.) (1921–2) *Libanii Opera* x–xi (Leipzig: Teubner).
Fontenrose, J. (1988) *Didyma: Apollo's Oracle, Cult and Companions* (Berkeley, Cal.: University of California Press).
Förster, R. (1921–2) *Libanii opera X–XI* (Leipzig: Teubner).
Gager, J.G. (1992) *Curse Tablets and Binding Spells from the Ancient World* (Oxford: Oxford University Press).
Gaselee, S. (1947) *Achilles Tatius*, Loeb Classical Library (Cambridge, Mass., and London: Harvard University Press).
Goldhill, S. (2001) ed. *Being Greek under Rome* (Cambridge: Cambridge University Press).

Goldstein, J.A. (1968) *The Letters of Demosthenes* (New York and London: Columbia University Press).

Goold, G.P. (1995) *Chariton: Callirhoe*, Loeb Classical Library (Cambridge, Mass., and London: Harvard University Press).

Griffith, G.T. (1935) *Mercenaries of the Hellenistic World* (Cambridge: Cambridge University Press).

Grube, G.M.A. (1961) *A Greek Critic: Demetrius on Style* (Toronto: University of Toronto Press).

Gruen, E.S. (1984) *The Hellenistic World and the Coming of Rome* (Berkeley, Los Angeles and London: University of California Press).

Guarducci, M. (1974) *Epigrafia Greca*, Vol. III (Roma: Istituto poligrafico dello Stato).

Gulley, N. (1971) 'The authenticity of the Platonic epistles' in K. v. Fritz (ed.) *Pseudepigrapha* I, Entretiens Hardt 18 (Vandoeuvre: Fondation Hardt).

Habicht, C. (1970) 'Epigraphische Zeugnisse zur Geschichte Thessaliens unter der Makedonischen Herrschaft' in B. Laourdas and C. Makaronas (eds) *Ancient Macedonia: Papers Read at the First International Symposium* (Thessaloniki: Journal of Near Eastern Studies).

Halleran, M.R. (1995) *Euripides: Hippolytus* (Warminster: Focus Publishing).

Hammond, N.G.L. and Walbank, F.W. (1988) *A History of Macedonia*, Vol. III (Oxford: Oxford University Press).

Hands, A.R. (1968) *Charities and Social Aid in Greece and Rome* (London: Thames and Hudson).

Harris, W.V. (1989) *Ancient Literacy* (Cambridge, Mass., and London: Harvard University Press).

Harward, J. (1932) *The Platonic Epistles* (Cambridge: Cambridge University Press).

Hercher, R. (1873) *Epistolographi Graeci* (Paris; reprinted Amsterdam: Hakkert, 1965).

Herford, C.H., Simpson, P. and Simpson, E. (1925) *Ben Jonson* (Oxford: Oxford University Press.

Hölbl, G. (2001a) *A History of the Ptolemaic Empire*, trans. T. Saavedra (London and New York: Routledge).

Hölbl, G. (2001b) 'Ptolemaic Egypt' in Donald B. Redford (ed.) *The Oxford Encyclopedia of Ancient Egypt* (Oxford: Oxford University Press), Vol. III, 76–84.

Holland, T. (2005) *Persian Fire* (London: Abacus).

Holzberg, N. (1994) *Der griechische Briefroman* (Tübingen: Niemeyer).

Hooker, M. (2003) *Paul: A Short Introduction* (Oxford: Oneworld).

Hopkins, K. (1980) 'Brother–sister marriage in Roman Egypt', *Comparative Studies in Society and History*, 22, 303–54.

Hornblower, S. (1991) *A Commentary on Thucydides*, Vol. I (Oxford: Oxford University Press).

Horrocks, G. (1997) *Greek: A History of the Language and its Speakers* (London: Longman).

Innes, D.C. (ed. and trans.) (1995) *Demetrius, On Style* in *Aristotle, Poetics; Longinus, On the Sublime; Demetrius, On Style*, Loeb Classical Library (Cambridge, Mass., and London: Harvard University Press).

Inwood, B. and Gerson, L.P. (1994) *The Epicurus Reader* (Indianapolis/Cambridge: Hackett).

Jaekel, S. (ed.) (1964) *Menandri Sententiae. Comparatio Menandri et Philistionis* (Leipzig: Teubner).

Kennedy, G.A. (1963) *The Art of Persuasion in Greece* (Princeton, NJ: Princeton University Press).

Keyes, C.W. (1935) 'The Greek letter of introduction', *American Journal of Philology* 56, 28–44.

Kindstrand, J.F. (1981) *Anacharsis: The Legend and the Apophthegmata* (Uppsala: Uppsala Universitet).

Kirk, G.S. (1990) *The Iliad: A Commentary*, Vol. II (Cambridge: Cambridge University Press).

Konstam, D. and Mitsis, P. (1990) 'Chion of Heraclea: a philosophical novel', *Apeiron*, 23, 257–79.

Koskenniemi, H. (1956) *Studien zur Idee und Phraseologie des griechischen briefes bis 400 n. Chr.* (Helsinki: Suomalaien Tiedeakatemie).

Kühn, C.G. (ed.) (1965) *Claudii Galeni Opera Omnia* (reprint, Hildesheim: Georg Olms).

Lane Fox, R. (1973) *Alexander the Great* (London: Penguin).

Lang, M. L. (1990) *The Athenian Agora*, Vol. XXV, *Ostraka* (Princeton, NJ: Princeton University Press).

Lewis, D.M. (1977) *Sparta and Persia* (Leiden: Brill).

Lewis, N. (1974) *Papyrus in Classical Antiquity* (Oxford: Clarendon Press).

Lewis, N. (1983a) *Life in Egypt under Roman Rule* (Oxford: Oxbow).

Lewis, N. (1983b) 'Papyrus and ancient writing; the first hundred years of papyrology', *Archaeology*, 36(4), 31–7.

Lewis, N. (1986) *Greeks in Ptolemaic Egypt* (Oxford: Oxford University Press).

Lewis, N. (1992) 'Papyrus in classical antiquity. an update', *Chronique d'Égypte* 67, 308–18.

Long, A.A. and Sedley, D.N. (1987) *The Hellenistic Philosophers* (Cambridge: Cambridge University Press)

Long, A.A. (1999) 'Antisthenes and Diogenes – Cynic ethics' in K. Algra, J. Barnes, J. Mansfeld and M. Schofield (eds) *The Cambridge History of Hellenistic Philosophy* (Cambridge: Cambridge University Press), 623–32.

Maier, F.G. (1959) *Griechische Mauerbauinschriften* I (Heidelberg: Quelle and Mayer).

Malherbe, A.J. (1970) '"Gentle as a nurse". The Cynic background to 1 Thessalonians 2', *Novum Testamentum* 12, 203–17.

Malherbe, A.J. (1977) *The Cynic Epistles* (Missoula, Montana: Scholars' Press).

Malherbe, A.J. (1988) *Ancient Epistolary Theorists* (Atlanta, Georgia: Scholars' Press).

Meiggs, R. and Lewis, D.M. (1988) *A Selection of Greek Historical Inscriptions*, revised edition (Oxford: Clarendon Press).

Merkelbach, R. (1975) 'Nochmals die Bleitafel von Berezan', *Zeitschrift für Papyrologie und Epigraphik*, 17, 161–62.

Miller, A.P. (1975) 'Notes on the Berezan lead letter', *Zeitschrift für Papyrologie und Epigraphik*, 17, 157–60.

Mitchell, S. (1993) *Anatolia: Land, Men and Gods in Asia Minor* (Oxford: Clarendon Press).

Moles, J.L. (2000) 'The Cynics' in C. Rowe and M. Schofield (eds) *The Cambridge History of Greek and Roman Political Thought* (Cambridge: Cambridge University Press), 415–34.

Montevecchi, O. (1953) *Papyri Bononienses*, I (Milano: Editrice Vita e Pensiero).
Montserrat, D. (1996) *Sex and Society in Graeco-Roman Egypt* (London and New York: Kegan Paul).
Morrow, G.R. (1962) *Plato's Epistles* (Indianapolis, Ind.: Bobbs and Merrill).
Navia, L. (1996) *Classical Cynicism* (Westport, Virginia and London: Greenwood).
Parássoglou, G.M. (1985) 'A roll upon his knees', *Yale Classical Studies*, XXVIII, 273–5.
Parke, H.W. (1933) *Greek Mercenary Soldiers* (Oxford: Oxford University Press).
Parke, H.W. (1967) *The Oracles of Zeus: Dodona, Olympia, Ammon* (Cambridge, Mass.: Harvard University Press).
Parke, H.W. (1985) *The Oracles of Apollo in Asia Minor* (London: Routledge).
Parkinson, R. and Quirke, S. (1995) *Papyrus* (London: British Museum Press).
Parsons, P. (1980) 'Background: the papyrus letter', *Didactica Classica Gandensia* 20, 3–19.
Parsons, P. (2007) *City of the Sharp-Nosed Fish* (London: Weidenfeld and Nicolson).
Penwill, J.L. (1978) 'The letters of Themistocles: an epistolary novel?', *Antichthon*, 12, 83–103.
Pestman, P.W. (1981) *A Guide to the Zenon Archive* (Leiden: Brill).
Pfeiffer, R. (1968) *History of Classical Scholarship* (Oxford: Clarendon Press).
Preisigke, F. (1907) 'Die Ptolemäische Staatspost', *Klio* 8, 241–77.
Reardon, B.P. (ed.) (1989) *Collected Greek Novels* (Berkeley, Cal.: University of California Press).
Reed, R. (1972) *Ancient Skins, Parchments and Leathers* (New York: Seminar Press).
Reinach, A.J. (1910) ' Bulletin epigraphique', *Revue des études grecques* 23, 312–13.
Reuters, F.H. (1963) *Die Briefe des Anacharsis* (Berlin: Akademie-Verlag).
Reynolds, J. (1982) *Aphrodisias and Rome* (London: Society for the Promotion of Roman Studies).
Reynolds, L.D. and Wilson, N.G. (1991) *Scribes and Scholars*, third edition (Oxford: Oxford University Press).
Rist, J.M. (1972) *Epicurus: An Introduction* (Cambridge: Cambridge University Press).
Rosenmeyer, P.A. (2001) *Ancient Epistolary Fictions* (Cambridge: Cambridge University Press).
Rosenmeyer, P.A. (2006) *Ancient Greek Literary Letters* (London and New York: Routledge).
Rowlandson, J. (ed.) (1998) *Women and Society in Greek and Roman Egypt: A Sourcebook* (Cambridge: Cambridge University Press).
Russell, D.A. (1983) *Greek Declamation* (Cambridge: Cambridge University Press).
Sanmarti, E. and Santiago, R.A. (1987) 'Une lettre grecque sur plomb trouvée à Emporion', *Zeitschrift für Papyrologie und Epigraphik* 48, 119–27.
Schenkeveld, D.M. (1964) *Studies in Demetrius on Style* (Amsterdam: Hakkert).
Schneider, J. (1954) 'Brief' in *Reallexicon für Antike und Christentum* (Stuttgart: Hiersmann), 564–85.
Schubart, W. (1961) *Das Buch bei den Griechen und Römern*, third edition (Heidelberg: Koehler and Amelang).
Sherwin-White, S.M. (1978) *Ancient Cos* (Göttingen: Vandenhoeck and Ruprecht).
Skeat, T.C. (ed.) (1974) *Greek Papyri in the British Museum*, Vol. VII, *The Zenon Archive* (London: British Museum Publications).

Skemp, J.B. (1976) *Plato*, New Surveys in the Classics No. 10 (Oxford: Classical Association).

Smith, W.D. (1990) *Hippocrates' Pseudepigraphic Writings* (Leiden: Brill).

Stirewalt, M. Luther (1993) *Studies in Ancient Greek Epistolography* (Atlanta, Georgia: Scholars' Press).

Stowers, S.K. (1989) *Letter-Writing in Greco-Roman Antiquity* (Philadelphia, Penn.: Westminster Press).

Swain, S. (ed.) (1999) *Oxford Readings in the Greek Novel* (Oxford: Oxford University Press).

Sykutris, J. (1931) 'Epistolographie', in A. Pauly, G. Wissowa and W. Kroll (eds) *Real-Encyclopädie der klassischen Altertumswissenschaft*, Supplementband 5 (Stuttgart: J.B. Metzler), 185–220.

Sykutris, J. (1933) *Die Briefe des Sokrates und die Sokratiker* (Paderborn: F. Schöningh).

Thierfelder, H. (1960) *Die Geschwisterehe im hellenistich-römische Ägypten* (Münster: Aschendorff).

Thraede, K. (1970) *Grundzüge griechisch-römischer Brieftopik* (München: Beck).

Tod, M.N. (1913) *International Arbitration among the Greeks* (Oxford: Oxford University Press).

Tod, M.N. (1948) *A Selection of Greek Historical Inscriptions*, Vol. II (Oxford: Oxford University Press).

Trapp, M. (2003) *Greek and Latin Letters* (Cambridge: Cambridge University Press).

Turner, E.G. (1980) *Greek Papyri. An Introduction*, second edition (Oxford: Clarendon Press).

Turner, E.G. (1984) 'Ptolemaic Egypt' in *The Cambridge Ancient History*, second edition (Cambridge: Cambridge University Press), vii.1.118–74.

Usher, S. (1976) 'Lysias and his clients', *Greek, Roman and Byzantine Studies*, 17, 37–9.

Usher, S. (1999) *Greek Oratory* (Oxford: Oxford University Press).

van den Hout, M.P. (1949) 'Studies in early Greek letter-writing', in *Mnemosyne* 2, 18–41 and 138–53.

Van Hook, L. (1945) *Isocrates*, Vol. III, Loeb Classical Library (Cambridge, Mass., and London: Harvard University Press).

Vinogradov, Y.G. (1971) 'An ancient Greek letter from the island of Berezan', *Vestnik Drevnei Istorii* 118, 74–100 (English summary, 99–100).

Wehrli, F. (1952) *Die Schule des Aristoteles vi – Lykon und Ariston von Keos* (Basel: B. Schwabe).

Weichert, V. (ed.) (1910) *Demetrii et Libanii quae feruntur 'Typoi epistolikoi' et 'Epistolimaioi charakteres'* (Leipzig: Teubner).

West, S. (1985) 'Herodotus' epigraphical interests', *Classical Quarterly* 35, 278–305.

Westlake, H.D. (1977) 'Thucydides on Pausanias and Themistocles: a written source?', *Classical Quarterly* 27, 95–110.

White, J.L. (1986) *Light from Ancient Letters* (Philadelphia, Penn.: Fortress Press).

Whitehead, D. (1990) *Aineias the Tactician* (Oxford: Oxford University Press).

Whitmarsh, T. (2005) *The Second Sophistic*, New Surveys in the Classics No. 35 (Oxford: Oxford University Press).

Wilcken, U. (1899) *Griechische Ostraka*, Vols I and II (Berlin: Von Gisecke and Devrient).

Wilson, J.P. (1998) 'The illiterate trader', *Bulletin of the Institute for Classical Studies*, 42, 29–53.

Woodford, S. (1994) 'Palamedes seeks revenge', *Journal of Hellenic Studies*, CXIV, 164–9.

Woodhead, A.G. (1981) *The Study of Greek Inscriptions*, second edition (Cambridge: Cambridge University Press).

Yunis, H. (2001) *Demosthenes: On the Crown* (Cambridge: Cambridge University Press).

INDEX OF LETTER WRITERS

Quotation marks indicate a fictitious letter composed in the name of that person or persons.

INDEX

For Product Safety Concerns and Information please contact our EU representative GPSR@taylorandfrancis.com
Taylor & Francis Verlag GmbH, Kaufingerstraße 24, 80331 München, Germany

www.ingramcontent.com/pod-product-compliance
Lightning Source LLC
Chambersburg PA
CBHW071513110726
47908CB00003B/821

* 9 7 8 0 4 1 5 5 1 8 3 7 6 *